YO-EKR-835

Ellen & Mike —

You'll recognize this kid.

He lives in each of us.

Enjoy!

Frank

Given to us 2013. Fall,
at Elder Hostel at North
Arizona University. Enjoyed
talking to Frank. A fellow
elderhosteleer.

E.

SAILOR, WRITE YOUR MOTHER!

A Teenage Boy Comes Of Age
Despite The Rigors Of
The United States Military

Frank Herbert Spittle

Copyright © 2001 Frank Herbert Spittle

All rights reserved. No part of the material protected by this copyright notice may be reproduced or utilized in any form or by any means, electronic or mechanical, including photocopying, recording, or by any informational storage and retrieval system, without written permission from the copyright owner.

ISBN 0-972877-0-8

Published by
Ocean Breeze Productions
PO Box 3421
Laguna Hills, CA 92654

For information on obtaining additional copies
see order form in the back of book.

Printed by
Maverick Publications, Inc.
Bend, Oregon

...Half of this is fact;
Half of this is probably not fact...
Don't hold it against me if I add something
Or miss something
I'm telling you the way I remember it...

paraphrased from the epic poem *Manas*

There is a difference between fact and truth.

Shelba Cole Robison

Any man who may be asked in this century
What he did to make his life worthwhile...
Can respond with a good deal of pride and satisfaction,
"I served in the United States Navy."

President John F. Kennedy
1963, Annapolis, Maryland

l. to r.: Richard Boulanger, Jimmy Gargas, and Bob Howie
onboard USS OZBOURN, 1950

CONTENTS

WE REGRET TO INFORM YOU

Bert's Worst War — 1

Alice, A Gold Star Mother? — 5

The Facts Come Out — 8

COMING OF AGE THE NAVY WAY

The Quickest Way Out of Town — 11

Good-Bye Yard Work--Hello Adventure — 15

The Games Begin — 19

Boy Scouts Ain't Prior Service — 24

Kickin' Ass and Takin' Names — 30

Cinderella Liberty — 34

The Anchor is Aweigh — 37

SEAMAN SECOND CLASS, NON-SWIMMER

Two Steps Backward — 41

Give Me Liberty — 45

Who Gets the Worm? — 49

Mail Call — 55

Wouldn't Want to Live There — 60

THEY ALSO SERVE

You Got Orders — 63

Finally I'm Somebody — 67

A Brush with Death — 71

Boy Toy — 74

Grounded — 80

AT LAST, THE BLUE WATER NAVY

Sea Duty	83
A Change of Scene	86
Getting Sea-Legs	89
Welcome Aboard	94
Underway	101
Lessons to be Learned	105
Help Wanted--Typist	110
Let's Meet the Natives	113
Gettin' Inked	116
Goin' to the South Seas	120
Neptunus Rex Onboard	125
Where in the Hell is Korea?	131
Good Liberty	137
On Bird-Dog Station	143
"You Come My House"	148
When My Bunk and I Parted Company	154
Cold, Cold Everywhere	158
A Folk Hero for the Little People	164
My View from the Open Bridge	168
The Lucky Strike "Brown" Market	174
All Mucked Up	181
Owens, One--Delaney, Zero	185
Lost Steering--Found Hong Kong	189
I Only Came to Dance	196
Bon Appetite	202
Afternoon Delight?	207
Last Japanese Liberty	214
Making Homeward Turns	221

FROM TIN CAN TO HEAVY METAL

Everything Onboard But a Bowling Alley   225

What We Have Here is an Epidemic   229

This Could be Trouble   234

Lock Him Up   237

Swimming in an Unauthorized Area   242

"WE'LL TELL YOU WHEN"

Contagious   245

I'm Out   253

Glossary

WE REGRET TO INFORM YOU

The author, Korea, 1950

BERT'S WORST WAR

. The USS Ozbourn was taken under enemy fire in Wonson Harbor, North Korea. The following day Bert Spittle sat alone at The Hide-Out bar in Alameda, California, pulling on a cold beer and savoring the tang of pickled egg. It was all just the way he liked it, served up with a few onion and beet slices from the purplish mess floating in the large-mouthed jar behind the bar. As usual he ignored the half dozen loyal customers, remnants from the times crowds of thirsty civilian employees, and carrier-based sailors, packed the neighborhood joint.

He reached across the mahogany bar, poured his second brew into a fresh cold glass, and watched the bubbles glide up through the bright gold toward the surface. As he day dreamed, he wedged a thumbnail under the top of the wet label and tore down through its center, taking out the spread-eagle Eastside Beer logo.

He had always been something of a loner, more an observer, but for him The Hide-Out was like a private club--it was *his* place. He'd spend some of every Saturday and Sunday here and made it his first stop on the walk home after his shift at the Naval Air Station. A man worked up a thirst pounding the skins of damaged fighter aircraft, getting them ready to re-enter service.

The pugnacious little limey remembered the old times. How many years since he'd moved onto Alameda Island from across the bay when the Navy sold its housing project to civilians after the war? He let his thoughts drift to his son. Frank would be kicking around somewhere in the Far East right now, in the Korean Conflict--that phony name the United Nations gave to the action. He felt the old bitterness rise again within him. *When your ass is gettin' shot at, and kids are coming home in body-bags, that's called a war.*

Forty years ago he'd done his own teenage hitch, in the British Royal Merchant Marine. How many gin mills had his shore leaves taken him into? Maybe thousands. The Mediterranean ports, and on to Panama where he'd jumped ship toward the end of World War I and joined the U. S. Army with the promise of citizenship.

He had nearly finished his glass when he looked up and barked an order toward the departing bartender. "Blackie. Bring that back here. I want a bottle in front of me, always. Only take it when you bring a fresh one. You know the drill."

The ex-Marine shook his head and retrieved the empty from the trash, carefully positioning it before the five-foot, four-inch banty rooster. With a hint of sarcasm he mimicked, "You going to lay it across somebody's eyebrows, Bert?"

"Pal, when you've been loggin' time in beer joints as long as I have, you pick up a few tricks. Like the other day you gave that grifter change for a twenty when he faked you with a ten. Bet you won't get caught like that again soon."

"Shit." Blackie snarled through clenched teeth.

Bert drained his glass. "I'll have another Eastside. Then you can take away this guy." He motioned toward the empty.

"And open one for yourself," he called after him.

Buying him a cold one might settle him down--never a good idea to piss off the bartender. He tilted the new glass and carefully ran the sparkling brew down its side to create just the right head.

"Scotty." Someone was calling to him from down the bar.

Bert started at the sound of his nick name. He had encouraged it since his traveling youth, trying to avoid getting his ass kicked by Irish toughs if his true Manchester heritage was discovered. Nobody hated Scots. Everybody gave them plenty of room.

Across the five empty stools separating him from the source, it reached him again. "Scotty."

Bert turned to look toward a red-faced customer wearing a short-billed plaid cap, pulled down nearly covering his right eye. He recognized Tim, leaning on one elbow, hunched over a brimming shot glass. His acquaintance worked in another department at the Station.

"Scotty, what's the name of that tin-can your son's on?"

"Ozbourn, Tim. USS Ozbourn."

Tim lifted his glass, ignoring the spilling Bushmills, and moved tentatively, as though not sure it was okay to approach.

"Scotty, I picked up an *Oakland Tribune* on the way out of the Station, and read that two of our ships were shelled and sunk by the Commies in Korea. Ozbourn was one of 'em." He pushed his hat to the back of his head.

"Had you heard anything like that?"

A heavy curtain of silence dropped across the room and all movement in the bar froze into a still photo. The only sound in the room, a background hum from the refrigerator. Everyone's attention

2

fixed on Bert. That common denominator bonding them had kicked in. This was a Navy bar, in a Navy town.

Bert was trying to process the startling information. He couldn't think straight, unable to speak.

Jumping from his stool, he whirled around, sending the seat crashing to the floor. Forget his Navy peacoat hanging by the bumper pool table. He was out the back door running.

Oh my God. Frank. The only thing in this life that holds any meaning for me. Oh my God. He covered the 90 foot distance from The Hide-Out to the front door of his cramped one-bedroom apartment in a dozen beats of his pounding heart.

The venetian blind hanging on the front door banged loudly as he exploded into the living room. Startled by the commotion, Mabel scurried from the kitchen.

"Brother! You're home early. Did you lose your job?" She laughed. She never saw Bert after work until he'd had his couple of beers. This was a first in their six-year marriage.

"Where's tonight's paper?" He gasped for breath while his eyes darted frantically about the small living room.

"Right there beneath the coffee table. What the hell's got into you? Are you all right?"

On the second page he found it.

Navy sources would not confirm the reported sinking of two United States destroyers in Wonson Harbor, North Korea. Associated Press carried the story on the wire earlier today. At Twelfth Naval District Headquarters, San Francisco, spokesman Lieutenant Commander Lloyd Bixon promised a definitive statement by morning.

Bert's voice quivered, "Morning? Tomorrow morning? The greatest country in the world and they can't tell me if my kid is alive." The words, barely audible, seemed to choke him.

He saw the concern on Mable's face, as if she wanted to reach out, offer some consolation. But she stood motionless, like someone shell-shocked. After a moment she stooped to pick up the newspaper where he'd dropped it and quietly returned to the kitchen. Bert watched as she turned and stood gazing toward him.

"What time is it?" He shot the question toward her.

She strained to focus her teary eyes on the rooster-shaped ceramic clock above the sink. "Six forty-five."

Bert exhaled audibly. "Too late. Oh geez. First thing tomorrow morning at the Station, I'm going straight topside and walk right into the

Skipper's office. He says his door is always open. Well, I need him now. He'll get me answers."

Bert shook his head and collapsed into the worn recliner, not tipping back in his usual way.

"Oh, no. No. No." He sat bent over, head down. His arms hung lifelessly between his legs.

She moved her attention to the brief article. She'd often expressed her fondness for the blonde stepson she thought so resembled her husband.

From his chair Bert watched as her legs seemed to turn to rubber, and she steadied herself down into a kitchen chair. He guessed it had finally hit her too. She buried her face into her bent elbow and her entire body trembled as she quietly sobbed.

ALICE, A GOLD STAR MOTHER?

Her favorite time of day, five-thirty, quiet and still dark outside. It always began the same, sitting alone at the kitchen table. First saying prayers, with her son the centerpiece of her morning thanks. Thoughts of Frank in the Navy, thousands of miles from home, heading her list of petitions.

Steam curled from the inviting teapot's spout. The comely ceramic container displayed tiny yellow roses about its sides, each held by a short green stem. Alice couldn't describe the feeling of comfort, the satisfaction each early morning when she filled the little pot with scalding water to cover the four substantial pinches of Earl Grey she'd deposited. She gingerly cupped her hands about the hot china and drew the warmth into her body. Even Southern California mornings could be a bit crisp. She'd practiced this ritual since she had been a young woman in Canada. Montreal's biting winters were deeply etched in her memory.

She visualized Frank as he appeared in a favorite photo, taken when he was two. He stood in short pants, his blond hair tousled, holding a toy truck and looking down at it as he pouted. She had interrupted his playing to snap the moment, using the large black Kodak camera, a gift her brother George had sent from Toronto in the '20's.

With her head bowed she pleaded, "Please bring my son home safely from this insane war."

This part always produced tears. She wiped them away, across each eye and down her cheeks using long, deep strokes with the small hankie, one of several always in her apron pocket. Returning the little wadded linen cloth, she adjusted her apron straps and briefly arranged the sides of her hair with soft pats, then returned each hand to its station on the radiating teapot. Reclined into the slit-backed kitchen chair, she closed her eyes for a few quiet moments.

The sound of her husband Larry's voice interrupted her far away thoughts. She looked up with a faint smile.

"You were a million miles away. I've been standing here for a full minute. Let's see if I can finish some coffee and cornbread before 'the Misses' gets up." Larry made it sound like a pleasant request.

He was a male nurse. Several years earlier, after discussions that carried long into the night, the two of them agreed to move into the home of an elderly, widowed patient--to become full time care-givers. There had been unwritten promises made about them gaining the house upon the death of the owner, in return for their commitment. That had made the deciding difference in moving. Alice cooked and cleaned for the three of them. Larry took care of the physical needs of their eccentric patient, who mostly kept to herself in the two bedroom home. Hopefully the old lady would sleep late this morning and the two of them could have some quiet time together.

Larry went out to the front lawn for the morning paper while Alice removed the reheated cornbread from the oven. She inserted the tip of the ice pick into the yellow, clogged hole of the small Carnation evaporated milk can, clearing it for pouring. Putting it beside a hot cup of instant Nescafe coffee, she brought butter and the beehive shaped honey dispenser to the center of the small table, and waited.

The ready breakfast things began to cool. *Where was Larry?* Alice looked out the front window, but the yard was empty. She went to the entry door, quietly turned the knob, and eased the door open, not wanting to disturb the sleeping woman. Larry stood before her, just outside, the morning paper opened before him. He glanced up, not expecting her, his ashen face holding an unfamiliar expression.

Removing his glasses with one hand, he reached out and softly pulled his wife into his arms. She felt his body begin to tremble and heard sputters of sobbing. He couldn't look into her face. After what seemed an eternity, he cleared his throat a second time.

Still holding her close, her face smothered against his chest, he groaned, "Frank's destroyer has been sunk. His ship and another were hit by North Korean shore batteries yesterday. It's too early to know about survivors."

He felt her go limp in his arms.

In an attempt to learn more about the news story, Larry phoned the *Los Angeles Examiner* at 8:30 A.M. After being passed along to several sympathetic, but unhelpful listeners, he connected with Walter Goodfellow from the editorial staff. Goodfellow explained that he had a boy in the Army, fighting in Korea. He spoke to Larry at length and tried to answer his concerns.

"Mr. Taylor, you understand this is not an *Examiner* story. We took it off the AP Wire. Most printed news comes off the Wire Services. As the story points out, 'Peiping reported the sinking of the two destroyers, their hull numbers would have identified them as the OZBOURN and the SPERRY.' But you know those Commie bastards lie like hell at every opportunity, Mr. Taylor. They enhance engagement situations and inflate numbers, it's that way in every military conflict.

"My suggestion for Mrs. Taylor and yourself is to sit tight. The Navy will confirm or deny this as soon as they can--and that will be soon. My guess is it's all a bunch of bull.

THE FACTS COME OUT

At 11:30 the evening of the newspapers story, Frank's mother picked up the phone with a shaky hand before it could ring a second time. She hoped it hadn't awakened the old woman.

"Mrs. Taylor? Walter Goodfellow, L.A. Examiner. Sorry to call you so late, but I knew you and Mr. Taylor would want to know. The Navy confirmed your boy's ship *was* in action, and hit. Three men were wounded, but no one was killed. And no U.S. vessels were sunk. Your boy was not among those injured--he's okay. You'll get more particulars in tomorrow morning's paper.

"I know you and Mr. Taylor will be hearing from Frank soon.

"Mrs. Taylor, are you still there?"

Fighting back tears of joy, Alice struggled to whisper, "God bless you, Mr. Goodfellow. You're a caring man to follow through for us like this."

At 5:30 the following morning, fog hadn't begun to lift across San Francisco Bay. A ship's horn sounded somewhere out in the estuary. Bert walked toward his dripping wet parked car, in a daze after tossing all night without sleep. The Italian grocery would still be closed, but the newspaper stand in front should have the morning *Chronicle*.

He didn't wait for the engine to warm up, but ground into reverse and moved out. The arc of the Nash's steering wheel intercepted Bert's line of vision. His height wouldn't allow a full view through the front window of his oversized four-door sedan, but he'd angrily declined Mabel's suggestions to sit on something to raise himself.

"Yeah, right. Like the Yellow Pages, maybe? What bull shit."

As he cruised up the deserted street toward town, each click of the windshield wiper blade brought him a different childhood image of his son.

In front of Stellino's Market he left the car running and fumbled for a nickel as he trotted toward the news stand. The tall fresh stack of papers meant the morning edition had arrived.

Front page, lower-left. He read aloud in a rasping whisper. "Yesterday Peiping reported the sinking of two U.S. Navy destroyers in North Korean waters. The hull numbers identified them as the USS OZBOURN and the USS SPERRY. In war, combatants exaggerate engagement results to boost fighting morale. The Communists continue their lies at every opportunity. Washington confirmed late last night that the destroyers had engaged in enemy action. Three of our sailors were wounded, their families have been notified. No U.S. personnel were killed. No U.S. ships were sunk."

Frank's name was not among the list of wounded sailors. Bert began to reread the story, but the paper shook uncontrollably. He let it fall to his side and leaned the length of his body against the cold brick store front to steady himself. Tears coursed through his stubby whiskers and dripped off his chin down to the gray concrete.

Damn it, I want my son home.

⚓   ⚓   ⚓

Weeks passed before any of the crew onboard the OZBOURN knew of the communist's propaganda account of the action, making it into their hometown newspapers.

But it was decades later, after I'd gotten enough years under my belt, before I could appreciate the horror those hours brought into my parents' lives. First hearing the frightening misinformation, and finally gaining the truth--I was alive.

Of course Mother always harbored a fear, and perhaps Dad also, that their youngster might someday fall into harm's way. Most parents forced those thoughts into the background, they couldn't bear to deal with the daily anxiety.

But at just seventeen and entering my life's greatest adventure, I viewed the military as a vehicle to independence. Combat, personal risk, and certainly fear of death, never held any conscious meaning--until four years into my enlistment, during those surreal moments in Wonson Harbor, when communist artillery locked my ship into their sights.

Even then, allaying Mom's or Dad's concerns didn't seem an issue. I just didn't get it.

From the instant I entered my local Navy Recruiter's office, other considerations crowded out any thoughts of why my country maintained a standing force made up of individuals like myself. My plate was full trying to process the changing parade of events in my new life, and mastering the art of buttoning thirteen buttons, two at a time.

COMING OF AGE
THE NAVY WAY

Teenage Salt--Boilerman Al Pugh,
snipe liberty buddy, U.S.S. OZBOURN

"Sol" Blessing
U.S.S. OZBOURN crew member
visiting Christmas Island

THE QUICKEST WAY OUT OF TOWN

The stretch of mowed grass and palm trees ran from Inglewood's City Hall several blocks down past Tom Kelley's house. Tucked in behind the old bandstand stage, the Navy Recruiting Office sat in the center of Grevillea Park, one of the remaining city concessions to the recent war effort. I waited quietly in the open doorway, apprehensive and unobserved, listening to one side of a telephone conversation.

"You bet your ass it's good shore duty. The best." The Navy recruiter, his desk name plate indicated a First Class Torpedoman, sat with his back toward me.

"Hell yes, I know we're behind our quota for this cycle. The chief in L.A. reminds me every morning."

On a colorful wall poster, mounted above the "no smoking" sign, two sailors enjoyed liberty somewhere in the Orient. White hats pushed to the backs of their heads, they strode out through a crowded alleyway-bazaar, garnished on both sides with exotic birds on perches and two wide-eyed, long-tailed monkeys tethered with leashes. Food stalls featured steaming unrecognizables and a threesome of sultry ladies, long slits up the sides of their silken dresses, were reclining sensuously against dim, dilapidated, doorways. Everything in the poster shouted, "IT'S PARTY TIME."

Now *that* was the kind of life I was scheming for.

The recruiter's telephone conversation brought me back. "Randy, the best part of this cushy assignment is break time at that Sunburst malt shop across from here, you know, up on the corner. Between the high school bobby soxers and that Cuban waitress, you saw her there last week, I'm throbbing like a steam engine. What's with that black mole on her cheek? Do you think it's real? I'm sure going to find out before my tour here is over."

He bent over and, with his free hand, pulled one of the new, long Pall Malls from an open pack tucked into the top of his black sock. Their extra length was the theme of an advertising blitz covering local billboards and the backs of every *Colliers* and *Saturday Evening Post* magazine for the past three months. He fished in his breast pocket for a lighter and lit up his smoke with an impressive flame that would have singed his eyebrows had he not cautiously snuck up to it from the side.

Exhaling the first deep drag, his words puffed into the phone's mouthpiece, "Me too. I'd kill to keep this billet forever."

Suddenly, as if sensing a presence behind him, he slid his castered chair back from the desk and spun around in one smooth motion.

"Hold on, I've got a customer. I'll call you back."

Without looking, he placed the black phone into its cradle and smiled directly up into my face--the same smile the Hoover vacuum cleaner salesman had tried on my mom through the screen of our front door.

It was my umpteenth visit. Usually the recruiter hadn't paid much attention to me. I was just another skinny kid who wore a white sailor's hat and collected brochures or begged for a poster to put up on the garage wall. I didn't have a bedroom wall of my own.

But on this day, when I told him I'd be reaching the magic age of seventeen in just two months, he turned on the charm.

"You bet. You'll have your choice of any one of these ratings," he gestured toward a wall poster I'd shown an interest in, displaying the logos of dozens of different Navy career specialties, "after you're out of boot camp and you've had a little time to settle in.

"Frank, let me tell you about Navy food. It's the best of all the services. No worry about ever having to eat C-Rations aboard ship. Always a clean, warm bunk and hot food. You can have seconds, even thirds. No problem. And Frank, *all* the milk you can drink. I mean it, no limit.

"Three hots and a cot, buddy. That's what the Navy can do for you. You'll be gone from this little Dogpatch town and on your own, wearing service dress blues like the fellas in that picture on the wall there. And doing business with all the ladies." He smiled and shot me a wink.

Leaning forward, he reached out, slid a chair toward me, and assumed a more serious tone, "You know, Frank, you're a minor. You're too young to enlist without your parents' consent. Now I'd be happy to talk to your mother and father about all the advantages the Navy offers a young fella like yourself. Or we can leave it up to you to do the selling." He nodded slowly and assumed a look that communicates understanding between male equals.

He didn't have to use his sales pitch to close me. W.W.II had just ended, but propaganda from the war years had taken hold of my teenage mind. I'd seen Gene Kelly and Frank Sinatra in *Anchors Aweigh*, a second and third time. John Wayne, Randolph Scott, Aldo

Ray, and every other male star in Hollywood appeared on the Granada Theater screen Saturday afternoons, confirming the fun I could expect, and the adventures I'd experience as a man in the military--the camaraderie, the excitement of travel to foreign ports, beautiful girls loving me in my new uniform.

. And the freedom! No more teachers nagging me to "work up to my ability," whatever that meant. No more yard work around our house every Saturday before being allowed to go meet my friends. I hated mowing that damn lawn more than all my other chores put together. I had blisters from squeezing the clippers around the edges of our flower beds. It took all of my 122 pounds to move the rusty old mower up and down one way, then, to satisfy my exacting stepfather, back and forth across in the other direction. The broken grass catcher slipped off every couple of yards and spilled the cuttings. I was the unhappiest kid in the world.

Now I had a chance to escape. Not just run away. This was more. That uniform would transform me from a boy into a man, an independent man. I could replace the lawn mower with.... maybe a Harley Davidson?

But I needed that signature on the consent form.

For the next two weeks I made my mother's life miserable, pleading and arguing. Finally, complaining I was "making her daft," she threw up her hands. I'd done it. She actually signed off on the consent form.

But she was, like all moms I suppose, concerned about the Navy overpowering her boy, "thrown in with all those mature men." I sat on the back steps hugging old Tire Biter and scratching his ears. My stepdad and mother talked in the kitchen, unaware I was within hearing distance.

"Larry, I'm afraid Frank's going to get swallowed up, trying to cope with all those older men bullying him around. My goodness, he's never been away from home more than a week at summer camp. He's hardly more than a child. And we're sending him off to military service? I'm really having second thoughts over this whole thing.

"You know, yesterday I noticed in the window of a house just two blocks down our street, one of those gold stars on a little white flag, like the ones we saw in windows during the war. She's a Gold Star Mother. Her son didn't come back! Don't you find that unnerving? It frightens me to death."

Not waiting for an answer, she powered on. "And don't tell me again that the war's over. World War I was over when World War II started--and it was even worse. I'm becoming unhinged. We *could* have another war.

"Larry, please speak to the person in charge when you take Frank for his induction. Ask him to look after Frank. Surely he'll recognize the situation and show some consideration."

My dog panted beside me, his dangling tongue limp out the side of his mouth like a strip of red ribbon. I moaned and looked into his glistening black eyes.

Oh brother. That will go over like a bull-frog in a punch bowl.

GOOD-BYE YARD WORK
--HELLO ADVENTURE

The pre-induction physical was like some nudist convention choreographed in Hell, only colder. The whole place gave me goose bumps.

I stood with seventy-four other prospective enlistees, completely naked, in a cavernous room deep inside the Federal Building in downtown Los Angeles . The scene was worse than the high school shower room after P.E. The cold marble floor had the same antiseptic odor as a men's room after mopping.

Even the benches were marble. I eased my naked buttocks onto a seat and immediately jumped up. In that brief moment of contact, before my brain could register C O L D, the icy granite shocked Mr. Johnson, and "my boys" retreated high up somewhere near my navel. No wonder no one else was resting on the polished stone seats.

I hoped my gymnastics had gone unnoticed, but some joker hissed, "Hey, Bones." I weighed 122 pounds. "I'll give you a quarter to warm me up a spot."

There was measured laughter from the people within hearing distance. No one was sure if it was okay to appear to be having fun. We soon found out. It was not.

We stood around waiting, curiously sneaking glances here and there, careful not to get caught appearing too interested in someone else's "business." *So much for the US History class lessons on Jefferson's writings about the equality of all men.*

A tall, tanned man wearing a freshly pressed khaki uniform with a tailored fit, strode to the center of the room. His clipboard, and the fact that he was the only one in the room dressed, labeled him an authority figure. He looked like a misplaced movie actor with his perfect white teeth and jet black hair combed straight back, parted just a bit off the center.

"All right, people, let's form up in one line. We're going to draw some blood."

Moans rose all around me.

"We'll also need a urine sample. See those bottles on the shelf across the room? After we take your blood, fill one up."

"From here?" a stage whisper from the kid with the long skinny face who had offered me a quarter. "What's he think my Roscoe is, a fire extinguisher?"

"AS YOU WERE," barked the man in the center of the room.

Three people in white smocks entered through a door in the far corner. Each carried a mug of coffee and a partially eaten donut. All were laughing. We'd missed the joke.

Their hands are full. How are they gonna do whatever doctor stuff they do?

"Good morning sir." The man in khakis greeted the lead doctor. "Are you ready to inspect them sunny-side up?"

"Yes, Chief. Get them into position."

The Chief began barking orders. "Okay, people, turn around and face the wall. Separate your feet the width of your shoulders, bend over and spread your cheeks. Remain in this position until you're told to stand up.

"Not those cheeks, Nimrod, THE CHEEKS OF YOUR BUTTOCKS.

"HOLD IT RIGHT THERE. Something funny here, son? You. The guy with the big grin, standing next to the stanchion. Yes, you. Come up here. NOW. MOVE IT."

I remained bent over, afraid to look behind me.

"What's so funny?" The chief's tone made me grateful I wasn't in the center of the room being dressed-down.

"Nothing," a nervous New York accent replied.

"I can't HEAR you."

"Nothing, SIR."

"Don't call me Sir. I work for a living. Now get back into that line and put a sock in it.

"Okay, people, everybody over. Don't be bashful. You've got to really spread those cheeks. Good. Now hold it like that while the doctors have a look-see."

I faced the wall with the others. I could only imagine the doctors' view as they walked from opposite ends of the line toward each other, inspecting, over the tops of their jelly donuts, seventy-five mooning teenagers. For what, I still don't know.

The physical exam lasted most of the day, with a break for lunch. Without much enthusiasm, I dressed with the others to go eat. Somehow lunch in the middle of that physical business seemed unappetizing. But down in the cafeteria the variety of offerings, and a government chit paying the bill, kick-started my usual teenage hunger.

16

Throughout the day I was poked, prodded, and quizzed. Every orifice looked into.

Our eyes were examined, teeth counted and their individual conditions recorded. The medical people seemed particularly interested in our feet. Evidently they wanted to insure we were able to march. "Flat feet could exclude you," one of the older nudies shared with those of us nearby.

"But we're going into the Navy," offered Long Face.

"Not if you don't pass this physical. Navy rejects go into the Army."

"Ours?" Standing beside me, my new acquaintance from Pico Rivera inquired in a voice only those near him heard.

Finally, after running in place for several minutes and having our hearts listened to, it was over. We dressed. The clothing restored some dignity. Now I could allow my eyes to scan normally, without forcing my line of vision above everyone's shoulders.

The movie actor, I had tagged him "Boston Blackie," made a final announcement. "Listen up. The next communication you receive will come from the Chief of Naval Personnel, Washington, DC. It will inform you where to report and at what time. Bring only the civilian clothing you wear, no other. Do not bring *any* medications, prescribed or otherwise. That includes aspirin or any poultice or snake oil remedy your granny may have tucked into your bag. The Navy will issue you everything you need. When you report, be prepared to continue on to your recruit training. You will not be returning home that day.

"Your training will probably take place in San Diego, California, but it could be Great Lakes Naval Training Center."

Great Lakes--travel across the country. Yes!

"I know you people all joined the Navy to see the world, but believe me, Great Lakes is no place to be in the winter. Pray for San Diego, sailors. You're dismissed."

Not returning home that day? It was actually happening.

I felt like a balloon whose string had been cut.

On November 29, 1946, in downtown Los Angeles, I raised my hand and swore the oath along with fifteen other city boys--young wise guys, Zoot-Suiters, hustlers, trouble-makers, and dropouts. But mostly just teenage adventurers.

To my relief, Larry had taken me aside as we entered the building. Reducing our stride, we walked toward the assembled group. His hand rested on the back of my neck, coordinating a slower pace.

17

He leaned toward me and said, "Son, believe me, it will be better if I don't say anything to the lieutenant about watching out for you. We won't tell your mom. Women just don't understand these things."

This guy might know more than I've been giving him credit for.

He stopped and came around in front of me, extending his hand. Until that day we had always kissed good-bye. This time we shook hands. He seemed in a hurry, turning and starting back toward the entrance. His voice cracked as he walked away, calling over his shoulder, "We'll come to visit you. Write your mother. You know how she worries."

It all hit me at once. I couldn't speak past the lump in my throat. I wanted to say something to let him know the gratitude I had never expressed. But his eyes had told me, when we shook hands, that he understood.

Before I knew it, we new recruits had joined others on the huge silver and blue Greyhound bus, headed for San Diego. I leaned back into my seat, believing I was prepared for boot camp because I had been to Boy Scout Camp during summers. I could handle whatever they threw at me.

So I thought. But nobody on that bus could have anticipated what the United States Navy had up her sleeve.

THE GAMES BEGIN

Disappointment awaited us at the Recruit Training Center in San Diego. Our formal training couldn't begin until there were enough of us to form a company of 120 men. We spent the next few days sitting around, enjoying the Southern California sun, resting for hours at a stretch on green benches worn shabby by thousands of W.W.II recruits before us. Until chow time we'd read comic books when we weren't policing the area under the watchful supervision of the duty petty-officer, searching for scraps of paper and parts of field-stripped cigarette butts.

We were directed to memorize the "General Orders" outlining the responsibilities of Navy watch standers, and a few days later began standing night fire watches in our barracks. We committed the General Orders to memory, but some of them were puzzling. "Salute all officers and standards not cased" gave me some trouble. But I didn't want to show my ignorance by asking what the heck *that* meant.

The anticipated recognition, to be gained by wearing a web duty-belt and carrying a night stick, soon wore thin once on watch. As the only person awake in the cavernous berthing compartment, I strolled the building, upstairs and down, checking into every remote part. Sounds of farting, snoring, and hacking made for a dull four hours. After an hour of my first mid-watch, midnight to 0400, I hoped I wouldn't see much of this watch-standing business during the rest of my enlistment. Oh, brother. How dumb can you be?

The smoking lamp was lit only at the bench area in front of the barracks. That meant we were allowed to smoke nowhere else but there. I had tried smoking in high school, sharing a cigarette around a small circle of pals, but I didn't really enjoy it as much as I did the "sophisticated" image I thought I presented. I had never owned a new pack of cigarettes.

Twice each day we were marched to the exchange where there were toiletries, magazines, candy, and ice cream. This got us off the benches and offered a little exercise, plus a break in the monotonous waiting. And we were given complimentary cigarettes in little packs of four. Free smokes, and the poster of John Wayne in his Camel ads, hooked most of us wannabe warriors within the first few days. Taking up smoking meant buying the obligatory Zippo lighter with its distinctive Navy logo, a supply of flints and a tin of Ronson lighter fluid. Hot Dog! Flipping out that Zippo and torching my smoke really gave me the feeling of having arrived.

In less than a week enough recruits arrived from other parts of the country to form our company. The new boys from the South were fun with their stories of stills and "white lightning." The fellas from Georgia, Tennessee and neighboring southern states kept us less mature West Coast youngsters entertained by trying to outdo each other spinning tall tales. Living in "dry" counties back home, they claimed the "old boys" would spit tobacco juice into the bottles of bootlegged "peach squeezin's" to brown 'em up, satisfying the visiting Yankees' preference for bourbon.

What the hell am I going to share with these guys? How my dog Jerry would chase me down the hill when I'd ride wedged inside an old car tire? That just won't hold-up against the South Carolina boy's story about "haystack humpin'."

With the forming of the company came the introduction of the two scariest characters ever to walk across the stage of my life--Chief Gunner's Mate Alvin Young and Chief Boatswain's Mate Kie Zikowski--our company commanders. I now had new parent figures.

For the first order of business, the chiefs took us to the barber shop. Four barbers would cut 120 heads in 92 minutes. As I watched the customers in chairs before me, I thought of the length of time required to regrow that hair falling to the floor. I remembered being eight years old, in the secrecy of our dirt-floored single garage behind the house, Wendell Fuller and I helped each other chop off our hair. Who needed barbers at twenty-five cents a session? In the semi-darkness, softened by diminished sunlight seeping past the edges of the two closed swinging front doors, we used scissors to scalp each other. Seemed like it took most of the third grade to grow back. At that rate my shipmates and I would be skinned well past our time in Boot Camp.

The floor of the barber shop was hidden by the scattered colors sheared from people who sat down as individuals, and in seconds their identities fell to the floor around their chairs. That was the idea--strip away all of your individuality. Trance-like, I watched the pompadours, duck tails and long sideburns drop. In complete shock I waited silently for my turn while the uninterested barbers carried on a four-way conversation as if they were alone in the room. We were just nameless pieces of meat moving through their *dis* assembly line.

"Want your sideburns?"

"Ye..."

"Catch 'em." The sheers sped upward. My sideburns flew off and out in an arc.

Only Sid Ballard, the New Jersey bookmaker's runner, ended up with a little semblance of length and form on the top of his head. We all wanted to know how he persuaded the barber to leave something.

"My brother Nathan was in the Navy during the war. He warned me about this slaughter house. Said when I was called to the chair to slip the man a quarter before I sat down. And not to let anyone see me do it."

I determined to stay close to Sid Ballard. I didn't want to miss anything else his brother's experiences could protect me from in the weeks ahead.

It was time to get rid of our civvies. The chiefs marched us to the clothing locker for uniforms. I felt the rush of excitement--this was what I'd waited for. Uniforms, along with our military haircuts, would move us into full Navy mode, my whole reason for leaving home.

Each of us took our turn standing on a raised platform while storekeepers flailed yellow tapes about our bodies, measuring us for everything from hats down to socks and shoes. As each finished a measurement, he called out the reading to an assistant recording at lightning speed.

"Waist, 32."

"I'm a 30."

"You'll grow into it."

We carried the paper lists of our recorded measurements down the long issuing line.

Elbow to elbow, we eased along the counter, manned on the opposite side by storekeepers who read our individual sheets, turned and removed uniform parts from the bins behind them. They slammed the items onto each man's quickly growing pile. The smell was of things new, and the number of items was overwhelming. Dungarees, dress blues, undress blues, whites, skivvies, black web belts, white web belts, brass buckles. *Why so many different types of the same thing?* Blue flat hats with "United States Navy" written in gold across the front on a silk band looked great with our new, heavy wool, peacoats. I removed one of the three white hats from my pile to try it on. It rested on my ears--too large. I risked asking, in a low voice, "Are you sure this is my size?"

"It will be, if your hair grows back. KEEP MOVING."

Work shoes, canvas shoes, dress shoes, bedding, with mattress covers that the storekeepers called "fart sacks", rounded out our seabags. Most of us were at an age where the word fart still elicited a snicker.

The final station in the long line had a storekeeper operating a punching machine that created our stiff, name stencils. He handed each man his stencils accompanied by a blue covered book--*The Bluejacket's Manual.*

"This is your bible, boy. All the readin' you'll be doin' for the next few, fun-filled, weeks. Move it. MOVE IT."

The Bluejacket's Manual codified *everything* a sailor would ever require to be a success at his job. It was the source from which we learned, among a thousand other things, how to create semaphore signals using hand-held flags. Later, each time we performed our calisthenics, we snapped out a routine, using our hands rather than the flags, A-through-Z. We'd shout out the letter names in unison as we physically demonstrated the signal. Soon the entire drill was etched in my memory.

Everyone in authority (that would be anyone other than a recruit) prodded us along with the concern one holds for cattle. Our newly issued gear was loosely folded and hung out everywhere as we fought to keep it all together. It wouldn't fit into the new seabags, even after filling our smaller ditty bags.

We hurried down the stairs and out of the building, struggling to keep up with the two chiefs who strutted out in front, leading the way toward our new barracks. Stopping to retrieve dropped items, nearly stumbling, we all took turns contributing to the comic scene.

With everyone finally inside, upper and lower bunks were assigned in alphabetical order, positioning me down the row a considerable distance from my new resource person, Sid Ballard. I'd have to seek opportunities to gather more of his brother's hints for making Navy life easier.

The next activity had the potential of a mass nightmare. It was time to stencil our names onto the inside of each item we had been issued. The danger here was, unfamiliar with the different pieces, a recruit might inadvertently stencil his name onto the outside, rendering the item unusable. The inks, both black and white, were the messiest stuff I'd ever handled and, of course, permanent. The chiefs really had their hands full directing so many of us greenhorns through the exercise. But they were up to it. While standing on the writing table in the center of the long dormitory, Chief Young explained the process in a manner that sounded scripted. Chief Zikowski added, "Any one of you shitbirds that ruins a piece of your new government clothing will see a picture of it on your first pay envelope."

We were shown how to tie our bars of soap, wet after showers, beneath the springs of our bunks to dry. This required using clothes-stops, string like cotton pieces we were issued for tying clothing onto the drying lines.

That first night together as a company, each man wore his new white skivvy shorts and shirt, and collapsed onto his rack, exhausted. We were all too high after the day's activities to fall asleep. A scratchy recording of a bugler blowing taps crackled out of load-speakers across the base. The distant sound came from all directions. Uncle Sam was telling thousands of boys "night-night." The fire watch turned off the lights.

But a long, restful sleep was not part of the plan. Before daybreak we were jolted out of our warm sacks by an ear splitting noise. Reveille was being performed by Chief Young. With the stub of a cigar clinched between his teeth, he rotated a night stick around the ribbed inside of an empty metal trash can at maximum RPMs. The stick paused and he bellowed, "REVEILLE. REVEILLE. HEAVE OUT. TRICE UP." The individual words were new to me, but their meaning left no room for confusion. I later learned the expression was a hold-over from the times of sleeping in strung hammocks. Over and over he attacked the can with the night stick.

What kind of an animal is this?

No wonder Mother always had a tough time getting me up in the morning. Wrong technique. Immediately, everyone's feet hit the cold barracks' floor. No sleepy-heads getting a couple of extra winks.

That morning marked the change of my lifestyle from playing pinball at Russ' Donut Shop back home, to hardball Navy style. My *new* life.

Chief Zikowski paraded, like a feisty rooster, down the line of bunks screaming, "Let go of your cocks and grab your socks! Form up outside in 12 minutes, clean skivvies, faces shaved, and ready to march to chow. And I don't want to see any peach fuzz on those rosy cheeks--put a blade in your new razor.

Chief Young added, "There's a special treat for the last man falling-in. Sailors, you don't want to be that last man."

My foggy brain tried to prioritize: which piece of my new clothing should I begin with? Where would I find it? Or should I go into the head and shave before dressing? *These guys mean business.*

I determined not to be the last man to formation, ever.

BOY SCOUTS AIN'T PRIOR SERVICE

Chill from the San Diego marine layer filled my nostrils with each inhaled breath. We formed up in six ranks and waited. Through the semi-darkness the base loud speakers crackled a recording of reveille. Wacky timing, we'd been awakened much earlier by Chief Young's night stick banging in the trash can.

The Chief removed his stogie, smiled and spit a direct hit into the butt kit at the bottom of the stairs. From his elevated position on the entry porch of the barracks, he half turned toward his shorter partner.

"Looks like we rolled 'em out a little early this morning, Mr. Zikowski."

Some business had to be completed before marching to chow. Chief Young explained we needed a "Recruit Petty Officer," a man from our ranks to be designated as the senior recruit. The job sounded good to me, I'd been the Senior Patrol Leader in my scout troop. This might get me out of some unpleasant details.

"Any of you men had prior military service?" Mr. Zikowski barked.

At this point I made my first tactical error. I raised my hand, along with one other man.

The chief asked the first man, "What service; how long; what rank?"

He answered smartly, "Army; 18 months; PFC, SIR."

I was asked the same question. Seeking to impress, I sounded off, "Boy Scouts, SIR. I am an Eagle Scout, SIR."

The two chiefs exploded in unison. They were bent over laughing uncontrollably. Had I missed something in the exchange? Possibly. These days I was experiencing a lot of confused feelings.

Chief Zikowski was the first to gain partial control and in his Brooklynese, one laughing word at a time, declared, "LA," his name for me, " Boy Scouts ain't prior service.

"Oh shit, Mr. Young, I give up on these clowns."

The gang at the CPO club must have roared that night over my story. The chiefs felt the first man better qualified. He was ordered to leave ranks and march us to chow. I was to stay in ranks and remain, as Mr. Zikowski was fond of saying, "California dog scrap."

I liked Navy chow. Desserts that were new to me, like prune whip and fish eye tapioca, headed my list. At breakfast, creamed chipped beef or ground beef in a tomato gravy were served onto your tray, poured from a large ladle atop a waiting piece of toast. A mess cook with a filled ladle suspended from each hand rasped to individuals as they approached, "Foreskins or shit on a shingle?" Many sailors complained about the food, but our newly appointed Recruit Petty Officer asked if he could have both.

Outside the mess hall we fell in and double-timed to the Personnel Office to have our pictures taken for ID Cards.

"No smiling, people. This is not your high school graduation picture."

The short kid from New Jersey inadvertently signed his new ID card in the wrong place.

"Manfredi, you Guinea bastard, you are not the 'Issuing Officer.' Are you?"

"NO, SIR, CHIEF SIR. Oh Geeze."

"Then, Pea-Brain, why did you sign in the Issuing Officer space? Look shithead, your signature goes on the front, like the Yeoman told you. Now he has to make you a new card."

Manny moaned "I didn't write my whole name, can't we just use some white-out?"

"Your whole name? Your hole name is 'butt hole.' Now get your ass back to that camera. PEOPLE, these official documents can have no corrections, erasures or strike-overs. Keep that in mind when you wise guys think about changing that date of birth to make yourself old enough to do business in some gin mill. You'll end up in the brig on piss and punk," the Navy's slang for bread and water.

"Now listen-up. While Petty Officer Justine is laminating your ID cards, we're going next door to get your dog tags made-up. Stay together and NO TALKING. Got that Manfredi? NO TALKING."

Even with the windows open, the small room was hot with stale air. A gray-haired First Class Carpenter's Mate rested on his elbows behind the counter.

"Hi, Ski," he greeted Chief Zikowsky.

"Hi, Whitey. What's the word?"

"Ain't out yet, Chief."

"This here cream of America's youth needs their dog tags. Watch the little guy from New Jersey." He pointed toward Manfredi. "He'll screw you up like a Christmas goose."

25

Manny tried to hide behind Able Tina, the East LA heavy weight prize fighter. We handed "Whitey" our information sheets, complete with our blood types and religions filled in. On his left sleeve, beneath his crow, Whitey wore seven long, red stripes. Hinkley, our guy with 18 months in the Army, explained in a whisper that each 'hash mark' meant 4 years of service.

"But how come he has his crow on the wrong sleeve?" someone wondered out loud.

"Our chiefs have 'right arm rates,' this guy has a left arm rate," our new Recruit Petty Officer enlightened us.

I decided I'd try to figure that one out later and moved down just past the First Class. He handed me two metal dog tags attached to a beaded chain. I noticed little indentations on the two ends of each stamped oval and asked, "Sir, what are these niches?"

"Son, you don't call First Class Petty Officers 'sir.' The indentations are there so when they find you, dead, they open your mouth and position a dog tag between your teeth. That way those smelly decomposing gasses can escape and you won't look all blown up. Move it down now."

This is the first civil fella I've met in the past week and a half. How refreshing.

I hope he isn't serious about the gasses.

"All right Hinkley, double time 'em to the armory."

"The armory. Our guns. We're going to get guns!" Excitement rippled throughout the trotting ranks.

Mr. Young calmed us down. "You're going to be issued your PIECE. Got it? PIECE. Your 'gun'--that's something else."

At the armory we were introduced to Chief Gunner's Mate Turpin. "They're all yours, Bull Dog," Chief Zikowski joined Chief Young over to the side and they lit skinny cigars.

Like many older Navy men, Chief Gunners Mate Turpin's stomach paunched out so far he couldn't possibly see his shoes. His web belt was slung down around the "melon" and secured just above his crotch, the glint from its shiny brass buckle barely visible. Because his trousers were low at the waist, they broke at his shoes into deep indents. In his neatly pressed, short sleeved khaki shirt, I could see that every inch of his arms, right down to his wrists, was covered with tattoos. From the distance, his arms appeared solid blue.

While we stood at parade rest, Chief Turpin began to drone a speech he'd probably delivered, to recruits before us, hundreds of times.

"In a minute you will enter the armory." He motioned over his shoulder. "The armory is a no bullshit place. We store weapons here. Weapons are designed to kill people. So listen up.

"You will be issued a bolt action, Springfield ought-three. These are old World War I pieces. You will not fire them, but you will keep your piece in ready condition, cleaned and oiled. Later in your training you will go to the range and fire M1's and .45's.

"When you return these weapons to me, before you leave Boot Camp, they had damn well better be in the shape you've received them. If you drop this piece you will damage it. Dropping the piece will result in you sleeping with it, beside you, under the covers, for so long you'll think she's your old lady. Never lay it down, anywhere, except to clean it. When outdoors, if it must leave your hands, stack your piece with two others in a tripod fashion. DO NOT DROP THIS PIECE, or your ass is grass and I'm the lawn mower.

"Always consider a weapon armed. Handle it accordingly. If I see any of you jerkoffs pointing that weapon at anybody, I will stick it up your ass and cap off a round. There's only one time you ever point a weapon at someone.

"Now file in, single file, no talking. Petty Officer McGiver will issue you your piece." He raised his voice, "Here they come Jim, I hope you're ready for 'em."

"No sweat, you bet, Chief," a faceless voice replied from somewhere inside the armory.

I was a city boy. There were no guns in my home. I had never fired a gun. I *had* secretly handled Mr. Fitzgerald's .22 rifle after school one day, when Jack and I were alone in his house. Now I was holding one I would carry every day.

Back in ranks, with our guns, we waited, excited, for the last man to leave the armory.

"One more word from me," the Chief Gunner's Mate got our attention again, "then I'll turn you back to Chiefs Young and Zikowski.

"Hold up your piece in your right hand. In your right hand, shitbird. The one you throw the ball with." Chief Turpin moaned.

"Man-fred-i," Chief Zikowski sang the syllables. Manfredi changed hands.

Chief Turpin paused and ran his eyes over the assembly, registering scorn. "That's right."

We were as still as a photograph.

"Now grab your dick with your left hand and repeat after me.

"This is my piece." He shook the ought-three in his right hand.

Everyone responded.

Not satisfied, Chief Turpin screamed, "I can't HEAR you. AGAIN."

We all screamed back, "THIS IS MY PIECE," as we shook the ought-threes in our right hands.

"Good. Now. This is my gun." He shook his left hand that had enclosed his privates.

"Let's hear it."

"THIS IS MY GUN!" We were getting caught-up in the silliness.

"Now we're going to put it all together. Listen. Then repeat. And I want to HEAR ya. Then you can get the hell out of here.

"This is my gun. This is my piece. I shoot with my gun. I fire my piece. ROAR IT OUT, SAILORS."

We responded and Chief Turpin seemed pleased. He smiled and nodded his red face up and down.

"Now, I don't ever wanna to hear any of you refer to this weapon again as a gun. Give it to me one more time."

We filled our right and left hands and screamed one last time, "This is my GUN. This is my PIECE. I shoot with my GUN. I FIRE my piece."

Nothing about these procedures reminded me much of school, teachers, nor learning classroom lessons, but "Bull Dog" could have taught me the square-root algorithm just using his intimidation.

After being shown how to hold our *pieces* while marching, we put them onto our right shoulders and stepped out toward the barracks. Marching along, I felt every inch a fulfilled military man.

We arranged clothes-stops beneath the bottom bunks to suspend our pieces off the floor while indoors. Chief Young barked, "With another man, study the Manual of Arms illustrated in your *Blue Jacket's Manual*. With your piece, each of you practice 'right shoulder arms,' 'present arms,' and 'parade rest,' while the other observes.

"Also review the seabag layout for tomorrow's inspection. Your clothing will be clean, rolled and tied with clothes-stops--tighter than a bull's ass in fly time, or you'll spend the weekend at the clothes-washing racks with a kieyie brush."

Tomorrow I'll really get acquainted with my piece.

My piece. Piece. I'm going to have to remember that.

To prepare us for life aboard ship, where space is a premium, part of our training involved rolling and tying our trousers and jumpers to minimize individual storage space. We would buddy-up, straddling a

28

bench in the barracks. Facing each other, one man held the end of a pair of trousers tightly while the other rolled his end toward the holder. We'd continue until each man's entire seabag was ready for inspection. These rolls were *very* tight, with the stenciled name of the owner exposed on the hem. They were uniform on one end, as if cut with a sharp knife. For inspection we would lay all of our gear on individual mattress covers, placed on the deck, every item in its designated position--*exactly* as illustrated in our *Blue Jacket's Manual*.

During the next morning's seabag inspection, I stood next to my gear, laid out near my rack. Mr. Young stopped before my display and picked up a pair of rolled white trousers.

Holding one end and shaking the roll as if it were rubber, he proceeded to beat me about the upper body with it while roaring, "Mr. Zikowski, look at this shit. This looks like my dick on a Monday morning."

He attacked me like a madman, jamming the end of the trouser roll deep into my abdomen, knocking the wind out of me and forcing me to bend over.

I'd never heard a grown man, especially an authority figure, use that kind of language. My mom would have liked to wash his mouth with soap. It really shocked me. Or was it the combination of the yelling and the pummeling? And, I could make no connection with the "Monday morning" business.

The two of them struck out down the inspection line, kicking and throwing our clothing about like madmen. They hollered and screamed at us "boots" their displeasure with the appearance of our gear. We stood ram-rod, our shaved heads pink and shining with nervous perspiration.

When dismissed, everyone ran to the head, trying to insure getting a commode before they were all occupied. That's how upset we were.

Our entire unit of "shitbirds," as the two company commanders referred to us, was highballing its way into manhood. We had each figured out that crossing either of these two characters would mean our worst nightmare.

They soon validated our fears.

KICKIN' ASS AND TAKIN' NAMES

The two company commanders trooped the line, stopping periodically to berate one of us. Mister Young stopped before me and moved his head around to inspect my face from every angle. I held my breath. Finally he declared, "You did not shave this morning."

"I do not shave, sir," I replied.

"The Navy issued you a razor. Use it. Shave tomorrow and every morning. Keep that fuzz off."

"Yes SIR." *Swell, last week I started smoking. Now I start shaving. Welcome to manhood.* The two of them continued down the ranks, watching for men smiling or looking around, rather than forward at attention. Unshined shoes, Irish pennants, those threads that sometimes hang from seams, buckles not polished or not buckled "brass on brass," white hats not squared evenly on the top of your head or, heaven help you, a dirty skivvy shirt. That earned special attention.

Chief Zikowski swaggered down the ranks we'd formed on the black-top drill area. Sticking his index finger under the collar of a skivvy shirt, he would pull it toward him and expose the inside. Everyone held his breath, waiting for the outburst. He didn't disappoint us. "You crumb. You filthy scum. You shitbirds will be scrubbing this grinder with your tooth brushes if you can't wear clean clothing. Every day you will put on clean clothing!"

The message was beginning to settle in.

Back at the barracks we fell in beneath the giant clothes lines that punctuated the open space separating dozens of barracks. They resembled May poles with their lines streaming down from the top. Our two leaders stood, elevated before us on the steps that led inside, and shared their thoughts at the top of their voices.

"Things didn't look good out there today, did they Mr. Young?"

"No, they did not, Mr. Zikowski. That shitbird Lowery will have to have a "kieyie party" to get himself scrubbed down nice and clean, since he can't take care of it himself." The kieyie brush was a 6 inch, wood backed, stiff bristled brush that was issued to each of us for scrubbing our clothing. We suspended it to dry, using a clothes-stop, next to our soap bars, beneath our bunk springs. A kieyie party meant that a group of men took an individual into the showers and scrubbed him with their brushes until his body was ruby red.

The next few minutes were likely to become seaman recruit Leroy Lowrey's most agonizing lifelong memory. A chubby lad from Oklahoma, he took a lot of ribbing and heat from the company commanders. Now he had earned us bad marks at the personnel inspection. The chiefs were unhappy and that always meant trouble for somebody, or everybody.

"Lowrey, you Oklahoma shitbird, get your fat ass up onto this porch.

"Turn around and face your shipmates, you filthy crumb. I'll bet your skivvy shorts are dirty too, just like your shirt. Drop your pants. You heard me shitbird drop those pants NOW!"

Oh my gawd. The poor guy.

"Now take off your shorts."

"But Chief..."

"Don't give me that 'but chief' shit; take them off NOW!" Chief Young took Leroy's shorts and manipulated them around to expose the inner rear. "Look at this, Chief Zikowski, hashmarks on his skivvies. I figured as much."

Chief Young then performed a little exercise that I, and I know Leroy too, have never forgotten. He worked the shorts around until he had formed a protrusion, with the "hashmarks" at the very forward part of the extension. "Open your mouth, you son-of-a-bitch."

Leroy moved like a man in a trance. He had been standing at attention before the company, fully exposed from the waist down, for some minutes now. He obediently opened his mouth wide while his eyes were fixed straight ahead. Chief Young rammed the offensive section of the shorts into the gaping target.

"Now chew that. Every day your skivvies are not clean, this is going to be the drill. Understood, sailors?"

"YES SIR," we screamed in unison.

We stood at rigid attention, numb with shock. It was so quiet you could have heard a mouse pissin' on cotton.

Leroy obeyed orders. After half a dozen chomps, he mumbled past the shorts, "How long do I do this?"

From either side of him the two Company Commanders leaned toward his face and screamed in unison. "Until I tell you to stop."

The "chiefs from hell" were doing what they did best--teaching lessons.

One hundred twenty young men had been correct. We were independent now, on our own, and no longer had to do what our unreasonable parents and school teachers demanded.

31

But we had new parents and teachers now, and no one questioned *their* directions.

Our chiefs were very interested in our personal hygiene. After being together for a week we had our first "short-arm" inspection. I don't think my mother would have signed the papers if she'd been aware I would be subjected to this old military ritual, performed in an open setting. Compound this with the gutter language from Zikowski and Young, and it's a given she'd want me out of there. And at this point in my short career, I'd have gone with her.

For the uninitiated, a short-arm inspection requires participants lining up and one at a time approaching a seated hospital corpsman. The subject drops his pants and shorts and when directed, "milks it down." The corpsman, with flashlight in hand, watches for any discharge. Then, shining the flashlight around the entire pubic area, examines for crabs (another new one for me) and/or visible sores. Hence the examiner's nickname, "Pecker Checker."

I made a mental note to remove Hospital Corpsman from my list of potential Navy career paths.

Weeks passed and I suppose the Navy figured we needed a little treat before we all suffered nervous breakdowns. Our first liberty was announced, but no one went into town before viewing the traditional "VD Movies." I gave the Navy credit. There was some professional acting up there on the screen. I recognized some of the characters on the screen from "B" Westerns I'd seen at home. There was some humor, but I suppose most of our laughter was of the nervous sort, caused by our discomfort seeing this slice of life for the first time. The use of a prophylactic kit was illustrated, in its entirety, with a live actor.

The laughing stopped when the actor removed a tube from a small package printed with the nostalgic W.W.I name "Doughboy."

I wondered if they were left over from 1917?

Unscrewing the top from the tube, he inserted the end into his penis. A moan went up in the darkened theater. After squeezing out the contents, the tube was removed. The Academy Award performance ended with the star holding the end of his Johnson, while, with his free hand he externally directed the contents along the length of his urinary canal. All of this done while he sat on a bicycle seat style contraption at a "VD Station." The exercise was followed by some real footage of male and female private areas infected with ugly sores or discharging disgusting fluids.

I got the message. Another lesson learned. I never dreamed this sex business involved all the craziness.

We were told there were VD Stations at the Tijuana border, in the event we purchased more than the traditional wallet and large finger ring, so popular in Mexico with the tourists. The Navy medical representative cautioned that the best method was to carry a pro kit and use it immediately after sex.

"Condoms are available at the liberty gate. Use 'em!" we were directed. Posters in the heads reminded viewers to "Put it on before you put it in." Match book covers advertised, "Caution. Use cover. Don't get burned." Some of my more creative shipmates designed their own slogans. The effeminate Robin Wells surprised us with, "Don't be silly, protect your Willie," while "Big Ben" Washington followed in his usual form with, "Cover your stump before you hump."

This was more laughs than my high school sex education class.

CINDERELLA LIBERTY

The excitement of that first liberty remains a vivid memory. New Dress Blues, wool, with a smell that was, well, special, good, Navy. The jumper was without insignia or rating, only the seaman's stripe circling the right shoulder. Slick sleeves. No suggestion of rank since we were, as Chief Zikowski often reminded us, "lower than whale shit." But the white triple piping and two stars on the collar still made us stand out as men-o'wars-men. The thirteen trouser buttons, each with its small anchor insignia, completed the nautical costume we had all yearned to show off in town.

Chief Young taught us to dampen our thirty-inch square silk neckerchiefs and, with a partner, hold the four corners and waft up and down with a snap until the wrinkles disappeared. Hours of spit shining had brought each man's liberty shoes, with their clean, new leather soles, to a mirror finish. Everyone had his own technique for guaranteeing an inspection-perfect shine. Fail inspection -- no liberty. There was no concern over clean skivvies. We had learned that lesson well. And interestingly, no one razzed Leroy any longer. We were all bonded brothers now.

After the chiefs inspected each of us outside the barracks, we marched to the reviewing field. There, in formations by companies, was the entire enrollment of the Naval Training Center. The Navy band was playing *The Colonel Bogey March* as we wheeled onto the grinder to take our position before the reviewing stand.

We smartly swung our arms, and with a proud bounce in our step sang, to ourselves, our made-up words to *Colonel Bogey*, "Horseshit, it makes the grass grow green. Horseshit, ..."

The different company commanders reported. The base commander introduced some dignitaries and recognized several companies for outstanding performance during the past week. Ribbons were awarded to fly from the winning companies' standards. Our company hadn't been in existence long enough to qualify for any commendations.

Up in the review stand, the senior officers rose.

"Pass in review," barked over the loud speaker.

The company commanders marched their wards in review. As we approached the stand, chief Zikowski barked.

"Eyes right."

The band was playing my favorite march, *Stars and Stripes Forever*. For the first time in my rebellious teenage life, I felt the pride of belonging to something worthwhile, something with a grand tradition. Finally my life was settling into a direction.

Downtown San Diego in 1946 was still geared for wartime business. First stop was the USO for homemade cookies and playing the free juke box with Glenn Miller's *Pennsylvania 6-5000* or Benny Goodman's *And the Angels Sing*. And drinking lots of cold milk. We were acting like the seventeen year olds we were and, of course, this activity didn't require any of that goofy Doughboy Pro Kit business.

Next, on to visit the arcades on Broadway. Pitch men, and women, vied to separate us from our money with bets on interesting skills like covering the interior of a circle with three hand-dropped disks.

"Just take a look. See how easy it is?"

The wagers could be substantial for throwing darts at balloons, tossing coins into saucers or shooting .22 rifles down an encased tunnel to a target, returned by a pulley so you could see why you were unsuccessful.

"Here Hawkeye, take it back to the ship with ya." A target souvenir of your close win.

We each bought some flashy memento. What new navy recruit didn't get his mother back in Topeka a beautiful fringed pillow with gold fabric and the words "Mother" or "San Diego California" printed in bilious lavender script across the front?

We had been paid and the $30, hidden in the secure inside pocket of my jumper, was the most discretionary money I had ever held. I had my shopping list firm in my mind, and the first item of business was a tattoo. I had begged my mother to let me get inked while I was still in school and now damn it, if I wanted one, I'd get one. I'd get 6, if I wanted.

I decided on my forearm for the location, so it would be more easily seen. An eagle pulling a banner from his beak with "U.S.N." Just for good measure, in case I was out of uniform and some observer challenged my Navy involvement, I had my service number inked in above the majestic bird, just to make it official.

After our Cinderella Liberty, expiring on the base at midnight, we gathered in the barracks to compare experiences. Bandages came off new tattoos and we shared their designs along with other purchases.

Casper "Slim" Waldritch was a six foot, four inch, moonshiner's son from Jonesboro, Arkansas. He was so thin, his issued uniforms had required the Navy to perform special tailoring. His shape looked like he'd been squeezed from a tooth paste tube.

"Lookie here," sang Slim as he dramatically, slowly, pulled from his pocket a silver knife with ebony handle inlays. Flipping a lever, the shiny blade charged forward. Our eyes opened wide.

One of the older fellows commented, "That there is illegal. If they see it they'll take it and put you on report. What the hell do you want a toad sticker like that for anyway?"

With that Slim reached into his other pocket and brought out a half-dollar. Tossing it onto the table with his left hand, he brought his right hand down through a high arc and drove the knife point right through the coin.

Looking up smilingly at the challenger he boasted, "I got everything now that I ever wanted. A gun at home, a knife with me here--everything."

I was happy with my first liberty, too.

THE ANCHOR IS AWEIGH

The dark blue government bus passed through the main gate, out from the Recruit Training Center in San Diego. Every newly graduated "boot" let out a cheer. Smart aleck comments about never coming back, or kissing a part of our anatomy, were offered by excited passengers, each trying to outdo the other with outrageousness. Then, spontaneously, as if on cue, this bus load of kids in their new dress blues burst out singing *Anchor's Aweigh*, just like in some movie.

We were all headed for our first duty assignment, Naval Air Station, Corpus Christi, Texas. With my seabag packed, I slid the heavy tan envelope containing my orders, pay record, service and medical records, deep inside the front of my trousers, and covered it with my jumper. My train ticket and meal vouchers went into a new, hand tooled, "genuine cowhide" wallet. This was to be my first time out of California, my first train ride.

I had boarded the bus giddy with excitement. For the best view during the short ride to the Santa Fe depot at the foot of Broadway, I took the aisle seat behind the driver.

No longer a "slick sleeve," I was now Seaman Second Class *and* I wore a "designated striker" badge above my new stripes. I loved my job. I loved my country. I was ready for anything.

The bus stopped across the street from the Santa Fe train depot in downtown San Diego. I was first off and pushed my seabag ahead of me out the door. It was heavy with everything I owned. After descending the steps, I grasped the seabag by its top and slung it over my shoulder. Not onto my shoulder, over my shoulder. It landed on the sidewalk behind me. But I was still holding on. I landed on the sidewalk, flat on my back. The bus passengers roared. At 127 pounds, I just couldn't handle those heavy maneuvers. I jumped to my feet, gathered up my seabag and hurried toward the depot to lose myself in the crowd.

On the trip through Texas we played cards, tried to top each other's jokes, and teased back and forth the way seventeen year olds do. But we were sailors. Sailors had a reputation to uphold, even if we were teenagers.

A knowledgeable "older" shipmate tipped a porter to bring beers for everyone. My first long neck. It was wonderful drinking like a grown man, rather than sneaking a bottle around a circle of boys in somebody's half-lit garage.

Even now, years later, every time I hold a cold, long-neck that train ride replays in my head.

Day two on the train, Ralston, the West Virginia coal-miner-turned-Navy-Seaman, came up to our car and informed everyone there was a "hooker" three cars back.

"She's with a little boy, but she's hot to trot!" he announced. "She put the make on Hobart."

I was next to a window, sitting beside Jimmy Watts and watching the open plains pass, enjoying the view from the unfamiliar backwards position. I felt a nudge at my side and Jimmy challenged, "Let's go check it out, Spit."

This was a new one on me, but I tailed along.

We didn't have any trouble finding her. She had her deep-red lips wrapped around the neck of a bottle of orange drink. One bare leg was hiked up onto the arm rest of the chair in front of her, her dress buried down between her widely spread legs. A small boy, with a missing shoe, was stretched out on the seat beside her, fast asleep. His foot barely held its little sock, half pulled-off. One high-top, black tennis shoe was on the foot tucked beneath him, the other on the floor.

The sticky heat had straightened her lifeless hair and brought it down close to her head with only a suggestion of curls. Three buttons of her print dress were open, allowing some ventilation, I supposed--and plenty of exposure. She looked about my mother's age, which put me off a bit. But Jimmy carried on, acting like he knew the drill from a hundred past experiences.

"Where y'all from, sweet cheeks?" Jimmy teased.

"San Antone soldier, and the name's Flo." Glancing back toward me, she purred, "What you and your little pal up to?" Little Pal set the record straight, "We're sailors, not soldiers." Now I could leave the next few lines to Jimmy. He leaned over so nearby passengers wouldn't hear, "You know, Peaches, I'm feelin' so wiggly. Think anybody in this neighborhood's turnin' tricks?"

Without moving her head, only her eyes, Flo looked to both sides and smilingly offered, "Who wants to know?"

It was my turn. I knew I would have to contribute if I was ever to face the others later. *But what do you say to a hussy like this?*

"How much, how much for all night?" I tried to appear comfortable.

Flo broke into a big smile and looked from my face to Jimmy's face then back to my face again and cackled, "You fellas just work for the Navy, you don't own it." She took another pull from the orange drink and the youngster stirred in his seat.

Jimmy bantered, "Well, if you're ever in Corpus Christi, Honey, look me up--Seaman Second Class, Non Swimmer, Jimmy Watts." Tossing her a wink, "I'll buy ya an orange drink."

I cleverly offered, "See ya," and we both hurriedly turned and swaggered up the aisle toward our own car. I was holding back a laugh so hard that air was bubbling out through my eye lids. I opened the door that led us out into the area between two cars. It slammed closed behind us with a whoosh and we stood alone, facing each other in the noise of the wind and clacking wheels. Together we let out a warhoop.

We didn't need to say it. We were inexperienced kids in men's clothing. But we had pushed the envelope, danced close enough to the flame to satisfy our curiosity--for the moment. Holding onto each other's shoulders with both hands, we bent over laughing till we cried.

On the Odyssey from San Diego to Corpus Christi, I ate in the dining car, slept in a Pullman berth, flirted with women and had a grand old time.

This Navy business was okay.

Okay, that was, until the first day aboard at Corpus Christi Naval Air Station.

SEAMAN SECOND CLASS, NON-SWIMMER

The author

TWO STEPS BACKWARD

I'd never thought much about it, but even Naval Air Stations have lawns and landscaping. That fact brought with it a demonstration of the lesson, "rank has its privilege," or in my case lack of privilege. I enlisted in the Navy to serve four years, not just to do and see exciting things, but to get away from chores at home--yard work. What I got was an assignment to Grounds Maintenance.

The extensive lawns on the base looked as though they hadn't seen fertilizer since seeding. Sporadic watering left them a neglected patchwork of light yellow-green, like drying corn silk, with isolated patches of darker green that only nature could explain. The Navy, however, did understand keeping the grass trimmed. It would be mowed and edged regularly. That was to be my job. Yard work. Lawn mowing. In the Navy only four months, I found myself back behind a stinking lawn mower. From the first minute I grasped the handles and pushed against the beast I schemed to be transferred.

At morning quarters we'd each yell "Yo" when our names were called. Then came the dreary military style announcements. But the longer the announcements took, the less I would be cutting, clipping, mowing, and raking.

Now the uniform of the day is undress whites. Dungarees for work details.

It has come to the attention of the Executive Officer that some individuals are not wearing caps when out-of-doors. Remain covered or face disciplinary action.

All personnel are reminded that allowing yourself to become sunburned is a court martial offense. Take precautions in this hot sun. Shirts are to remain on during work details.

Request Mast 0830.

Sick call 0900.

Dismissed. Ship's company turn-to.

I would fall out and slowly stroll, alone, to the maintenance shed located at the far side of the base. This was good for eighteen minutes. After assembling my garden tools and the push style lawn mower, eleven more minutes, I found a concealed spot to hide-out and wait for noon chow.

The first order of business when hiding-out behind thick bushes was to prepare for the possibility of discovery. I'd fill a bucket half full

41

of bush trimmings. With a hand trowel I'd loosen and pull enough weeds to fill the remainder of the bucket, making sure to pile them over the rim. Once concealed, I settled into the comic or paperback I'd stashed in my rear pocket, a thin one which didn't bulge and draw attention. If approached while hiding, I planned to wait until the enemy was about twenty feet away, gather up my bucket and trowel, and proceed to crawl out toward him as if I'd been cleaning the area behind the shrubs.

"Som bitch, sure hot ain't it. What's up?" I was ready.

Afternoons on the Gulf Coast were the worst because the temperature was much higher when the sun was well overhead. That required a hideout with overhead shade, a place to wait for 1630, time to secure from the day's work.

The Navy called this disappearing act " Shirking Duty." No one had discovered me while I hid. However, my division leading petty officer had described, on the charge sheet when he placed me on report, that he frequently couldn't locate me.

On this particular day, when I returned from hiding to lock up my equipment, he was waiting at the maintenance shed with the completed charge sheet in his hand. He had spent the afternoon searching for me, he said, with no success.

Exasperated, he thrust the paperwork toward me, "Read this. Sign it. Captain's mast is at 0900. Report tomorrow after quarters. Wear your dress whites."

"And Spittle, don't try to bullshit the Old Man. He's heard it all. He'll hang your ass if you try to jerk him around."

When I shared my misfortune with my shipmates at chow that evening, they offered all kinds of advice.

"Iron your whites and make sure they're clean."

"Get a regulation hair cut."

And the best one, "Wear your ribbons."

I had been awarded one medal, the World War II Victory Medal. It was given to everyone who served within a prescribed time frame. We thought of it as something of a joke because it was so automatic. Dress up and show up sort of thing. We referred to it as "Alive in '45." No one ever wore it unless there were other ribbons to accompany it.

The next morning I wore it, for the first time, all alone on my left breast. I couldn't imagine what possible influence this little multi-colored bar could have on the skipper's decision. But I'd try anything. At quarters I stood out among the others, dressed in my whites. Everyone else wore working dungarees. They razzed me, suggesting punishment from confinement, reduction in rank--I was already at the bottom, restriction to base, extra duty, or a fine. I prayed for a reprimand.

Strange how in moments of stress we sometimes make observations that otherwise would go unnoticed. At mast I realized that the officers, all being fliers, wore brown shoes with their khaki uniforms. The rest of the Navy wore black shoes with their khakis. This added another item to the list of Things Different About 'Airedales,' as we referred to anyone in Naval Air.

The first man called before the captain was charged with "Absent over liberty for three days."

Stern, the no nonsense Captain demanded, "Where were you?"

Sporting a black eye, scuffed red hands, and appearing on the verge of collapsing, the sailor moaned, "Matamoros, Mexico, Sir."

"Deck Court Martial." The Captain motioned the Master-at-Arms to take the man away, probably afraid he might lose his breakfast onto the blue carpeting.

Second man.

"Disrespect toward a superior officer. What exactly did you say to Lieutenant Sandsom when he directed you to purchase regulation, non-bell-bottomed, trousers?"

"Nothing, Captain. I wasn't talking to the Lieutenant. I had turned around and was walking away. I even saluted him."

"But Lieutenant Sandsorm indicates you were disrespectful in your manner of speech. What exactly, then, did you *not* say to him?"

"I was talking to myself. I said, 'When donkeys fly. When donkeys fly out my ass.'" He was barely audible.

"I didn't quite hear that. Please repeat it."

"When donkeys fly out my ass. Sir."

"Tell me son, where does an expression such as that originate?"

"Greenville, Sir. Greenville, Mississippi."

"Three days confinement on bread and water."

My turn.

The captain looked down at the charge sheet the yeoman placed before him on the lectern and read aloud. "Shirking duty." His face showed no emotion as he raised his eyes to mine. "Seaman Spittle, this is a large reservation. All personnel cannot be directly supervised every moment. I expect you to be where you have been directed, performing the job you have been assigned. Do you feel that your leading petty officer did not understand the situation when he put you on report?"

Here was my chance, if there was one.

"There is no excuse for me not doing my work." I paused to catch my breath. I was gathering my thoughts to begin the explanation of how I hated the assignment and how that took away my motivation to perform in my usual way. Good work history, conscientious, reliable, give me a break I'm a good guy--those sorts of things. I paused too long. The skipper was left with only hearing the part about "no excuse," if he even heard that. He was into his "dispensing swift justice" mode before I could outline my extenuating circumstances.

"I am awarding you twelve hours of extra duty." He wrote some notes onto the charge sheet, "to be performed this Saturday and Sunday. You will report to the Chief Cook at the galley for two hours after each of the six weekend meals."

His steel eyes drilled into mine. "Spittle, do not appear before me again. Understood?"

"Yes sir." I decided there is a universal law in the world for fathers and commanding officers. You can't play with your friends on the weekend until the damn lawns are mowed.

GIVE ME LIBERTY

The audible click alerted every experienced ear to stand by for an announcement over the base public address system. A bugle sounded colors. All personnel out of doors stopped, faced the direction of the flagstaff, and saluted the hoisting of the flag until the final note faded.

"Now hear this. Now hear this. Starboard section air bedding. All mattresses, pillows and blankets are to be removed from barracks by 0810."

If we could find them. Who needed blankets in this twenty-four hour a day tropical sauna? Half the crew gathered the bedding from their bunks and hung it in the sunshine. Tomorrow the port section would air bedding. Then we'd all have nice, fresh, lice-free blankets, mattress covers, mattresses and pillows.

Heat and the humid climate of the Texas Gulf Coast, compounded by my lousy work assignment, kept me longing for somewhere better. Liberty shoes, left in my locker, grew green with mold on their inner soles by the time I wore them next.

Any physical movement brought profuse sweating. Body parts that rubbed against one another chafed and were constantly irritated. Like all the lawn maintenance men, I walked with spread legs, like a range rider from Montana. "Jock itch," red and raw, flamed down my inner thighs, half way to my knees. "Athlete's-foot" caused angry canyon-like cracks between every pair of toes except in the space next to the big one, where a little air was able to sneak in. Regardless of the number of showers, the problems persisted. Discomfort was the order of the day.

Dewitt Raleigh's mother was a practical nurse in Mobile. After she received his distress call, she wrote about the wonders of petroleum jelly. We were disappointed that, in her excitement to come to our rescue, she neglected to include her regular batch of raisin cookies. But the proposed remedy was better than any cookies.

Each of us bought a pint jar of Vaseline petroleum jelly, raced back to the barracks and applied it liberally everywhere there was friction. We had found a miracle drug. And, as a bonus, it worked beautifully to keep my hair in place.

The following week, I was shaving at a bank of sinks lining the wall of the large, wide-open head. I noticed Duane Willoughsby standing in front of a sink beside me, nude. I cautiously glanced at him in my mirror (one could quickly get an unwelcome reputation checking out naked guys in the head). I had just finished grooming my hair with the new petroleum jelly.

Wayne had gone to junior college for a year and I wanted to see what this sophisticated role model put on *his* hair. Digging into his toilet kit, he produced a tall, slim bottle--Brill Cream. When he laughed out loud to no one in particular, and sung "A little dab'll do ya," I recalled the current radio commercial. Since the eighth grade I had been using a rose scented, pale, pink oil. It left a sheen everywhere it made contact and migrated down from my hairline during hot days.

After grooming his hair, Duane really got my attention when he held a small, flat jar full of white ointment in his left hand. He put his right fingers into the jar, then spread the contents under his left arm, changed hands, and repeated the process under his right arm. I'd never seen a *man* do that before, and here was Duane, risking the wrath of a barracks full of guys, carrying on as if this was standard male procedure.

That morning I was introduced to a new product. My teenage mentality labeled it "female cosmetics." The label on the jar read "MUM." Duane then explained the importance of combating body odor with regard to female types.

After work that afternoon, searching through products at the base exchange, I found MUM. Yep, it was stocked on a shelf in the cosmetics section. At Duane's suggestion, I had also decided to upgrade to a more expensive after-shave lotion--Musk. I found the after-shave in a box illustrated with the silhouette of a standing nude couple kissing. This one I found in *male* toiletries.

I liked Duane's style. I didn't know if it was because he was twenty-one, came from New York City or his education, but I began emulating him. Tomorrow, if the opportunity presented itself, I wouldn't want him to misunderstand, I'd ask him about that powder he sprinkled from a green tin, all around his pubes and wacker. Like the physical changes with reaching puberty, I was now experiencing some major decisions regarding my body, such as grooming it successfully for social situations--liberty.

All thoughts during the workday were directed toward Saturday liberty. In crisp dress whites, we waited just outside the main gate for the city bus. Off the station the air seemed cleaner, the sky bluer and the day held an offer of something better than hiding out behind a bush to avoid work. Once in Corpus we proceeded to whatever out-of-the-way bar was serving underage sailors that particular weekend. The word always got around--scuttlebutt the Navy called it.

In these dives we drank beer, ate peanuts and threw the shells onto the floor. After flipping coins to determine teams, we sprinkled the long shuffle-board table with fresh wax and arranged our teams at opposite ends to begin demonstrating individual styles of puck sliding. Enthusiastic players would send the pucks flying down the oak surface, exploding everything in their path. All of this took place with the constant background accompaniment of bells, whistles and the other racket from players finessing and jostling the ubiquitous pin-ball machines.

Next stop was food. We were all about seventeen years old and anytime was time to eat. I took a stool in the diner, near the pass-through door to the bar. The waitress placed the pork chop special in front of me. She remained, examining and adjusting the artificial flower pinned against a large, folded, ornate hanky, high on her left chest.

"Ma'am, what's this stuff over here?" I pointed my fork toward the glob of snow white bulbous lumps on my plate .

"That's grits."

"What's grits?"

"It's hominy. It comes with every order."

"But what *is* it?"

"It's like corn that's been soaked till it all swells up."

"I don't think I like grits. Got any mashed potatoes."

"We don't serve mashed potatoes. Everybody in the South eats grits."

"What are these beans, next to the grits?"

"Them's black-eyed peas and next to them is collard greens." She smiled and cracked her gum in three staccato bursts. "There's Tabasco and jalapenos over here on the counter, next to the napkins. Y'all enjoy."

"I guess you Californians don't eat anything besides fruits and nuts?" On the stool next to me, Dewitt emptied the tiny little glass bottle of milk that had rested on the saucer against his coffee cup.

"Pass the sand," he pointed to the sugar. A soda cracker stood up inside the glass, chrome topped, sugar dispenser. "The grits are really good with gravy over 'em." Dewitt reversed his circular motion and stirred his coffee in the opposite direction.

I held a forkfull of the grits in my mouth. They felt funny. The consistency was odd. I was finally able to swallow. They didn't have much taste, but they weren't really bad. I liked mashed potatoes better. After trying grits with salt, pepper and even gravy, as Dewitt suggested, I

47

decided grits and I could get along. We had to anyway, because they came on your plate regardless of what you ordered.

Our liberty horizons broadened considerably when Bernard Lutzski's grandmother died in Hamtramck, Michigan. His daddy telephoned that Grandma had wanted Ber to have her 1939, four-door Packard. It took five days leave for Ber to hitchhike up to Detroit and drive his inheritance back down to Corpus Christi.

After that, no more public buses for us. Now we had wheels to take us anywhere, even down South to Brownsville and across the line into Matamoros, Mexico.

We would find out for ourselves if what they said about the goings-on in that "hell hole" were true.

WHO GETS THE WORM?

The next Saturday after Ber returned to Corpus Christi, we gave his grandma's Packard a test drive. The minute liberty was called six of us hurried over to the car.

Ber motioned us forward, up to the front bumper where he waited. Taking out his handkerchief, he caressed the hood ornament as if it was a treasure, and began working up a brilliant silver glow. He removed the cloth, exposing the art piece for all of us to enjoy, "Check it out. It's the best part of this buggy."

The figure was a nude woman with prominent breasts. Her body extended forward in a prone position, her head lifted upward over the hood into the wind. Long hair flowed down the length of her body. Her arms lay against her sides. Even with the car parked, she communicated fleet, forward motion.

"Nice melons," observed Sweeney.

We piled onto the plush, maroon, cut-velvet seats. We each chipped in fifty cents toward a tank of gas and an additional dime for two quarts of cold Blatz beer to keep us cool on the trip. After showing the gate-guard our liberty cards, we were through the main gate, the gleaming, elongated chrome hood ornament pointing South toward the Mexican border. We picked up beer at the first store, one quart went up front, the other remained in back.

The boys sitting in front searched the radio stations for "non-western" music. Most of the offerings were unfamiliar Mexican tunes or country. Diller suggested we crank up one of the Mexican numbers and start getting into the salsa mood.

In a few short hours we were in the middle of the action of the wide-open border town of Matamoros. It looked like everything we'd heard about. The atmosphere of the cow-town was so bizarre, so rowdy, so sin-filled that it fascinated us--even as non-participating observers. Over the months to come, we returned and witnessed this slice of life again and again, like children captured by the carnival set-up on the outskirts of town.

Our introduction that Saturday morning began when a hustler on the sidewalk playfully blocked our way and, with both arms extended, directed us toward a black curtained barroom entrance.

Here, he promised with a lecherous smile, we would see "nude dancing. She takes off everything but her tattoo."

We exchanged smiles, nodded in agreement, and executed a column left in single file. Separating the curtains, we trooped into the darkened, cave-like room. I made out three musicians at the rear of an elevated platform. They began to play just as we opened the curtains. A chunky young woman, wearing only a bra, panties and heels, stretched a leg upward to climb onto the lighted stage and began to slowly grind her hips to the beat.

Sweeney gave a low whistle. "That little tamale looks like she could suck the chrome off a trailer hitch."

Though my eyes still hadn't completely adapted to the darkness, I could see that we were the only customers. Not wanting to appear like country boys new in town by staring at the dancer's large tatas and beckoning cleavage, we turned away and bellied up to the bar. "Gypsy" and the boys in the band continued their set.

It was important to project an experienced, nonchalant attitude in these kinds of adventures. We were "cool" even then. And under the drinking age.

Sweeney took charge and ordered double mescals for our party.

"This stuff will make you guys crazy as hell," he laughed.

The barman set six double-shot glasses in front of us, salt shakers and two larger glasses filled with slices of fresh Mexican limes, thin skinned and juicy. He reached around into the lighted back-bar. Its ranks of different sized and configured bottles held liquids of every color, including red, green, and blue. Some were clear as water. As if his hand was directed by radar, it went directly to the mescal. He brought it up and began pouring. Our glasses were filled so full they could not be lifted without spilling. This required the old "lowering the head to the glass" drill, so as not to lose a drop.

"Hey, wait a minute. Isn't that something at the bottom of the bottle?" Ber squinted and brought his eyes closer to the amber liquid.

The barman stopped pouring and righted the bottle, holding it before us for closer examination.

Sweeney chuckled, "Yah. The guy who drinks the last of the bottle gets to eat the worm. At the distillery, they put one into every bottle, for flavor. First he does the backstroke for awhile, but he soon settles down."

I glanced toward Ber. We rolled our eyes.

As the barman finished filling the last glass, Leland invited him to have one himself. He didn't require much encouragement. He faced us, his ample belly resting half on the bar, and filled his glass to overflowing. With a slice of lime in his left hand and the salt shaker in his right, he licked the back of his left hand, poured salt onto his dampened skin, and encouraged us to follow along with him in the ritual. He raised the glass in his steady right hand toward us.

"*Saludo.*"

He licked the salt from the back of his left hand, expertly emptied the contents of the full glass in one quick pull, without spilling, and immediately bit into the lime slice he had been holding.

"Ayeee, Chihuahua," he squealed, and did a little in place jitterbug.

Sweeney, always the showman and never to be outdone, took the Zippo lighter from his breast pocket and expertly flipped back the top, lit the wick and brought the flame toward his glass. The liquid surface jumped into a little dancing blue flame. He snapped the lighter closed with a flourish then stared, admiring his pyro demonstration.

"You'll blow the roof off this place, Brian," I joked with a nervous half laugh.

The barman exposed a mouthful of huge, white teeth through a wide open grin and we all stared at the burning alcohol. I wondered if maybe we should have ordered cold Dos Equis beers instead. But this cactus juice was going to "set us free," if Sweeney could be believed. He blew out the flame.

"Brian, are you sure this stuff's safe to drink?" I was having second thoughts and feeling a little uneasy. This was the first time I had been served hard liquor at a bar.

"Hell yes. You saw Zapata here handle it."

"Let's do it." Mikey sounded as if he had to hurry or he might not be able to pull it off.

Sweeney arranged salt and a lime slice.

"*Erin go bragh..*" He grabbed for his glass to toast his Irish ancestors, but immediately released it with a scream. It was still hot from the flame.

The barman laughed and couldn't seem to stop. He handed Sweeney an ice cube for his fingers and refilled his glass.

I was determined to stall as long as I could. I didn't want to finish my glass, then be poured the last of that bottle, with its little "treat" as my reward.

I eyed the mescal bottle resting on the bar, with its motionless occupant curled into a ring at the bottom. Less than an inch of liquor remained.

I tensed unexpectedly. From nowhere a sensuous play of finger nails traveled up, then down my back. I turned and faced three "working girls" smiling into my face, all flashing their gold dental work. Each pushing up so close the trio was "violating my space." And I felt the tingle of excitement. Six practiced hands were teasing the six prospective "Johns," and set up a chorus of pleading, like kittens, for us to buy them drinks.

"You buy me drinkey, okay?"

Sweeney reached across the bar for the mescal bottle and handed it to the size 38 double-D who had been gently dancing her long finger nails across his shoulders and up into his hairline. Maintaining her smile, she grasped the neck of the bottle and proceeded to gurgle down the entire remains. When she removed the vacated bottle from her mouth, there was that damn worm--she was holding it between her pursed lips for all of us to see. When satisfied we'd all witnessed the exhibition, she inhaled the fat little grub with a snap.

Brian Sweeney took 38 double-D into his arms, placed his lips squarely onto hers, and pulled her up close with both hands spread wide over the cheeks of her ample buttocks. When they finally broke for air, Sweeney was chewing the worm she had transferred to him during the lip lock. He looked around at his admiring shipmates as he chewed and smiled, his arm tightly encircling 38 double-D's waist. Throwing his head back, he delivered an ear splitting rebel yell and swallowed the prize.

We boys-on-the-town applauded the two of them, then turned to our own attack on the demon mescal. Each of us deftly positioned salt and lime as we'd been instructed.

In our excitement over the worm crunching exhibition we'd forgotten the solo stripper on the platform. The musicians had continuously played *Harlem Nocturne* since we arrived. The dancer's unenthusiastic motions suggested she was pacing herself for a long afternoon shift of delivering bumps and grinds. But the pace of the music announced the time had come now for this number's finale.

She had removed her bra earlier, without any of us noticing, and now she was stepping out of her panties. I hoped no one heard me suck in my breath

Out of her panties? All attention shifted to the platform lighted in purple.

With the toe of her high heeled shoe, she caught the panties and flipped them over toward the side of the platform. After a long, reedy, low note, the sax man increased the tempo.

Before any of us understood what was happening, a new image erupted from the shadows and sped toward the illuminated stage.

52

Mikey Livingston had left the bar and was racing toward the stripper. Like a startled animal, she stood immobile. Recovering quickly, she bent over into a slightly squatting position. First she covered her dark triangular muff with both hands, then reconsidered and wrapped one arm across the large, black aureolas that capped her breasts.

The boys in the band froze in mid-note.

The house lights surged up. The barman hurried his large frame around the far end of the bar, waving a "billy" high over his head. His new, evil expression said he meant business.

"*Policia, policia,*" he yelled as he dashed toward Mikey. No one was smiling now.

The five of us sprang from our stools, nearly knocking over the hookers who had formed a velcro bond with us. Thirty-eight double-D made the sign of the cross over her upper chest.

We sprung forward to stop Mikey from whatever the hell he had in mind. The women screamed.

In their scramble to evacuate the action area, one of the musicians accidentally hit the strobe light switch. The unworldly scene was then complete.

In my excitement, wonder, fear and physical exertion all mixed together in a rush. *This is a good thing? No, this is a bad thing. Why am I laughing? Oh boy.*

Before we could reach Mikey El Nutso, he had bent down, on the run, and scooped up the trophy panties. As he attempted to change course, his momentum carried him forward, toward the startled sax man and his polished golden instrument, resting in its holder on the floor beside him. Mikey plowed through the man, the holder, and the sax. In the mayhem one foot landed squarely on the F-key, severely altering the configuration of the man's musical livelihood and sending it flying. The musician scrambled after it, cursing words I recognized from Able Tina in bootcamp. One of them, Able had cautioned, "*never* use"--*cavrone.* The sax player yelled it over and over as he rocked back and forth cradling his badly bent instrument.

Mikey turned as quickly as his forward speed allowed and dashed toward the drape covered entrance, shouting, "Let's get the hell out of here."

In Keystone Cops fashion, the six of us tumbled out onto the bright sunlit sidewalk.

Oh God, please, no Mexican police. No Mexican jail cell.

Sweeney had been right. That damn mescal *will* make you crazy as hell.

After five minutes of running and executing diversionary maneuvers, we looked over our shoulders and could no longer see the bartender nor the insane sax man in pursuit.

We stopped to catch our breath. In our little circle on the sidewalk, huffing and puffing, Mikey reached under his jumper and removed the pair of panties that had started the whole commotion. We all looked at them, looked at him, looked at each other, and burst out laughing. We were bent over holding our sides. Passers-by looked curiously and gave us wide berth.

"Let's get a beer," I gasped, and we were off. Refocused--the past two hours already a memory.

MAIL CALL

Two weeks after the mescal worm incident in Matamoros, some of us sat around on bunks, reading mail and eating from a fresh box of Dewitt's mom's cookies.

Mikey slowly set down his cookie and looked up from his letter. Staring out into space, he moaned, "I'm a dead man."

"What's up pal, bad news?" Questions and comments flew between everyone in the circle of pals.

"She's missed her period, right?"

"Not a Dear John, Mikey?"

"They're goin' to repo his motor scooter."

Mikey held out the letter to Leland, seated on the bunk across from him. Leland took it and began reading aloud.

Dear Mike,

It was wonderful having you home on leave, sleeping in your old room. Roscoe is spending a lot of time on your hooked rug, looking at the roller skates, wanting to pull you down the sidewalk again. The days just went by too fast. We all enjoyed your stories of Navy life. It sounds like you've made some fine Christian friends there at the Naval Air Station.

Mother and I were so proud of you in your uniform, when we went to Donolley's Chicken House. I couldn't help but notice that little waitress, Jenny. She took quite a liking to you in those sharp looking dress whites. Mother said she noticed too. Reminded me of when I was in the army out on the West Coast at Fort Ord. All day busting down tires on semis in the motor pool. Then dressing up real smart to go into Monterey in the evenings.

It was perfect us running into the Harringtons and them seeing how fine you turned out. They're always bragging-up their Owen and his hoity-toity position as an Executive Trainee with Encyclopedia Britannica. I often see him walking door to door. Some kind of job. I've had the feeling that kid was a loser ever since he got you into trouble when he brought those trashy girlie magazines to Boy Scout Camp and passed them around in your tent.

Son, since you left, some unfortunate happenings have developed here at the house. First your grandmother discovered what she described as vermin living in Fort Bushy. Sissy was next. She told your mother about her horrible little creatures, and she's still crying herself to sleep at night. Says no boy will ever ask her out if this gets around Lexington High School.

I had to rescue your senior picture from the bottom of Lady Bird's cage, where Sissy must have slipped it to collect the droppings. I'm telling you, that girl is upset.

By the time your mother thought she might have some activity in her eyebrows, I knew we had a full-on problem. I'd been scratching around for a couple of days myself, but hadn't wanted to say anything cause your mother might have gotten the crazy idea I'd been

56

over to Hamptontown, seeing them
floozies Uncle Rex likes to
visit after paydays.

We have a damned epidemic
here in the house. Doc Liston,
down at the Owl Drug Store,
recognized the symptoms as crab
lice when he read the folded
note I handed him at the
pharmacy counter. I couldn't
risk anyone overhearing me tell
him how the whole family's
infested. He gave me some salve
to bring home for everyone.
After a few applications the
little demons are finally giving
us some peace. But Sissy still
cries at night.

Your grandmother says
you're darn lucky grandpa isn't
here to see her suffer. He'd
take the strap to you. What a
sense of humor that woman has.
I guess that's where your mother
gets her's.

I'm afraid that Mother has
taken it worse than Sissy or
Grandma. It was her having to
shave her pubic area, on
Grandmother's recommendation,
that demoralized her. It was
only later we learned folks no
longer need to shave. But by
then it was too late. Last time
I saw her this upset with you
was when you and your cousin
Alfred put the garden snake into
Grandma's crochet basket.

She says she'll never be
able to shop at the Owl and hold
her head up. I hope you'll
understand if you don't hear
from her for awhile.

I was sharing the problem
with my pal, Ray, down at the

Elks Lodge Friday night, him
being a professional barber and
dealing with hair all day long.
He asked me, as a personal favor
to him, to keep it under my hat.
Seems he felt if the word got
out it could hurt his business.

Anyway, we're all going
around here with shaved private
parts. The salve gave Sissy
quite a rash. She left it on
too long. Damn fool kids
anyway. Think they know
everything. If seven minutes is
good, twenty will really get the
job done. She'll think twice
before she does that again.

Mother had to write her a
note for school, to excuse her
from dressing for P.E., and
having to shower in front of all
those other girls.

Well, son, what concerns me
almost as much as these women
whining, is that you realize
your condition. I told your
mother that you must have got
those crabs off of a toilet seat
there on the base. Left, I
suppose, by some rascal who'd
been out carousing with the kind
of chippy you'd never cotton to.
Then you unknowingly brought
them into this house and, well,
you know the rest.

Get yourself over to
sickbay, Buddy, and let that
pharmacist mate shine his
flashlight around (if you get my
drift). I'm sure the Navy has
something as effective as this
Blue Butter Doc Liston
prescribed for us.

And please, please don't
surprise us, for a few weeks

```
anyway, by coming home.  Let
things settle down a bit.  In
fact, I'm thinking maybe we can
drive down there for our next
visit, on my vacation.  Save you
the bother of coming way up
here, and all.
     I'll end now.  I  want to
get Roscoe to the Vet's before
closing time.  Poor dog's been
rubbing himself raw, scooting
around on the living room
carpet.
     Take care of yourself,
Mikey.  Your mother will come
around before long, you'll see.
                    Love,
                    Daddy
```

Mikey dragged his thoughts back from his father's horror story to the attentive little circle of friends, and wondered aloud, "I've been itchin' a lot down there lately, too, but I just wrote it off to this damn Corpus Christi heat and sweat. Guess I'll make sick call tomorrow."

"I wouldn't wait, Mikey." The advice started flowing from all sides.

"The first order of business is for you to shit-can those panties you stole from the little Chiquita down in Matamoros the other day. They got creepy-crawlers in 'em."

"Real funny. Stop crackin' my nuts. I said I'd take care of it."

"Better burn 'em."

"Man, you're puttin us all at risk for gettin' VD."

"Crabs ain't VD, you dope."

"You should have stayed awake during those movies in boot camp."

"Crabs, geeze."

"Your grandmother!"

"Oh boy. You *are* a dead man."

WOULDN'T WANT TO LIVE THERE

On return trips to Matamoros we discovered several of the bars, located on what passed for a main street, featured live sex shows. Rowdy audiences packed into small clubs and their eager volunteers, though rarely allowed to participate, were continually being pushed back into their seats by hefty house bouncers. On the select occasions when volunteers were allowed to come onto the stage, the audience worked up to such a frenzy that the proprietors had all they could do to keep them from tearing the place down, a kind of amateur night with a questionable first prize. It was bedlam, and we loved it.

Occasionally a donkey or a dog would be worked into the menagerie. The special donkey act required a dollar cover charge. I supposed there was a shortage of trained, cooperative animals. But word traveled fast and it was always a special draw for the curious. Stories describing the show circulated around the station for weeks afterwards. Each version got farther from the facts, as the donkey was an unreliable performer who often simply would not cooperate. The donkey didn't like it much with all the hooting and hollering distracting him.

B-girls hustled drinks, and more. For the price of an amber-colored water, one was entitled to heavy petting and groping. If you could afford a little more expense, you'd be led by the hand to one of the booths in the darkened rear. Here you were restricted only by your imagination, dexterity, and your pocketbook.

Forget about ID cards and the problems of being served as a minor. Waiters kept everyone's glass filled, carrying small pen lights held in their mouths, for navigating the darkness with their two hands occupied by trays. A continuous stream of drinks arrived at the tables--sometimes ordered, often not.

One Saturday night we watched a crew-cut young man rise from his showroom table and stroll onto the stage. By his age and haircut, I knew he must be a serviceman in civvies. Who else came here? He wore sun glasses in a half-hearted attempt to conceal his identity. Either the bouncers didn't notice him, or they weren't concerned. The performers welcomed him with smiles and laughter and folded him right into the act. Dancing around him to the beat of the music, they began slowly taking off his clothes. In seconds he was an active part of the raucous demonstration of no-holds-barred debauchery.

After a wild afternoon and evening, Ber drove all of us north in the Packard, back toward Corpus. Off to our right the sun was beginning to pink-up the sky over the Gulf. It was quiet in the car as we headed up Highway 77, with most of us half asleep. Out of nowhere Leland Mosley, sitting in the middle of the back seat, broke the silence.

. "I don't care what anyone says, you'll never convince me that guy wasn't a plant."

All the passengers moaned.

My daily routine at the Air Station, life in Corpus Christi's "brown shoe" Navy with all the Airedale atmosphere, was wearing me down. Airplanes screamed their ear-splitting noises, airborne and on the ground. At any time of day you could always hear an engine howling from some direction. Enormous hangers and busy runways commanded every view. And what was it with all those logos of pilots' wings pasted on every building, every piece of letterhead paper, even fired onto our eating crockery? Talk about total immersion. Surely this was a different life from the real Navy, the one I'd hoped for when I took the oath.

Sea duty looked like it offered better possibilities for adventure. And definitely no lawn mowers to push around.

My mind was made up. The Third Class Boatswain's Mate at the Master at Arms shack explained how to fill out the "dream sheet" requesting a transfer and where to deposit it.

"But you just got here three months ago." He quizzically observed.

"Really? It seems like three years." The hiding out every day had made time crawl.

This Seaman Second Class wanted a change of scenery.

THEY ALSO SERVE

Author, Naval Construction Battalion Depot,
Port Hueneme, California

YOU GOT ORDERS

I listened up as the base loud speaker blared, "NOW THIS MAN, SPITTLE, SEAMAN SECOND CLASS, LAY UP TO THE STATION ADMINISTRATION OFFICE."

Hey, that's me. They want me to leave my work detail. A break from gardening. Regardless of what they need, I can stretch this time to at least an hour and a half. It'll take a long time just to find the place.

With the rake, hoe, and gunny-sack of clippings mounted on top of the lawn mower, I pushed the mess back toward the gear locker, then proceeded to find 'Admin'.

In minutes I turned a corner and there was the flag pole. Damn, I had found it quickly. I pushed through the double doors centered on the street side of the battleship gray building. Just inside, a pock-marked seaman first class sat behind a desk. This receptionist's complexion looked like somebody had beaten him about the face and neck with a track shoe.

A large green blotter covered half of the desktop, looking as if it had recently been set there, new and clean. An in-basket, arranged above the out-basket, held a lonely mimeographed sheet announcing Sunday church services--last week. The out-basket was empty. *Nothing* on the desk showed the clerical activity for which the furnishings had been designed. He reclined back in the swivel chair's maximum position, making him almost horizontal, and looked over the top of a little Jiggs and Maggie Tijuana Bible.

"I'm Spittle. Someone here called for me."

Whistling In The Whiskers-- I caught the title of the porno booklet as he eased himself upright, slipped the small sexual primer into the center drawer, and removed the opened paper clip he'd been using to probe between his teeth. Turning slightly, he hollered over his shoulder, "Reggie, did you call for a seaman deuce, Spittle?"

"Yeah. Come on over, Spittle."

Reggie began fingering his way through a tall pile of papers as I approached. When he reached what he wanted, he slid the stapled packet out from the stack and perused the information on the top half of the sheet. Looking up at me, without raising his head, just his eyes, he announced,

"You got orders."

Orders? Orders! Wow. Where am I goin'? Who cares, I'll take it. Thank you Lord.

He handed me the packet of a dozen sheets with the ink signed original on top. I flipped through them. Each was a mimeographed copy. Smiling, I half fell into the chair beside his desk and began digging into the treasure I held in my hands.

```
        Upon receipt of these
orders, and when directed by
proper authority, you are to
secure the first available
surface transportation and
proceed to Port Hueneme,
California.
        Report to the Commanding
Officer, US Naval Construction
Battalion Center, for permanent
assignment.
        Travel time of five days is
authorized...
```

It wasn't sea duty, but it would get me away from my yard work hell-hole. I looked up at Reggie.

"Spittle, if you died at this moment, the undertaker couldn't wipe that smile off your face.

"Take your orders over to the dispersing office. They'll get you a train ticket and arrange special pay, if you need it. Here's your check-out sheet. You can start right here by turning in your liberty card to pizza face, up there in front. He'll sign you off. You'll probably be able to get out of here by day after tomorrow.

"And Spittle, you'd better quit smilin' like that. People'll think you don't have a full seabag."

That evening we skipped chow and I took my close buddies over to the enlisted men's club for beer and cracklins, the deep fried pig skins my Mexican friend, Emil, called *chicharrones*.

As usual, the line to order beer was so long that, when I finally worked my way up to the counter, I bought a whole case of long necks. Back at the table we each took a beer from the box and had a deep pull before drawing matches, torn from a book, to see who would get the next round. The loser grabbed an additional beer and got back into the end of the line to wait his turn to buy another case for the table. By the time he returned we were ready for another cold one. And so it went until closing at 2200 hours.

After breakfast on departure day, the guys walked me back to the barracks to pick up my packed seabag. Mikey was giving me that twisted little grin as he held out his hand. I thought, *this guy will never live to see the end of his enlistment, with his hell bent lifestyle.* We shook hands all around and each man shared his envy of my leaving for Southern California and all the dreams that magical place conjures up in a seventeen-year-old's mind.

On the final leg of the trip, the train from Los Angeles didn't stop in Oxnard, gateway to the Sea Bee base, but continued on to Ventura. A Greyhound bus back-tracked me into a downtown area that, judging from the number of bars, had been a hard charging place during the war years. But the saloons were barely hanging on now, crippled by the tamer, postwar economy.

At the bus depot baggage counter a lady with a man's short haircut and a heavy key chain that disappeared into her rear pocket, took my claim ticket. As she compared the claim check to tags on the few seabags, I asked her how to get myself and my gear out to the base. On my eighty-dollar-a-month salary, there wasn't money for a cab. She directed me around the corner to the "quarter snatcher," a van that took people out to Port Hueneme.

We rode past miles of tilled, dark earth while I breathed in the beautiful spring day. The humidity was at a comfortable level, and I flashed back to my sweating pals in Corpus Christi. A large billboard at the edge of a furrowed field announced:

OXNARD'S 1947 LETTUCE FESTIVAL
Featuring Slim Barnard and his Floor Busters
Carnival rides and 4H contests
Bring those pies, cakes and prize livestock
This will be our biggest celebration yet

I had wanted to see the world. I guessed, by today's scenery, you had to begin with baby steps.

The jitney left three of us at the main gate of the sprawling complex that was home to the Navy's builders of landing strips and Quonset hut cities. They were the movers of mountains--the Navy Seabees, from "C.B."--Construction Battalion. This part of the Navy had made its reputation during the war in the Pacific by going from

65

island to island, after each US invasion, constructing everything from mass enemy grave sites, dug with the blades of bulldozers, to warehouses, EM barracks, and officers' quarters.

The duty officer at the guard shack signed my orders and logged the time of arrival on each sheet, handing me one copy. We were directed to go with the duty petty officer, whom we followed to his jeep. As we drove to the Master-at-Arms shack, I thought how great it would be to sit in that driver's seat and tool myself around the base. Maybe I could get an assignment that required driving a gray jeep.

After a couple of my probing questions, the driver bragged, "You can't push one of these babies around without a Navy driver's license." He was the model of imagined authority.

I made a mental note to get that license first chance. I would be ready. Access to a military jeep would be like having my own car. I hadn't dreamed I was anywhere close to that.

At the M.A.A. shack we were assigned our racks and locker numbers. In the adjacent barracks I located my locker. For the first time since leaving Texas, I unlocked my seabag, hung the lock onto the locker door, and began storing my gear as I searched for fresh bedding.

Soft, light, and silky. What was my hand touching in the seabag? Curious, I pulled out a pair of women's panties. That darn Mikey. I hadn't seen that underwear since he stole it from the stripper in Matamoros. Remembering the last conversation we'd had about those red silkies, I sure hoped they'd been washed.

I changed into undress blues and reported to the Admin Office to receive my new assignment.

Ship's Company, Regimental Guard.

Now what the hell was that?

FINALLY, I'M SOMEBODY

Duck hunter night watch was especially lonely. I'd be dropped off at 2000, 2400, or 0400, depending upon the watch I drew. While I balanced my night ration and a paper cup of hot coffee, the man I'd relieve would jump into the jeep before I could get my second leg out. It was particularly dark in the remote area and I seldom saw another human being until the Sergeant-of-the-Guard checked back with me about midway through my watch and poured another coffee. I carried a weapon without ammo, sang every song I knew to amuse myself, and thought I saw trouble in each shadow. How many times had I bucked up my courage, assuming a voice more mature than my seventeen years, to challenge the empty darkness, "Halt. Who goes there?"

After four hours in this twilight zone, I'd be relieved by another reluctant warrior and be off watch for the next eight hours.

We also serve, who do these Mickey Mouse jobs.

The Regimental Guard was a part of base security. As watch-standers, we manned the gates of the reservation or were posted in remote parts to protect material, guard fences, and secure equipment.

The Navy saying, learned early on, ran through my head while on watch. "If it moves, salute it. If it doesn't, paint it." My right arm ached from saluting while on gate duty.

We also stood the duck hunter watches at Point Mugu Naval Air Station, about fifteen miles down the coast from the Seabee base. Hunters presented a problem by trespassing into the base's marshy areas, with weapons of course, in search of birds. This was unauthorized and we were directed to politely escort them back onto Pacific Coast Highway where they parked their cars.

The good news was, I was on duty for forty-eight hours in the watch standing cycle, then got forty-eight hours off for liberty. Two days off out of four. Now that was a schedule I could live with. It allowed me to go home to Inglewood on a regular basis to my old friends, my family, and a chance to get completely away from military routine.

Between watches one morning, I was reading the Plan of the Day posted in the Regimental Guard office. Opportunity reached out and smacked me square in the face.

67

```
---NON-RATED MAN WITH TYPING SKILLS---
    Train to become a legal yeoman
    and advance your Navy career.
    Inquire at Base Legal Office.
```

There never seemed to be enough typists to churn out all the government paperwork. This legal yeoman thing could mean inside work, regular hours, staying clean, dry, and warm. And I had seen young ladies working there in the administrative center.

I went directly topside and presented myself to Ensign Harry Locke, the base legal officer. As we spoke for about ten minutes, I explained I had learned typing in junior high school. *Typing.* He jumped at the word. His eyes telegraphed interest. His brows lifted slightly and a hint of a smile turned the corners of his mouth. His whole body transmitted the feeling of a coiled spring waiting to be released by the end of my sentence.

Pushing himself up from behind the desk, he ushered me into the larger office, separated from his by a glass partition, and introduced me to the secretarial staff of two. I sized them up. The first, an older lady probably 45, full bodied, with a permanent, sweet smile. *The motherly type.*

"Call me Peggy."

The second was elderly, probably 55, and British in her manner. She came from New England and gave the appearance of being frail, but capable with years of experience. She extended her thin, parchment like hand. *A pleasant Greer Garson.*

As I drew closer to her desk to take her hand, I recognized the scent of Yardley's lavender, and my thoughts slid-back to my grandmother's favorite scent.

"I'm Miss Treadwell."

At the far end of this larger working office sat a man with his head down, busy at work over a desk eclipsed by paper. The name plate read "Provost Marshal."

"Mr. Hicks, the cavalry has arrived. Meet our new yeoman, Seaman Second Class Frank Spittle." Mr. Locke actually sparkled with excitement.

The crusty old Warrant Officer behind the desk wore his jet black hair slicked back in a Dick Tracy style. I stole a glance at his wrist, checking for the watch-radio.

He brought me back to the scene with "Welcome aboard, Spittle, we can really use you here."

They all seemed to be genuinely delighted I was coming on staff. I hadn't thought the experience and talent of a young kid offered so much. A new, content feeling was overtaking me.

To each, Mr. Locke had described me as the "new yeoman." It seemed I was hired, without a typing test, reference check, or any other exercise besides the brief, initial interview. I was a warm body and they had serious needs. This was to be the first, but not the last, opportunity typing skills opened for me.

The next morning I reported to Miss Treadwell. She was to be my trainer. When the previous yeoman had been transferred, she was assigned his responsibilities until a relief arrived. I was the relief. Between sips of steaming tea from a bone-china cup, she made it clear that she was *very* pleased to have me aboard. I would soon relieve her of the added responsibilities that kept her from her regular assignment--typing proceedings of Summary Courts Martial. She made me feel an urgency to quickly learn my duties.

Everyone seemed caught-up in a hectic pace, everyone except Peggy. While she kept occupied, she seemed to be the only one on top of her job, not buried under it. And she showed that perky smile at every opportunity.

I soon learned that pleasant Peggy, due to her General Services rating, was the senior civilian in the office, and Miss Treadwell's supervisor. A situation not to Miss Treadwell's liking. I watched her show occasional objection by a facial expression, but you had to observe quickly. Other subtle body language, only briefly displayed, convinced me the two of them were not soulmates. All the work of the departed person stayed with Miss Treadwell. None flowed back to Peggy's desk.

I was assigned a desk outfitted with supplies of every sort. The upper left drawer opened to display sheets of bond, onion skin salmon, canary and powder blue and carbon paper, all arranged in a slanted configuration. A typewriter was positioned on an extension from the right of the desk. A phone with a bank of labeled buttons was within easy reach, and my name plate, sitting forward on the desk top, announced "Legal Yeoman." The in-basket overflowed. My out-basket was empty.

Sitting on the comfortable, roller wheeled chair, I manned the clerical cockpit and felt as if I should be fastening my seat-belt. The glass slipper had slid right onto Cinderella's foot. A perfect fit. I had a title. I had a good job. I had some meaningful responsibilities. Hell, I felt like an executive!

After two months as the legal yeoman, I was promoted to Seaman First Class, largely due to Mr. Locke's efforts on my behalf. I was eighteen and enjoying my new identity. There was talk that I would go to yeoman school in San Diego, as soon as the office work-load reached a manageable flow.

That meant I could make rate, Yeoman Third Class.

My life was taking shape. This legal business was okay.

"Oh Frank, why don't you go down to the exchange and get us some lunch? I'll buy." Miss Peggy warbled from her desk.

"I eat in the mess hall, Peggy."

"Well, I just can't get away from this desk today. Could you *please* make the trip? A hamburger and pie for me? I'll buy you a coke or anything you want." She threw that sweet pudgy smile at me again.

I consented and headed out on my errand. In the hall, "Snake" Taylor, the First Class Boatswain's Mate, Assistant to the Provost Marshal, crept up behind me. He had evidently overheard the conversation about getting Peggy some lunch. He softly jeered, "And, Oh Frank, can you help me with this itch I just can't scratch?"

"Snake," I said, " you're a sick man."

"Kid, that little butter-ball will have you in the kip before you know what's hit you."

A BRUSH WITH DEATH

Chef poured sherry into the small skillet, shook the pan, and threw its contents into the air, forming a two foot high streak of livers and mushrooms. With his professional expertise he recaptured every morsel, then tilted the contents onto the waiting plate in his other hand. This was to be my little treat.

I was working in the officer's club. The beautiful old residence sat on one corner of the sprawling base. It had been the family home for the former owner of the reservation property before being converted into a club. Ensign Locke had encouraged me to see the club manager, Mr. Britt, who was hiring part-time help. It was a chance to pick up some cash toward my dream of owning a car.

When we met for the interview, Mr. Britt leaned toward me from across his desk, "Harry Locke recommended you highly. Says you're reliable and trustworthy. Coming from Harry, that's good enough for me."

A guy doesn't mind giving 110% to a boss who shows his appreciation the way Mr. Locke does.

During my night shift at the club I waited tables for cocktails, served food, and joined the clean-up crew after closing. But the part of the job that I prayed would happen every shift I worked, was the occasional need for a driver. The club's jeep was sometimes needed for errands, like picking up supplies that had been unexpectedly depleted. I ached to drive that jeep.

Most of the club employees were civilians. This included the chef, Lamar Landrell, an interesting fellow. Helen, an experienced waitress who knew where all the club's skeletons were stashed, declared, "Lamar is experiencing a sexual identity crises. We must keep the windows closed in the galley or Chef will fly out."

This particular evening he was in his usual high excitement mode, sailing around the kitchen at top speed in his checked trousers and starched white smock. The tall toque pulled squarely upon his head, exposed just a peek of curly salt and peppered hair.

"Frankie, I fixed your favorite tonight, chicken livers. You must eat them while they're still good, sweetheart. But first go tell Johnny to fix my drink."

Out in the bar I gave his request to Johnny, who always rolled his eyes when Chef sent me from the galley. Seagrams Seven Crown and Seven-up poured into an ice-filled, stove-pipe glass. It never varied.

Back in the galley, I set the glass, sweating cool beads of moisture on its outside, onto the raised metal counter that separated the cooking area from where the servers picked-up orders. Chef wiped the edge of my plate of livers with a towel from his shoulder and placed the presentation next to his drink on the counter. He took the cold glass and drew half the golden liquid down in one long pull, as if to extinguish a fire. I found a stool to sit and enjoy my feast.

From behind his shirt collar, he pulled out a towel and wiped it across his sweating face, then over the back of his neck as he shook his head.

"Rolls. That asshole Britt didn't order my rolls." Turning toward the nearest waitress, he ordered, "Cecilia, go tell "the nitwit" to get in here *pronto* if he wants his customers to have dinner tonight."

Everyone liked this man's cooking, but I couldn't figure out why the waitresses and even the manager kissed his butt. The waitresses gritted their teeth as he constantly yelled at them for some transgression, not ordering properly, not picking up orders quickly enough, or neglecting little finishing touches he directed be placed onto the plate before serving. Mr. Britt tried to pacify him and satisfy his every whim. Years later I learned that a chef can make a restaurant great or bury it. At the club our chef was *the* person crucial to its successful operation. Management wanted to keep him happy.

The only people to whom Chef was pleasant were the young sailors on staff and Johnny the barman. He needed Johnny for his Seven-Seven coolers. And the boys--he couldn't keep his hands off the boys. He'd find a reason to hurry over to any group of young guys and have to "squeeze through" to the other side under the pretense of rushing to business that could not wait. His face was always as close as he could get it to you. He usually smelled like my old man on Sunday mornings, after a long Saturday night of drinking.

We made darn sure we were never alone with this guy. If we noticed a fellow worker in a potentially uncomfortable situation with Chef, it was agreed among us that we would tell the person he was wanted *elsewhere. Right now* !

Mr. Britt walked out the galley's swinging door toward where I was placing setups on a table in the dining room. He extended his hand, dangling the keys to the club jeep and moaned, "Get three dozen poppy seed dinner rolls and three dozen sesame seed. Better get two dozen plain for backup, just in case. If we run out Lamar will have kittens right there in front of his stove. Tell the baker who they're for; I want the freshest. And hurry back here; I need you waiting tables."

Wow! A chance to drive. I seldom got to drive alone, in charge, hot-dogging it my own way.

. The seats and steering wheel of the open jeep were damp from the night air and it was cold driving with the wind whipping all about me, but I had my mind on more important things. Heading out across the dark, barren base toward the far gate that led into town, I watched the speedometer needle move farther and farther across the lit numerals. Pedal floored; 40--50--60. The old jeep shimmied, rattled and vibrated its way toward maximum velocity.

The next few seconds brought so many frightening events I couldn't manage them all. The headlights failed to pick up the bump in time for me to react. The front tires, then the rear tires in quick succession made impact and that was all it took to catapult the old jeep airborne. I felt the unmistakable sensation of all four wheels being off the ground. The headlights now showed no black-top road before me, only open, starry sky. The experience was like I was part of a movie--surreal. I held on for my life and prayed that when I landed the wheels would be aligned so as not to roll the jeep or maybe even throw me out.

I held the steering wheel as true as I remembered it at lift-off. The jeep came down and like a bronco, veered off roughly. I swung the wheel, my buttocks bouncing hard and sliding around on the driver's seat. Finally we settled onto the road. My foot was off the gas pedal now. The car and I were still on the road, moving forward, 40--30--20. I slowed to a stop and set the hand brake.

Shaking and struggling for breath, I felt the night air chilling my damp skin. After my breathing approached normal, I slowly proceeded toward the town gate, still some distance away. Spasms shook my abdomen as I kept my speed well under the base limit for the completion of my errand.

In those ten seconds of takeoff, flight and landing, I learned a lesson that never left me. I realized I couldn't drive with the bravado of my favorite "wheel-men-Charlies," Bronson and Coburn, as they drove in their action films.

Forget personal danger, injury--even death. All I could think of was the Navy taking away my government license for reckless driving.

BOY TOY

He came to his office doorway as we moved past and greeted us cordially, atypical for "The Snake." An obvious charade for Peggy's sake. "Mornin', Miss Peggy. Mornin', Frank-boy. Where you takin' my leading seaman? He's got work to do." Snake was pouring it on. Peggy didn't suspect this closet lecher.

"Well, Petty Officer Taylor, I'm taking Frank down to show him my new Buick. Why don't you come along? We won't be long, it's just downstairs."

"Thank you, Ma'am, but I'll have to see it later. You two go on and have a real nice time."

Oh, brother. If you only knew this man.

Peggy led off down the administrative building's hallway. Snake shot me a rakish wink and darted his tongue rapidly in and out--his trademark--hence his nickname "Snake."

"Give me a break, Snake" I nervously whispered over my shoulder and hurried to catch up.

Light metallic blue. Four doors. Dark blue leather seats. A Roadmaster--top of the line. I didn't know anyone at home who could afford a machine like that. It came from another world, not mine. But her manner showed the new car didn't have the same effect upon her as it did me. She thought it was *nice*, I thought it was *bitchin'*.

"Let's take a little spin, okay Frank?" Peggy was like a proud new parent. I reached for the door handle in front of me, on the passenger side.

"No Frankie, you get in over there." She pointed across the roof to the driver's side. You're driving."

"But I don't have a California driver's license, Peggy, just a Navy license." My disappointment must have showed.

"That's good enough for here on the base. Take the keys." She dangled the shiny keys toward me.

I was eighteen. I sensed my eyes glaze over. Half-way in I was stopped, couldn't get past the steering wheel. Peggy had adjusted the seat as far forward as it would go and positioned a pillow behind her back so her short legs could reach the pedals. I moved the pillow over between us and shifted the seat back to accommodate my longer legs. Peggy took the pillow and tossed it casually over her shoulder into the back.

We were off. I was floating.

Cautiously I eased us down the base's main avenue, keeping within the 25 mile an hour limit. It seemed like every pedestrian's head turned toward the Roadmaster as we passed. A feeling of self-conscious took hold. Was it the new car? Was it the older woman beside the kid with the broad smile? Were those grins of "understanding," something like one receives from a wink, a nudge in the ribs--or a tongue darting in and out?

Get over it. She's just enjoying watching a boy having fun driving a new, expensive car. Snake's nuts, talking about her getting me into the kip. What the hell does an old seadog like him know about anything anyway?

"We'll have to get you a license, Frank. Find out the Department of Motor Vehicles' hours in Oxnard. We'll take the car into town one day soon and get you fixed up."

Now I was really soaring. Me, with a state driver's license.

Show me the car. I'll drive it.

Life was as good for me that day as any time I could remember.

Saturday the two of us were in Oxnard with the Buick, waiting my turn to be tested. I was squirming with anticipation, having studied the Department of Motor Vehicles brochures day and night for the preceding three days.

The examination went pretty well, with the exception of parallel parking. After the examiner rearranged the orange cones I'd knocked over for the third time, Peggy's powder-blue "box-car" was finally positioned into the designated spot.

I passed the test. The temporary license was secure in my wallet.

We left downtown with me behind the wheel, heading out through the farm lands toward the base. Peggy turned on the radio and searched-out a music station that surprised me. Women her age liked Guy Lombardo and Kay Kaiser. She began snapping her fingers to a Lionel Hampton beat.

"Let's stop at the base commissary for the makings of a celebration dinner." Her voice lit up. She was as happy as I with the morning's events.

Dinner? What the hell does she want to hang-out with me for? But it is a home cooked meal. Well, I guess that's the least I can do--she's been so good to me.

We drove out through a back gate from the base into the Hueneme sand dunes, the bag of groceries balanced on the back seat. Still piloting the Buick, I felt like we had established some sort of deal--whenever I was in this car, I was to be the driver.

Up ahead, the seaside area with its small, wooden-sided, week-enders, showed a part of the area I'd never seen.

"That's me, there where the wind is blowing the spinning daisy out front. Just pull it into the driveway, 'James.'"

The whole place was smaller than a two-car garage. I thought of Jack Benny's saying, "A room so small you'd have to go outside to change your mind."

"You grab the eats while I let us in." She rummaged through her yellow and orange, over-sized, purse as she climbed two steps up to the back door.

I set the groceries onto a table-for-two in the corner. From the tiny kitchen I looked directly into the adjacent living room. I could see the entire home from the doorway. Across the small living room were two adjacent doors. One, partially opened, exposed the white bathroom pedestal sink. The other was closed. I assumed it led to her bedroom.

"I have wine, bourbon, Coke, and Seven-Up. Sorry, I don't have beer. What can I get you?" My hostess bubbled as if there was no one in the world she would rather be entertaining.

Was she kidding? I was under-age. I never drank anything alcoholic, except for an occasional beer. The other stuff tasted like medicine to me.

"I'll have a Seven-Up, thanks. I don't drink much."

"Humph."

That seemed to knock some of the air from her balloon. She poured herself some Kessler's Bourbon and added Coke until it threatened to flow over. Two long sips and she exhaled through her pursed lips in a half-whistle. Things from the market lined the short sink-top and she began moving them about, opening packages and containers.

I was getting a little bored sitting there at the table, answering Peggy's questions about my past. What past? At my age that would be "childhood-past."

Shall I tell her about my dog, Jerry, or how excited I'd been to finally get my Bird Study merit badge for Eagle Scout?

"Here, make yourself useful." She handed me a large can and a hand-held can-opener. The plain label read, "Whole Chicken," but I didn't know what to expect from a can. I'd never seen a whole chicken come out of a can. At home when we wanted chicken, my stepdad got a live one from the back-yard.

I removed the lid and looked inside at "the bird." His crammed-in form filled the entire container.

How do they do that?

I shook him out onto a platter and stared down in disbelief. Without the protection of the can, it looked even stranger. The bird had kept the configuration of the cylindrical can. It lay there with grayish tinted gelatin clinging to its goose-bumped flesh. I felt an urge to look for an inflation stem to blow him up, like a balloon, back to his original form.

I wasn't much of a conversationalist that night, I guessed it was because I was so much younger than she. She couldn't be interested in the stuff a kid liked, or did, and I sure didn't care about her hobby of collecting thimbles from "all over the country," displayed in a special-made glass case that hung on the wall.

We got through the meal pretty much in silence. The canned peas and boiled potatoes rounded out the "chicken dinner." She sure didn't cook chicken like my mom. The meal tasted about as good as the bird's appearance promised when he slid with a plop from the can.

Peggy began clearing the table, putting the dishes into the sink. I helped carry some to the counter, but she motioned me away from the mess, toward the living room. They would be cleaned later, probably some time later. The mess would wait.

"I feel sticky after being out and about today," Peggy announced. "Think I'll take a shower. I won't be long.

"There are some magazines there in the rack. The radio is over here by the kerosene heater. Help yourself to anything you want."

She reached for a box of Blue Diamond matches resting beside a sleek, ceramic black panther crouched on the mantel. Partially sliding out the interior section, she removed a wooden match, and expertly struck it across the rough side surface of the box. Bending, she lit the tall, circular heater--an exact replica of the one in my grandmother's bedroom. In my mind I pictured her room in our house when I was a little boy. Granny would adjust the temperature so high you could hardly breathe when you came in to visit.

The yellow, blue, and orange flames were visible through the transparent band that encircled the heater's base. They produced dancing images on Peggy's furnishings and walls, lighting up the dumb display of thimbles "from around the country"--*big deal.*

She was back in no time, wearing a white chenille robe and drying her hair with a towel held in one hand, while the other hand guided a toothbrush in piston action over her teeth with the determination of a search and kill mission.

See, I have a nice, clean, mouth.

Peggy removed the foamy brush and motioned with a swing of her head toward the bathroom, "You can take a shower if you want. There's a clean towel on the sink. I left you some hot water."

Why in the hell would I want to take a shower--here? I hope I'll be back at the base before much longer.

"No thanks, I'm fine," I said, wondering how I could propose leaving soon.

"Well, I'm sure feeling the effects of a long day. Think I'll lie down for a few minutes."

She disappeared into another room around the corner. "If I doze off, call me in about fifteen minutes."

I thumbed through some of her magazines.

Saturday night. Eight o'clock. You'll never catch me doing this again. Sitting alone in this doll-house-sized living room, wondering what I'm even doing here. I don't like these Silver Screen and True Confessions magazines. If I play the radio it will disturb her. I'd like to get the hell out of here. Maybe just slip out? Nah, too far to walk.

"Frank?" Her voice floated from the other room.

Surprised, I shot up from the chair and walked to the open doorway.

"Yes?"

Peggy was lying on top of the covers in her robe, her head propped up on two pillows, reading a *Police Gazette* by the light of a small lamp next to the bed. A water tumbler half full of what looked like the white wine she'd had with dinner, rested on the bedside table. "Are you as tired as I am? Would you like to lie down and take a nap?"

"No, I'm fine," I remained standing in the doorway.

I guess I said the wrong thing. I was a little shocked by her transformation, reminding me of the movie *Jekyll and Hyde*. Her chubby facial features shifted into a hardened glare. Her arm brought the *Gazette* down beside her with a smack and she jerked herself upright, readjusting the pillows behind. She looked ready for serious business. Pointing her finger, her arm fully extended, she stabbed it in various directions while she rasped.

"Flip that switch beside you. Get that stack of materials off the bureau. Pull the chair over here." She indicated a spot next to her bed.

78

I complied with the string of commands, wondering why she had become so combative.

Old people, who can figure them out? She seems pissed.

"Sit down," she waved her hand toward the chair I'd placed beside the bed. "Ask me some of those practice questions off these." She thrust a collection of papers into my chest. I have two weeks to get ready for my GS-5 exam.

I can't waste this *whole* evening."

GROUNDED

Brain Donahue jogged into the bar. "Britt just pulled out! Yeooeeh--let the good times roll."

Brian began his rendition of the Dirty Boogie incorporating his exaggerated hip gyrations. It always put us on the floor. Laughing, Tiny and I began our end-of-the-evening clean-up chores.

After the last patrons left the officer's club each evening, it was time for us to prepare the club for the next day. When we were certain the manager had left, I took one of the quarters marked with red nail polish from the small dish by the cash register and selected six favorites from the neon-lit juke box.

Tiny, the six-foot-five-inch weight lifter, headed behind the bar. Securing the beer cooler was a spring steel rod crossing the top, with one end slipped into a receiver and the other padlocked to the box. Tiny's muscles bulged beneath his white skivvy shirt as he flexed and without much effort slowly bent the bar. He lifted at the center to release one end from its holding configuration. The other end of the steel bar was still locked to the box, but the bar was ineffective securing the lid in place with the second end not engaged. Up with the lid and Tiny played bartender, producing cold Blatz beers for our three man crew.

This was our usual drill. We sang along at the tops of our voices with Frank Sinatra and the Pied Pipers. By the time we'd finished "I'll Never Smile Again," "Oh! Look At Me Now," and the other four selections from the quarter, the beers were finished and the work was done.

This frivolity was punctuated by dropping nickels into the different "one armed bandits" stationed along the barroom walls.

Actually, we were not allowed to play the slots.

Nor were we allowed to do what happened next. We attempted to release the jackpot bank from the quarter slot machine by jamming the end of an opened coat hanger up the payoff channel. What possessed us to try this stunt, I still don't know. We had never attempted it before and it didn't seem such a big deal at the time. I can't even remember whose idea it was and we didn't have any luck releasing the quarters.

Had the quarters fallen, I don't know what we would have done because basically we were each pretty solid citizens. No one would have wanted to touch the ill-gotten coins. It would have probably been one of those "Well, *you* did it." "Bull shit, it was *your* idea." "Well, it was a dumb idea. Now how do we get the damn quarters *back in?"*

But we hadn't released the coins, and I didn't give it another thought.

At 1000 the next morning, Ensign Locke, my mentor, called me into his office. He motioned toward the door and asked me to close it. Turning, he crossed the room and closed the second door leading out to the hallway. Evidently this was to be a private conversation.

Probably another pat on the back for my continued dedication to the job. Ensign Locke was not stingy with compliments and recognition. This was one of the reasons I liked him so much.

I was half into a chair when Mr. Locke directed, "Do not sit down. Stand here before my desk." He motioned his hand toward a spot directly in front of him. I felt awkward in this formal mode that Mr. Locke had never insisted upon in the past.

"Tell me what happened at the club after closing last night."

I reviewed the night's activities, leaving out the free beer and attempted coin theft from the quarter machine.

Thank god that quarter jackpot hadn't fallen.

Ensign Locke picked up a paper from the desk in front of him. With a pained expression on his face, he informed me Base Security had looked through the windows into the bar last night and witnessed our "conduct." He explained that the Provost Marshall and Mr. Britt, the club manager, each had a copy of Security's report.

I glanced away from his eyes for a moment, shifting from one side of his octagonal, frameless glass lenses to the other. Little veins protruded from his forehead, just forward of each temple.

My stomach is cramping. I've got to go to the head. Oh geeze.

"Frank, Mr. Britt has asked me to inform you that you are no longer welcome in the club, not as an employee, nor as a guest. He does not choose to press charges and he asks that you do not discuss this incident with anyone.

"Mr. Britt is a gentleman and a personal friend of mine. I am *directing* you not to discuss what took place last night with *anyone*. No one else in this office, except Mr. Hicks the Provost Marshal, is aware of last night's activities."

He stood up and slowly paced behind his desk for a moment.

I shifted from one foot to the other. *I can't hold this much longer.*

"I have not determined what disciplinary action I will take. Perhaps, after you have had time to consider the gravity of what you have done, you will suggest something appropriate.

Right now the electric chair sounds about right. I must be nuts. Talk about "acting the jackass," this tops everything.

"But for now, give me your Navy Driver's License. You won't be needing *that* anymore."

I slowly removed my wallet from my trouser front. I was numb.

Oh no! How about--I don't have it? I lost it? It's in my locker, I'll bring it in later? He'll never go for more of my antics--too much like the old "dog ate my homework" pitch. Oh please, not my license.

I handed over my most valued possession.

There was no mention of how he had vouched for me in getting the club job. No talk of his disappointment, after going out of his way to make my assignment as his legal yeoman a fulfilling experience for me.

"Mr. Locke, I..."

"Place the license right here." He rested his index finger on his desk, immediately before me.

"You're dismissed, Frank. You have a lot of work waiting at your desk."

I hightailed it down the hall to the head.

The topic never came up again in the remaining year I served in the office.

Still, I wished I had that damn license back.

AT LAST,
THE BLUE WATER NAVY

l. to r.: author and "Gus" Gustafson,
U.S.S. OZBOURN, liberty in Formosa

SEA DUTY

If it hadn't been for Snake Taylor I probably would have slit my throat. The week after the "O Club caper" I took a mid-morning break and headed next door to the Assistant Provost Marshall's office. There was always coffee brewing and "Chaplain Snake" to tune up my morale.

I stuck my head inside, checking for permission. "Joe pot on?"

Snake looked up from his paperwork. "You skinny ass little goldbricker. Who said you could leave that pile of papers on your desk? They sure turned out more work in that office before you ever came aboard."

That meant I was welcome.

Snake stood and poured me a steaming mug. "Frankie, you're lookin' sorta shitty. You and Butter Ball have a little spat?" His fatherly smile seemed almost genuine. *Keep your guard up with this guy--for a joke he'll pull the rug out from under you.*

"My life's upside down, Snake. I've blown it with Mr. Locke and I don't know how to put it back together."

He poured himself half a cup of coffee and settled into his swivel chair. I stood looking out the window, wishing I was far away.

With the tips of his shoes he pushed his chair slowly one way, then the other, as if that brought his thoughts together. "We all screw up sometime. The important thing is to learn from it. Think about that. Would you ever make those same bad calls again? Hell no, I know you. You're a smart cookie. You're Snake trained."

He stopped swiveling and faced me. "Put it all behind you and show 'em you can do a good job. Everyone there in Legal likes you. You've gotten good performance marks since you came there. In a couple of months no one will even remember this little bump in the road."

"I wish I could believe that."

"Well, believe it, Bones." He shifted into a less serious tone. "Tell me, whatever happened with that idea of getting yourself a car?"

"I don't have the money, especially now that I've lost the extra job at the club."

"Hell, nobody pays cash for a car. You could get a loan. The people in the car business will line up financing for ya. You should go lookin' in the Oxnard lots this weekend."

"There *is* a '33 Ford coupe I've had my eye on. I'm going to talk over that financing stuff with the fella on the lot at home in Inglewood. Yeah, I'll do it." I was starting to feel better.

He stood. "Okay, get your ass out of here and let me do some work. I'm coming by your desk at eleven-fifteen and we're goin' to chow together, you and me."

Teasing, he rapidly darted his tongue in and out a few times. "Come on now, give The Snake Man a big smile."

Oh, brother. He's a character, but I sure needed that boost.

Me and the First Class going to chow together. I supposed when I walked into the mess hall the guys would call me a brown noser, but at that point I figured "screw it."

He was right about the car. I *could* get my own rod. Ensign Locke could take that Navy driver's license and stick it where the sun don't shine. I'd have my own wheels.

Two weeks later I was driving a black, two-door coupe. My life was renewed.

After months of working hard to reestablish myself in Mr. Locke's eyes, the heavens opened one morning when the mail arrived. I was given what had the feel of a reward for good behavior. Boom--I had orders to report for duty in ten days, to the USS OZBOURN DD846, a destroyer docked at Long Beach, California. SEA DUTY. I was finally going to be a real sailor.

During the next week I drove Snake wacky with a million questions, trying to prepare for my new sea-going assignment. Snake's years aboard ship made him the perfect mentor. But he was not beyond "forgetting the truth" in his advice, whenever he thought he could get away with it. He often mentioned during his tutoring how I must locate the "Golden Rivet" as soon as possible after reporting aboard. The Golden Rivet, he explained, was that strategic rivet holding the entire ship together. If it were to go, the ship would fall apart.

The idea of the exercise in finding it, I discovered later, was for the rookie to canvas the ship, asking crew members for directions to the Golden Rivet. This would hand all the knowledgeable sailors a good laugh as they sent me from one location to another, asking for help.

Snake assured me I could use my new car when stationed aboard ship because the ship operated out of one home-port and I'd be returning often.

Two days before my departure Ensign Locke called me into his glass office and invited me to sit. "I know you're excited about this new assignment of yours. I'll tell you the truth, I was on the phone to The Detailer in Washington the day your orders arrived. I tried to get them changed. I was unsuccessful.

"Frank, your performance here has surpassed anyone's expectations of a young seaman. Your family should be very proud of you, you've proven to be a fine young man." He stood and extended his hand. "I wish you every success. But let me give you one piece of advice. Choose your friends carefully. A man is known by the company he keeps.

"Now go into that office and see if you can calm those two ladies, they've been teared up all day with your leaving."

I returned to my desk. Before I could sit down the secretaries rose in unison from their desks, Mr. Hicks, the Provost Marshal, stood up and Mr. Locke came into the room. The four of them approached me, and Miss Treadwell held a gift-wrapped package. They were all smiling.

"We wanted you to have these. A little farewell gift from all of us." Miss Treadwell extended the package with one hand while she dabbed the corners of her eyes with a lace trimmed hankie.

I held the gift for a moment. I wasn't used to presents. "Don't you want to know what's inside?" Ensign Locke laughed, coaxing me to tear the wrappings.

They couldn't know, but it didn't matter what was inside. Just giving it to me meant they felt I was okay. I hoped *I* wasn't going to start crying.

With the paper off, I lifted the lid of the flat box and moved aside the tissue. "Gloves. Leather gloves." I held one up. "They're beautiful."

Peggy cooed, "They're pigskin driving gloves. Mr. Hicks found them. They'll be great for your new car."

I smiled a thank you all around to each of them. To my surprise, and delight, they all four began applauding.

As usual, Snake was right. It *had* been just a little bump in the road.

A CHANGE OF SCENE

Fumes from the departing bus burned in my nostrils. I held onto my hat and leaned my head back, staring up through the drizzling mist. A strange, confusing sight. There before me, shored up by massive timbers, the OZBOURN rested in dry dock. The entire forward section of the ship was missing. A gaping void presented itself as I focused my gaze, back into the interior. Tangled in a maze of wiring, pipes, and lines, it projected the image of an explosion in a spaghetti factory. Even during the daylight hours, powerful lights were noticeable, providing additional illumination. It would be awhile before this crazy aberration was going to deliver the sea-duty I'd had in mind. I felt like the victim of a cruel joke.

The entire day came together in a series of unexpected challenges. Earlier, when I arrived outside the shipyard at the large, unpaved, vacant lot across the highway, it looked full. But I turned in and began my search for a spot to park the rod. Twice around the wall-to-wall array of cars and I began looking for *any* bit of room I might shoehorn into. In desperation I headed up an inclined spot that had been passed over by previous, sane, drivers. The angle was about 45 degrees. I set the hand break and eased the driver's door open. If the door hadn't been hinged in the rear and opened forward, I probably wouldn't have been able to climb out. As it was I resembled an acrobat struggling past the door, holding it with one hand while pulling my seabag with the other.

Shouldering the seabag, I waited at the edge of the busy street, then dashed at the first traffic break, toward the other side and the main gate. Finally, arms aching and body exhausted, I let my 127 pound frame fall onto a bench for the base shuttle-bus. The skies began to darken. By the time the light-gray bus pulled to a stop in front of me and the driver swung open the door, rain drops had begun a pattern on the concrete sidewalk.

I positioned myself just behind the driver, steadying my seabag with one hand and myself with my arm wrapped around a hand-pole. The bus was crowded with sailors.

As we lurched forward in low gear, I asked toward the back of the driver's head, "Could you tell me when we get to the OZBOURN?"

"Sure, what's the hull number?"

I took a chance, assuming hull number might be the designation following the ship's name printed on my orders and crossed my fingers, "846."

"Boy, I don't remember seeing those numbers on any of the ships around here."

A faceless voice called from behind me, "Maybe it's the tin-can with the bow missing."

"Could be," the driver speculated, "that would explain the numbers not being visible on the hull."

"No shit, Sherlock," a second unseen voice mumbled.

After several stops, the driver pulled off and positioned the bus to look up into the area adjacent to a dry dock. Two hundred feet ahead, extending off perpendicular to a vessel, a canvas sided gangway held a polished mahogany sign with white letters spelling out "USS OZBOURN DD846."

"There she be, Pal. But it doesn't look like you'll be getting underway for awhile. She must have been in one hell of a collision." He hadn't over dramatized.

I eased my mind out of its reverie, picked up my seabag and walked around toward the side of the vessel, away from the forward view where the bow once fit. Unfamiliar, high volume noises held me in their grip as I made my way toward the gangway. Pounding, scraping, and pneumatic tools riveting out their continuous barrage offered an accompaniment to the dynamic scene.

Civilian shipyard employees and the ship's company moved like worker bees about the vessel executing their tasks, all alien to me. Amidships, up by the torpedo tubes, a yard worker in yellow hard-hat, goggles, and welder's leather jacket, guided a heavy disk grinder over the bulkhead's surface. His equipment caused a shrill scream as the abrasives bit into ship's metal at high speed. A shower of brilliant sparks bounced off the man, the deck and everything else in its path, ending only a few feet from my shoes.

I moved up the gangway balancing my seabag on my left shoulder, steadying myself with one of the hand lines that paralleled each side. Ready to step aboard, in my mind I reviewed the protocol one last time. Smartly saluting the ensign, aft, and the petty officer of the deck before me, I offered the words mariners had presented for hundreds of years when boarding a naval vessel.

"Request permission to come aboard, sir."

Facing me, a young man no older than I wore undress blues, white hat and work shoes, a .45, holstered in brown leather, hung from his webbed duty belt. The letters "US" were visible on the flap of the holster. With the weapon resting low on his right hip, he resembled a nautical gun-slinger.

My salute was casually returned. "Permission granted."

I stepped aboard, beginning to feel overwhelmed with anticipation, some apprehension, and a thirst for adventure. The rush flowed over me. This Seaman First Class was finally entering his *real* Navy career.

GETTING SEA LEGS

Frowning, he rolled his eyes and leaned his body forward, his mouth up next to my ear.

"The crew is berthed in a barracks while we're here. The messenger'll take you there." The Petty Officer of the Deck yelled above the cacophony. He shifted his chin toward the sailor leaning against the railing. The messenger was dressed in the same way as the petty officer of the deck, except he wore no .45 side-arm on his tan duty belt.

"Give your orders to the yeoman in the ship's office, right there in the mid-ship's passageway," he gestured over his shoulder with his thumb.

I followed the thumb into a large passageway. It extended to the opposite side of the vessel. I stood peering into a narrow compartment that grabbed my attention. A huge, rhythmically spinning, cylindrical washing machine dominated the scene. By my feet, large bags filled with crew-member's clothing waited outside for their turn in the rumbling beast. A sailor in dungaree trousers and white skivvy shirt stood before the mechanical monster. He carried a pack of cigarettes rolled into the sleeve at his left shoulder and perspired as if in a sauna. Farther inside a second man was lowering the top of a large pressing machine, using both hands on a bar, while his right foot engaged a lever, causing steam to hiss and rise all around him and the press. The first man stole glances at the gauges beside the noisy hulk. Our eyes met and he tossed his head back in a silent greeting.

This guy had the shipboard's equivalent to Corpus Christi's lawn mowing. How do people end up in these "jobs from Hell?" I guess Chief Zikowski in Boot Camp told it right. Seaman Second Class, Non Swimmers--lower than whale shit.

Behind me, on the other side of the passageway, was my destination. A yeoman leaned out from the top half of a double Dutch door that stopped foot-traffic from entering his compact office. He motioned me toward him. Taking my orders, the routine check-in formalities began. These were begun with materials placed upon a small, pull-up writing area hinged atop the bottom half of the door.

The yeoman spewed out information and directions. I was to report to the Executive Officer after I got my gear squared away. "The XO, Commander Ousey, is in his cabin, aft. We all work on board, but eat and sleep ashore. You're assigned to the starboard duty section; you have liberty tonight.

"Sign this liberty card after you read the back, and put the date next to your signature, March 17, 1949. That says you understand if you lose the card you're restricted to the ship for twelve days. No liberty--automatic. Be sure to place your liberty card in the box when you return aboard. That's also twelve days restriction. Too many wise guys trying to get themselves an extra liberty card.

"Check the Watch, Quarter, and Station Bill first thing tomorrow morning for your assignments."

He dropped the flat writing surface, hinged to the door, with a bang and slammed the top-half closed, briskly terminating my welcome.

The messenger helped me gather my gear for the walk to the barracks. "That's Harris. He's nuts, but he can be a lot of laughs when he's not so busy. When we're underway the yeomen have a little free time since there's no mail coming onboard for them to work on. Then you'll see Mr. Crazy in action."

Leaving the ship, I reversed the boarding ritual.

"Request permission to leave the ship."

"Permission granted."

After I saluted the flag, *have to get used to calling it an ensign,* I followed the messenger down the gangway, feeling its subtle bounce beneath our weight. I began to affect a slight swagger into my gait. Sea legs? Without a drop of water beneath me?

There's nothing like life at sea. Or at least aboard ship. Or being assigned to a ship. Well, pretty soon anyway.

"What are all those guys doing lined up over there?" I quizzed my guide, pointing to a single file of men barely inching forward.

"They're waiting their turn to get into the head. The heads aboard the ship are all secured while we're in dry dock. You'll have a problem when you really *need* to go to the head; it's always filled with goldbrickers. Everybody's doggin' it to stay away from the dirty, hard work of refitting the ship. The work isn't just a matter of replacing the bow. When we're in the shipyard there are always a bunch of 'ship alts' to take care of."

Another new guy question, "Ship alts? What's ship alts?"

"Ship alterations. Changes, remove obsolete things, add new state-of-the-art stuff. You know, keep us fighting ready." He winked.

"They pile up until CINCPAC decides it's time to come in and do some refitting." Smiling, he offered, "CINCPAC, that's Commander-in-Chief, Pacific Fleet. But I suppose you knew that."

He gestured toward the queue again. "You'll be in that line tomorrow, waiting for a commode to sit on and read your magazine. It gets so bad that sometimes they station a guard at the entry to collect books and magazines and another inside to keep people moving, not spending the morning with their pants down around their ankles.

"And you deck force guys are the worst," he looked toward me and smiled again.

I saw from the white stripe circling his right shoulder that he was a seaman. His comment pricked my curiosity, since I too was a seaman.

"You on the deck force?" I asked.

"Yep. Tomorrow you and I will be chippin' paint, elbow to elbow, with the rest of the deck apes."

As we passed the end of the dry dock I motioned toward the missing forward section of the ship. "Where's the bow?"

"Well, the new bow is waiting at the other end of the shipyard to be attached. The original bow is at the bottom of the Yellow Sea. Went down in the Tsingtao, China, area. Our destroyer squadron was conducting a training exercise for launching our Mark 15 torpedoes. We were four tin cans, abreast of each other," his hands and arms became animated. "We're steaming toward the target vessel. Something got screwed-up in the execution of the order to turn and launch the fish. We were rammed by the CHANDLER at the forward five-inch-thirty-eight gun mount.

"Sheared the bow right off, and down it went. Some guys on the bridge said you could hear screams in those seconds before the huge forward section slid beneath the surface. They watched the hull number on the bow disappear into the deep green. There was nothin' anybody could do about it. It all happened so fast.

"Two sailors did go down with it, Damage Control people, probably in the CPO quarters eatin' the chief's desserts. Wonder how the Old Man explained *that* in the letter to their mothers?

"Everybody eats their dessert first, before anything else." he advised. "In case General Quarters is sounded during chow time and you have to leave your meal unfinished."

Doesn't this guy ever come up for air?

"The Damage Control crews will clean those desserts up fast while you're at your G.Q. station. No one's safe from those DC chow-hounds. Guess the chiefs thought they were past that craziness.

"We're still waiting for the courts-martial to convene. Somebody's ass is really going to hang high on this one. I mean they're goin' straight to the top. All the brass are sweatin' it out. How'd you like to have been 'the man' and had the con during that little exercise?"

"How'd the ship get back to the states without a bow," I asked.

"Patched up a false bow in Tsingtao that let us steam to Pearl Harbor. What a rockin', rollin' ride that was. In Pearl they fixed it up a little more and we sailed across to the mainland. By the time we got here the new bow was under construction and nearly ready to patch right onto the old OZ."

"Here's our barracks," he pointed toward the two level, cookie cutter style, rectangular solid that seemed to be the universal Navy on shore berthing structure.

Inside, we stood at one end of the long rows of bunks lining the walls. Tall windows, one after another, flooded the cavern with the rationed sunlight that had begun to work its way through the morning's gray clouds.

"Take any rack you want. Don't leave any of your gear adrift or it will go straight into the Lucky Bag. We have a real "regulation" Master-at-Arms who loves to collect loose gear and put you on report. And keep a lock on your locker. There are so many people roaming around the area, half the time you don't even recognize them. They have fast hands, and I don't mean on the piano."

He placed his finger against the gigantic white bag tied to the end of the first top bunk. It was at least six feet long and looked as if it opened to a diameter of about 30 inches. It was the same type I'd seen in the midships passageway.

"Dirty laundry. It's returned clean to your bunk when Ike and Dale, the laundrymen you saw across from the ship's office, finish washing it. Remember, get it stowed away fast or you'll be buying it back from the Lucky Bag. Davis, the Second Class Boatswain's Mate, will haul it in *pronto*. With him it's like a game; the man has no life."

The flow of information continued from the one-man Chamber of Commerce. But it was good stuff. I appreciated being filled in. He must have known how it felt reporting to a new assignment. I didn't mention it was my first ship.

"Mess hall's over there behind that steam fitter's shack we passed comin' in. Chow's at 1130; early chow at 1115 for watch-standers. T-bones today. Good chow here. New movies every night, not the old trade-arounds they sluff onto us from other ships when we're underway."

I loved T-bone steak. Back home steak meant pounded round-steak, breaded and fried. Mom's stuff was good; but it wasn't a real piece of meat like those government T-bones.

I hoped we'd have French fried onion rings with 'em, another favorite I never got at home.

More indoctrination, "A little tip from the top, Pal. If you wear your undress blues when you check-in with the XO after chow, you'll have to come back here to change into dungarees afterwards, before you can go to work. That should take most of the afternoon, huh?"

"Thanks for the tour."

"Sure. Hey, lots of young stuff on the Long Beach Pike every night. They love the bumper cars and the thirteen buttons. Can open 'em faster than you can. Maybe I'll see ya."

He waved and was off. That little break had taken him away from his job for over an hour.

I was beginning to see how it worked.

WELCOME ABOARD

Officer's Country. The small, black sign on the bulkhead directed me toward the after officers' quarters and Lieutenant Commander Walter Ousey. Arriving at an open doorway, I peered from the passageway into an area that looked about the size of three phone booths placed side by side--the Executive Officer's cabin. Just inside the entrance a slight built man labored over a desk. The bright lamp next to his elbow offered the only light in the room. His khaki shirt was open at the neck, and gold oak leaves shone from each collar point.

Figuring he was aware of my presence, since I was standing directly beside him, I waited quietly. He continued working and I surveyed the snug little lair. Next to the desk, against the same bulkhead, a bed filled its allotted niche. A fresh, light blue, bedspread bearing the U.S. Navy seal in its center was tightly tucked all the way around. It sure looked nicer than my white fart-sack with the blankets, folded and stacked at the end so the owner's name showed. A stand-up locker occupied the rear bulkhead finishing the Spartan allotment of necessities. The remaining bulkhead was clear for passing, except for a few clothes hooks, one near the door holding a khaki-covered, black billed cap.

The sounds of the shipyard were somewhat muffled from the interior location, but they still demanded one's awareness. Appearing to finish with the document before him, Commander Ousey looked toward me. The physical situation was so confining I could remain in the passageway and still comfortably transact my business without attempting to enter. My left hand was holding my white hat. By way of introduction I extended my right hand, holding my check-in sheet.

"I'm checking in, Sir."

He took the sheet without responding and placed it in the illuminated area of the desktop. While acquainting himself with the new seaman described by the thumbnail sketch on the paperwork, he held at the ready a black ball-point pen with the familiar "U.S. Government" etched down the side in small white letters.

"So you had a tour with the Seabees at Port Hueneme, eh Spittle?"

"Yes Sir."

XO leaned back into his chair, tipping it a bit. He slid his forefingers behind his glasses and rubbed his eyelids.

"Well, as you can see from the condition of this vessel, we're going to be here in Long Beach for a few more weeks. We're scheduled to go to Pearl Harbor for anti-submarine warfare exercises later this year. Ever been to Hawaii, Spittle?"

"No, Sir."

"Good duty. Everyone loves it. I can't get enough of that climate." He smiled toward me, "Pineapple juice running out of every scuttlebutt." He grunted several times as his upper body undulated with a little laugh at his pineapple juice joke. Then he brought his eyes back to my check-in sheet, and slowly turned his head from side to side as if remembering some pleasant time in the islands.

Never seen a guy get so carried away with pineapple juice.

"And the salad bars, they're everywhere. Do you like salads, Spittle?"

"Yes Sss..."

"Keep you from getting scurvy you know."

He's really on a roll. Must get lonely back here in his cubbyhole.

" Wish they'd get that salad bar idea working here on the mainland." He readjusted his position and moved his attention back to the business of the moment--me.

"Well then, you're assigned to the first division. Lieutenant-JG Moriarty is your division officer. You'll find your First Class Boatswain's Mate back on the fantail. I saw him there drivin' the deck hands just a while ago.

Indicating my slick left sleeve, he encouraged, "Let's see if we can't get a third class crow on that sleeve of yours. Start working on your Practical Factors right away and you'll be E-4 in no time." His glance continued upward. "Did you get noon chow?"

"Yes Sir, T-bone steaaa...."

"I can't have my sailors not eating."

Is he even listening to me? I don't think so.

He initialed my check-in sheet and handed it back. "Welcome aboard."

With that he returned to his busy desktop, then seemed to remember something. Turning back toward me, he advised, "And Spittle, we're a happy ship. Don't believe anything you hear otherwise. Carry on then."

Before I turned to leave, his head was down again, attacking the piles of paperwork.

Out in the light of the main deck, I approached a crew member on his hands and knees tearing up no-skid-pads from the decking with a pneumatic chisel. Seeing my feet come into his vision, he stopped his noisy tool and looked up through large protective goggles.

"Where can I find Mr. Moriarty?"

"Forward, up that passageway," he gestured, "to the wardroom."

Entering the passageway, I came to a double Dutch door, top opened, with a sign, "Sick Call 0830." The wire basket stretcher secured to the bulkhead across from the door seemed out of place. Inside, two chiefs leaned forward in their chairs facing each other, nodding and deep in "Chief's talk." It appeared that the Chief Corpsman was scheduling a time for the fireroom gang to get over to the base dentists for long overdue exams and the Chief Boilerman was sharing his unhappiness with the Navy's dental-care system, specifically the results of *his* last dental experience--an extraction.

"Don't those sons-of-bitches ever give cleanings or fillings? It's like the only day they came to class at their dentist school was when they were teaching them how to pull molars. If I neglected preventative maintenance on my evaporators the way these dick-heads look after our teeth, this ship would never have fresh water. Forget steaming, cooking, showers, or the scuttlebutts. No water.

"These kids are walking around with teeth missing, and I think it's a damn shame. Those teeth won't be replaced until they're discharged and go to a real dentist.

"Come on Brownie, use your juice to get me a bridge made for this." He stuck his forefinger into his mouth and pulled back his cheek, revealing a void between two teeth.

Continuing my trip forward, before I was caught eavesdropping, I was surprised when I looked into the deserted galley. Like everything else I'd seen so far on the ship, it seemed too small and compact. Hardly large enough for turning out meals to feed over 350 hungry sailors three times a day. I imagined the cooks' and bakers' activity when everyone was living aboard. But this day it was strange to see the large kettles, permanently attached to the decking, sitting idle, and the ovens empty and cold.

Just past the galley, an elongated, narrow area designated "Officers' Pantry" was quiet, except for a coffee urn softly hissing just inside the entryway.

I had reached the end of the passageway and faced an eye-level announcement, "Wardroom. Knock before entering." Uncovering, I knocked, not really comfortable anticipating the mysteries of this unfamiliar officers' retreat. Being my first sea duty, I'd never been in a wardroom. A voice responded to my knock. I could not understand the words, but they had the rhythm of a positive acknowledgment. Easing the door open, I slowly entered and waited just inside. Dominating the room was a large table, surrounded by armchairs, and covered with a green, felt-like material. Officers were seated around the table, some with paperwork before them, while others were slouched in their chairs, just socializing.

Large Naval Academy rings were visible on some hands resting on the table. I wondered if they'd begin rapping, in unison, as I'd been told they do at any opportunity to show the solidarity and pride of Annapolis graduates. This was to needle other officers, who received their commissions through Officers Candidate School or the Reserve Officers Training Corps.

"Over here." The young officer was holding a coffee cup, not a mug like we enlisted used, but a real cup with a handle and a little blue anchor decorating the side. He motioned with his head for me to come to him. I saw no Academy ring.

"I saw your seaman stripe and check-in papers. You gotta be mine." He took my check-in slip, and as he reviewed it, I surveyed the room. Battery-powered emergency lights, mounted high on the bulkheads, surrounded the compartment. Each one pointed down toward the green covered table. Circular port holes in one bulkhead, their opened steel-covers secured upward, allowed the now brighter afternoon light to enter, sending shafts through the thick smoke generated by a pipe, two small cigars, and lots of cigarettes. Everyone appeared to be smoking and no one seemed to mind that the room needed a blast of fresh air.

Up above the centered table, attached to the overhead, additional, larger lights were directed downward. They looked to be strong, much more powerful than a dining area would ever require, but were not lit.

A Stewardmate wearing white trousers, white skivvy shirt, white belt and a highly polished brass buckle, had been stealthily attending to things about the wardroom. He spoke softly to me as he came nearby, "Where y'all from?"

"L.A." I mimicked his whisper. "I'm Frank Spittle."

"Leroy McNair, Stewardmate Second," he responded in a manner that was friendly enough, but carried the message that I was on *his* turf.

"What's with those large lights over the table?" My curiosity was up.

Glancing up at the powerful overhead lights he observed, "Oh, those," he kept his voice low and smiled exposing big, bright white teeth, "This here table is used as an operating table if they need one during action. This wardroom becomes Doc Brown's general quarters station."

"Spittle," my new division officer interrupted, "it's too late for you to get any ship's work done today. Finish checking in. Take this afternoon to familiarize yourself with the ship. First thing after quarters tomorrow morning check the Watch, Quarter, and Station Bill. You'll have a lot of different assignments listed there, from Special Sea and Anchor Detail and General Quarters, to Replenishment at Sea. Learn 'em. When the word is passed I want you reporting from your assigned station, 'Manned and ready,' *pronto.*"

Exiting the wardroom the way I came in, I filled my lungs with a couple of cycles of fresh air. Immediately outside and to my right, a large open hatch in the deck revealed a ladder disappearing to the mess deck below. It was time to familiarize myself with the area I enjoyed most--the chow hall.

So this is where we get our eats. Descending, I remembered how Snake Taylor at Port Hueneme had cautioned me in preparing for sea duty. "Face forward, don't look like you're a landlubber by backing down the ladder. You're not wearing a skirt."

The gleaming stainless-steel serving tables ended at the biggest coffee urn I'd ever seen. Plumbing brought in hot water to the semi-sphere, its legs attached to the deck, a hinged half-top, and generous spigot. I continued my investigation, raising a leg to clear the nine inches of bulkhead remaining beneath the next open hatch, and found myself alone in the crew's mess area. A cylindrical casement hung against the far bulkhead, a movie screen ready to be pulled down and change the multi-purpose dining space into a theater.

Tables, with their accompanying benches, were arranged fore-and-aft to allow a bit of stability, allowing individuals to more easily manage their trays of food while eating as the ship rolled from side to side. The tables were secured to the deck. The benches were secured to the tables. In the exact center of the compartment another large hatch opened in the decking. Kick plates surrounding the opening and the raised hatch cover prevented anyone from accidentally strolling into the hole. Looking down, I recognized a berthing area by its tightly-arrayed formations of racks. Although empty of bedding and partially darkened, I could hear conversation and a radio playing "country" somewhere.

Taking advantage of my free afternoon, I followed orders and continued to "familiarize myself."

It occurred to me as I cautiously lowered myself down the second ladder that I was descending farther and farther below the main deck. A couple of turns toward the sounds brought me to the source of activity--the sonar shack. This small area opened right off the sleeping compartment and housed electronic gear for detecting underwater activity. Submarines and other below-surface noises and objects, as well as unexpected ocean-floor formations that might be a navigational hazard, were reported and monitored. I had read about this place in my Blue Jacket's Manual.

Men in dungarees were drinking coffee and lounging, their legs swung over one arm of swivel chairs which were secured in front of circular electronic screens. These darkened screens would light up with a green glow when the ship got underway. Others sat behind them, chairs tilted against the bulkhead. I felt like I'd come across their hideout.

"Looking for a rack?" one of the coffee drinkers inquired.

"I don't know where I'm berthed yet," I said, "I'll be checking the Watch, Quarter, and Station Bill tomorrow."

"Well, there's a rack open there on the top, right behind you."

I turned and faced the tier of three racks, one closely arranged above the other. Aluminum tubing held the canvas forms, with cotton line threaded through brass grommets around the canvas' edge. The bottom rack was triced up with the same sort of chain that suspended the other two, exposing three deck lockers for the gear of those who slept above them. There were no stand-up lockers in sight for hanging things. It seemed everything went into the deck lockers.

But the top rack held my attention. Crossing the middle of it, close to the overhead and about a foot and a half above the bed itself, was a wrapped twelve-inch pipe. The word "STEAM" was stenciled at intervals along its route. It transversed the entire compartment and disappeared through the farther bulkhead.

Reading my mind, the fellow with the first class crow stenciled in black onto his dungaree shirt sleeve jeered, "You make up your mind before you slide in whether you want to spend the night on your back or your stomach. Cause that's how you'll stay until you slide back out at reveille. There's no rolling over when you're sleeping underneath that pipe."

The third class chimed in with a laugh.

"At least you'll be cozy and warm huggin' that steam pipe."

Another Sonarman added to the mix, "With the guy in the rack beside you so close by, I think you're safer sleeping on your back."

Chuckles. The ribbing escalated.

Someone out of sight, deeper in the compartment, laughed. "Not much privacy for choking the chicken."

"Beware of the one-eyed worm," chimed in a new voice.

More laughter.

"Unless maybe you're in the habit of wearing your skivvy shorts backwards."

The new guy razzamatazz.

A chorus of, "OOOOOOOOOH."

"Hey," spoke up another, "with movies and chow up on the next deck, so close to where you sleep, you can't have everything."

I wondered if I could really get any rest at night in a zoo like that.

They *were* kidding me. Right?

UNDERWAY

I was standing on the main deck, just aft of the second 5-inch mount, when the word came over the horn from high up near the bridge. "NOW SET THE SPECIAL SEA AND ANCHOR DETAIL."

Here I go. My stomach was doing flip flops in anticipation of my upcoming performance. I'd been to the head three times this morning and the announcement jarred loose a new set of stomach churning. But no time for that now. This had been on my mind since the Plan of the Day, circulated late the previous evening, announced the OZBOURN was getting underway at 0700--our shake down cruise, to put the new bow through its paces. A week earlier I had gone up to the bridge to familiarize myself with my Special Sea and Anchor Detail assignment--Captain's Telephone Talker. A sympathetic Quartermaster took me through the ropes.

Now, hurrying up the ladder, I entered the pilot house and removed the phone headset from its storage space. The area was abuzz with people, all efficiently on task. I folded the sides of my white hat into a roll to accommodate the ear phones and adjusted them to my head. After plugging my line into the jack-box on the bulkhead marked "1JV", I concentrated on calming down.

Is my line plugged into the proper circuit? Yeah. Okay. I moved in close enough to the skipper to hear and be heard, but left him enough room to maneuver. He was in almost constant motion going from side to side and forward about the pilot house, checking on anything nearby or moving. One man coordinating this mass of steel--I was impressed by his coolness.

My stomach was still sending messages caused from "show-time" for the new kid. I depressed the button and spoke into the transmitter, "All stations, Bridge," clearing my throat, hoping they hadn't noticed the quiver in my voice. "Report when ready to get underway."

The first reply came, "Bridge, Forward Engine Room. Manned and ready."

"Bridge aye," I indicated receipt of the message.

Then I relayed, "Captain, Forward Engine Room reports manned and ready."

And the procedure repeated itself with "ready" messages from the Firerooms, C.I.C. Radar Shack, the Forecastle, Amidships, Fantail, After Steering, and ending with Port and Starboard Lookouts.

Turning his head in my direction the captain ordered, "Single up all lines," then leaned over the starboard side to supervise.

I passed the word for the deck sections to take in one of each of the doubled lines and waited for them to acknowledge.

My nerves began to smooth out. I felt I had the hang of it, if no one threw me anything tricky.

Finally I reported, "Captain, all lines singled up."

He offered his usual response, "Very well." If I didn't hear some acknowledgment I would wait for the next opportunity to repeat the message.

"Hold fast the stern line; take in all other lines." The skipper's tone said he had probably been directing this exercise before I was born.

In the direction of the helmsman, he spoke in the most business-like manner, "Come left 10 degrees. Starboard ahead one quarter; port back a quarter."

Both the helmsman and lee-helmsman smartly repeated the part of the order that was directed to each of them. The helmsman turned the wheel to port; the lee helmsman moved the two brass annunciator handles. Down in the engine room, in the dark, steamy bowels of the ship, I visualized the snipes executing the tasks to start making turns, and ringing up an acknowledgment of the directions from the annunciator.

I felt the rumbling vibrations of the huge screws turning back aft as the fantail shuttered and I watched the bow slowly swing left.

"Take in the stern line," directed the captain.

Following his cue, the duty boatswain's mate sounded the ship's whistle and piped the word that brought magic to my heart, "UNDERWAY."

The ensign was struck from the flagstaff aft and raised up the mainmast. After months of sitting high out of the water in dry dock, the OZBOURN was back to doing what she was built to do--steaming. And that suited me just fine. That was what I'd been seeking for the past two years. "UNDERWAY" culminated my dream and announced that I too was now doing what I was meant to do--steaming in the *real* Navy. *Finally.*

When we cleared the breakwater the word passed, "NOW SECURE THE SPECIAL SEA AND ANCHOR DETAIL. SET THE REGULAR STEAMING WATCH." My relief arrived and I went below to fall into the rear of the chow-line forming on the port side of the main deck. Feeling I had carried off my first underway assignment pretty well, I was proud. Thoughts of my mother came to me for a moment. I recognized the association I sensed with my success and wanting to share it with her. I wished she could have seen her "Jackass" perform like an old pro.

. Al Pugh, a snipe buddy, fell in line behind me. "Frank, you know about the bread."

"What bread?"

He explained, "During the first days out, always take three slices of bread when you go through the chow line, every meal, whether you eat them or not. Throw them away if you need to. The idea is to get rid of all the bread they bought when we were in the shipyard. Once it's gone the bakers will begin to bake bread. And Frankie, you've never had bread like this. Good as my mom's. And I love my mom's."

"I can handle that, Pugh Man."

I still felt pretty frisky about the whole morning's activities and, seeing another buddy ahead in line, I reached past two people and "goosed" Jimmy Gargas. Jimmy turned around and looked back. Recognizing me, he left his place in line and came toward me, swinging a tight fist to poke my arm. He didn't return to his place in line, but stayed back with me, making sure he didn't let me get ahead of him and eat first.

Gargas smiled, "What's for chow, Bones?"

I related the menu I'd read earlier; I *always* knew what was being served. "Seagull, mashed Murphys and gravy. Hope there's a tit left by the time we get down there. I get tired of legs. Hell, there's two of everything. Why so many legs and thighs? You don't think they save the breasts for the officers, do you?"

After two weeks of shake-down trials the OZBOURN was pronounced fit for duty. We were detached from the Naval Shipyard, Long Beach, to resume the normal schedule of exercises that fill a typical destroyer's peace-time activities. These included firing at shore targets on San Clemente Island in the California Channel Islands area and at sleeves pulled by tow-planes. The crew's marksmanship had become a little rusty. During the General Quarters Drill for a firing exercise, I was on the bridge and heard the radio traffic from the tow-plane pilot complaining of rounds coming too near his plane. He reminded the captain that the sleeve, not his plane, was the target. After more errant firing, again closer to the tow plane than the sleeve target, a round parted the tow line and the sleeve withered down toward the water. Rather than string out another target, the pilot packed up and left the area for the safety of San Diego Naval Air Station.

We practiced anti-submarine attacks (the OZBOURN carried depth charges on her fantail), torpedo launching attacks (there were torpedo tubes amidships), refueling and taking stores while underway, and all sorts of onboard drills--General Quarters, Man Overboard and more General Quarters--always more General Quarters. Fires of all types were simulated in different areas of the ship from the forward paint locker to the after engine room. They'd be "fought" with water, CO_2, or foam depending upon the source of the fire and the physical circumstances. There were drills to meet every foreseeable situation that required quickly coordinated skills, and we practiced them until we performed our individual tasks by rote. No wonder we ate so much and slept so soundly.

For these few weeks I'd been doing the work of a man, and I was feeling the accomplishment and maturity. No "backing up to the paymaster" for me. I was pulling my weight--earning every penny of my $117 a month.

LESSONS TO BE LEARNED

My hands turned blue when I took them from my pockets. The afternoon had turned cold, with a wind biting my face that made it even worse. To get out of the weather and warm up, I ducked into the first passageway and hoped I wouldn't get caught goofing off. The Engineering Log Room had the top half of its door open. I stuck my head in and began a conversation with the yeoman. I asked him about his job and told him I too could type. He showed an immediate interest.

"Wait right here." He headed aft and disappeared down a ladder into the forward engine room. In minutes he emerged following a khaki uniformed Chief.

"Here he is, Chief, your new Log Room Yeoman."

"You type, uh?" He looked me up and down with a quizzical appraisal. "Hillinger here wants to transfer to Quartermaster striker; thinks he'd like working on the bridge."

He smiled toward the excited yeoman. "A brown-noser like him enjoys being around all that brass."

"Ah, Chief."

Turning back to me, "Do you want this job?"

I knew right away I'd be much happier putting down my chipping hammer and doing what this typist did in his tiny, but warm, work space.

My Deck Force assignment had lasted three months.

Living compartments and heads aboard ship had been secured, out of use for months while the OZBOURN sat in dry dock. Now everything was back on line. My sleeping assignment wasn't the top bunk I'd earlier been concerned about, with the steam pipe passing across it. I ended up with a bottom bunk, in the same tier, just outside the Sonar Shack. A disadvantage came with sleeping in the lowest bunk. It covered three deck lockers that could only be accessed by raising my bunk. But everyone planned in advance to minimize the inconvenience.

There were no commodes in the enlisted heads. You seated yourself on two short boards, one on each side of you. The boards were attached at their ends to a metal trough. This seating accommodated five individuals. The trough ran fore and aft with salt water constantly flowing toward a drain. My first time at the trough taught me to ALWAYS sit away from the drain but not on an end seat. The two end seats would be drenched if the ship was underway and the bow plowed deep into the water. This caused the trough water to move aft with some force, meet the end and slosh the hapless person sitting there. The same splashing occurred when the water then moved forward. At times we just couldn't use the trough until things settled down.

When they thought they could pull it off, pranksters would risk a possible soaking and sit at an end position. Forming pieces of toilet paper into a loose ball, they would set it afire and drop it into the trough. Swearing erupted as the pyrotechnic floated toward the drain, passing under the row of exposed anatomy. The stench of singed hair and the commotion of people jumping off their seats made it tough for the guilty at the originating end of the trough to keep from laughing.

Another underway lesson, learned early on, dealt with showering. Fresh water was converted from sea water and flowed through the shower heads. The crew was regularly reminded to conserve all fresh water. In fact, wasting fresh water was an offense.

I was curious the first time I saw all of the wash bowls, in the area adjacent to the two shower stalls, filled with water, but unattended. Pointing toward the bowls, I asked a sailor stepping out of the shower, "Hey, what's this for?" The procedure, he explained, was an insurance policy. There was a specified routine for taking a shower. We were directed to turn off the shower while soaping-up, then rinse off. No longer the civilian luxury of leaving the hot water running throughout your shower. Whenever the ship went to a flank speed mode, since the duration of the higher speed was unpredictable, ample fresh water for the boilers had to be insured. The evaporators used to produce the precious fresh water from sea had a limited capacity. The showers were secured--fresh water turned off at the main valve. If you were in the middle of your shower, all soaped-up, and the ship's water turned off, you'd have a sticky problem. The previously filled wash bowls served as a backup. "French douche," my mentor called it.

I soon learned that Al Pugh had been right about the bread. The wonderful fresh-baked bread, Parker House rolls, and breakfast cinnamon rolls, were popular with the crew. The cooks and bakers devised a plan to keep them from being devoured too quickly. Otherwise they would have been baking 24 hours a day and not have available space in the small galley to also prepare meals. The scuttlebutt was that they held the fresh baked bread back a day or two before serving, making it less appealing.

For me the bread situation resolved itself. I was blessed with a shipmate, Bob Howie, whose brother, Eugene, was a ship's baker. Late at night, when Eugene was on duty, we would go to the galley and enjoy one of the loaves fresh from the oven. Bob would tear a hot loaf into steaming chunks, and we'd smear a block of butter over the insides. That Arkansas smile would rise over his dripping handful, and he'd muse, "Ah, the simple things."

Time arrived for the OZBOURN to be deployed West to the Hawaiian Islands. First steaming up the California coast into beautiful San Francisco Bay, we sailed under Golden Gate Bridge and tied up at Treasure Island. This Bay Area was new to me and I was excited to get ashore. Everyone said San Francisco was good liberty. Tom Corothers and I made it over to the Barbary Coast on the first night. He promised to show me "the damnedest thing I'd ever seen." There were men in sexy dresses, and made up like good looking women. I would never have believed they weren't what they looked to be had I not been tipped-off.

Sitting together at the show-bar in Finoccio's, I was in mild shock. The performers on the stage above us sang, entertained with salty humor, and the crowd couldn't get enough. You had to scream to be heard. Tom cupped his hand to my ear and laughed above the din, "Just keep remembering what's underneath those dresses. They have the same equipment you have, so don't get any ideas. I wouldn't move on any of the 'girls' in this place. It's a hang-out for freaks."

I learned of so many places in the city I wanted to see. We weren't in San Francisco long enough. The day before the ship left we received a group of recruits fresh out of Boot Camp. Getting underway in the morning, we secured the Special Sea and Anchor Detail after clearing the Golden Gate, and went to noon chow. Sea conditions at the mouth of the bay were always choppy, since river waters met the ocean with tremendous force. This produced some green faces and upset stomachs among our new arrivals.

Down below in the mess decks, experienced pals directed me away from any table seating the new men. I soon learned why. First of all, we "experienced" tin-can sailors always put half a slice of bread under the forward edge of our trays where they rested on the table. This helped secure the tray from sliding as the ship rolled. Second, one never left his tray unattended--it could go flying. It always took the new fellas a few meals underway to remember that you get everything, your coffee, milk, or water before you set your tray down at a table.

There was no protection from some of the newcomers hurrying with their loaded trays to the scullery, trying to get topside for some air before becoming ill. Often they didn't make it and vomited onto the mess deck. Others slipped in their vomit, *their* trays flew, and the deck was covered with beverages and uneaten food. Soon the place looked like something out of a Keystone Cops comedy with no one being able to maintain his footing. More falls. More spilled trays.

But the worst experience was someone vomiting onto his tray while seated at your table, not uncommon with recruits. People seated around them, if they hadn't lost their appetite, would look to determine whether the contents of their own trays had managed to survive the results of the nausea attack. Could they safely eat the remainder of their lunch or had their food been tainted? A careful examination might reveal their food's safety--except when there was potato salad. You just couldn't see that stuff if it got onto your potato salad.

If a new man joined your table, well, that couldn't be avoided. When it happened, my friend "Chicken" Hansen, the ship's youthful barber, had a little routine we all enjoyed. Surreptitiously, he slipped his front partial plate into the mashed potatoes on his tray. Later he would "discover" the teeth. Holding his fork with its potatoes and shiny surprise for everyone to see, especially the new fellow (who might have to be nudged by someone nearby to look across the table at the odd find), Chic would announce, "Now what the hell is this?"

Taking the cue, someone answered, "Looks like Cookie's teeth, Chic." Chicken would shake his head and put the fork, with the teeth, into his mouth. He'd adjust the teeth into position with his tongue, swallow the potatoes, and declare, "I'm really gettin' sick of this shit."

The first time I witnessed this, sitting across the table from him, it made the milk I was drinking backup and explode out my nose. That *really* got the new folks' attention.

But the hoot was to see their faces the first morning cooks prepared either creamed chipped beef or the other treat, SOS. Poured from a large ladle onto a shingle, a piece of toast. The rust colored SOS, a mixture of ground beef, tomatoes, onions, pickles and spices, in its yummy gravy, created all sorts of images in the minds of the new guys.

"What the hell *is* this stuff?" a new fellow would ask the heavily tattooed mess cook behind the serving line holding a ready ladle-full.

"This here's shit on a shingle, son."

The boot would hurriedly extend his hand over the tray indicating he didn't care for any, "thank you." Shaking his head in disbelief he'd move on, with his tray still clean. For the first few weeks new recruits seemed to make-do with dry cereal and bananas.

The entry of new blood caused the pecking order on the vessel to be ratcheted up a turn. I was no longer on the bottom. It sure felt good.

HELP WANTED--TYPIST

I sensed a presence in the doorway, looked up, and saw YN2 Floyd Harris. "Pal, you're wastin' your time here in this dinky space, typing those same boring logs every day."

Maybe he was right. Each morning the hard-bound Engineer's Log would be waiting at my typewriter with the night's events inked in. When I wasn't typing from its hand-written chronology of the engine room's activities, I was out tracking down the authors of the illegible entries for their translations. To begin my day I'd often need to awaken senior petty officers, sleeping in after a mid-watch, and be prepared for verbal abuse. While my simple work routine lacked challenge, I was enjoying the absence of supervision and the comfort of an indoor assignment.

Harris opened my door and squeezed in. "Look at this; I can't even cram in here it's so crowded. I don't know how you do it; you're going to go Asiatic in this phone booth. And you'll never make rate pissin' around with this stuff. Come to work in the ship's office and I'll have a crow on your arm inside of a year. Come on, walk over with me right now and just check it out."

Harris, the leading yeoman, had his arm around my shoulder, guiding me from the Engineering Log Room, around the corner to the double dutch doors off the mid-ship's passageway. He opened the bottom of the half-opened doors and motioned me in. Two desks, holding typewriters that folded away to make a smooth work-space, covered most of one bulkhead. The desk chairs, with their occupants, were held in position by attachments on each side of the chairs which hooked onto the stationary desks when the ship was rolling and pitching. Four-drawer file cabinets for service jackets, correspondence, and directives, lined the opposite bulkhead, with red signs resting in the top drawer handles cautioning: "Keep Closed." Keeping the file drawers latched was imperative when underway, a roll of the ship could send them flying with a velocity and weight fatal to anyone they struck.

A pass-through 12-by-12 inch opening above the files created access to the adjacent storekeepers' office, with a basket on each side of the bulkhead for the two-way flow of paperwork pertaining to pay, uniform allowances, and bonuses. A porthole allowed some fresh air, light and a limited view. It was larger than my log room, but what happened when the entire staff was working inside?

I mentally clicked off the pluses of Harris' proposition. A warm office, out of the wind, well lit, and clean. There were coffee cups around--a good sign. It felt comfortable and seemed non-demanding. Important features because, in this space-efficient compartment, I'd be spending not just working hours but much of my "off-time." On a combatant vessel there is little space available for letter writing, reading, gathering for conversation, or other free-time activities--one goes to his own, or a buddy's, work space to relax. And I liked the idea of working in the company of others--it got lonely in my Log room cubby.

Harris shifted into a business-like mode. "In a little more than a year my enlistment is up. This operation could be yours then; you'd be the man. We've lost two people; I really need ya here. We control the liberty cards--they're on swing-out panels beside you near the door--dream sheets, also by the door. Early chow passes are locked up in my desk, and we prepare everyone's leave papers. This is a great spot to be working, in the middle of the action. For your part of it, you'll deal mostly with personnel work--maintain service and leave records, learn to do discharges, reenlistments and extensions, plus advancement in rating paperwork."

Does he ever take a breath?

"Our marching orders come directly from the Executive Officer. He wears the Admin Officer's hat along with the navigator's; he signs everything, even above the skipper's name, 'by direction.'

"Around here one hand washes the other. You want a 72? You got it--if the work's caught-up. Want to go to a service school? I guarantee you a reserved date at a service school within 6 months; that's the *date* I'm promising in 6 months, the class might be a little later."

Harris dug back into his rear dungaree pocket. "Look here. I have a request for change of assignment already filled out for ya." He flipped up the small writing area hinged to the door and slapped down the dream sheet. "Sign right here." Placing a black pen engraved "US Government" on the signature line, he gave me a look that said, "I know I've closed you."

I didn't need a lot of selling to convince me this was an opportunity. Besides, I'd had some dealings with Harris in the past and he seemed like an entertaining guy to work with. He had the reputation for being a cut-up, and from what I'd seen, I enjoyed his kick in the ass antics. We seemed to rub each other the right way.

I signed the request and he continued. "Now, take this to your division Chief Petty Officer and tell him you want to enhance your Navy career. Then get the Engineering Officer to sign-off. Don't worry about

111

a replacement, any Seaman Second Class-Non Swimmer can handle those logs. If it comes up, tell 'em I'll get 'em some limp dick to take your place.

"Don't worry about this end; I'll grease it with the XO. No problem. Get right back here with that sheet signed and we'll walk it to the Exec together."

What a lesson in wheeling and dealing. This guy's exhausting me just listening to him. He really knows how to get the laundry out.

The process for change of assignment went as smoothly as Harris had predicted. The next morning, in clean undress blues for my new job, I reported to the ship's office and met Richard Boulanger, the yeoman striker. He corrected Harris' pronunciation of his name during the introduction, rolling the name out with a foreign sound, and explained it was French, translated as "baker."

Harris grunted, "Should translate as goof-off. Don't pay any attention to Boulie; he's always got a stick up his ass about somethin'." For the remainder of the day Harris continued to mispronounce "Boulanger," as if for spite. With each mispronunciation, Boulie would exhale, raise his eyebrows, and slowly shake his head.

I was now a Personnelman Striker, and that first afternoon I began to explore, with Harris, getting my school assignment. Graduation from a "Class A" school was an automatic advancement to Petty Officer Third Class, and like every seaman, I wanted that crow on my sleeve.

Reaching up to the overhead rack of Navy Pubs, Harris removed the bar that kept them from spilling out when underway, and tossed me the manual *Fleet Training Schools*, saying, "Here's your first project. Put together a package requesting a billet to Personnelman's School in San Diego."

There's nothing like motivating, to nudge a trainee to tackle an assignment. I'M GOIN' TO SCHOOL.

LET'S MEET THE NATIVES

My first liberty in Hawaii I would go alone. I kept my plan to myself--hike away from civilized, developed areas and find island natives in their natural lifestyle. Hopefully, native women frolicking about would be taken with a blond, pink-skinned boy. But when liberty was announced in Pearl Harbor, a couple of hundred of us, wearing dress whites, crowded down the gangway. Public busses waited to take us into Honolulu. I saw from the development all around the docking area that native villages weren't going to be found nearby. Better to go into town with the crowd and rethink my plan from there.

The Honolulu Transit bus looked more up-to-date than the ones I rode at home in Inglewood. As we sped toward town anticipating foreign adventure, Boatswain's Mate Owens pointed out the Dole Pineapple plant. Above it loomed a huge pineapple-configured water tower.

"That's filled with pineapple juice, Spittle. You should take a tour of that place. There's pineapple juice running in the scuttlebutts." Several of the old timers laughed.

"Or you could go down on Hotel Street with Gunner and me for a strawberry malt."

He winked a smile toward his old liberty pal, and Gunner chided, "Why don't you fix him up with one of your floozies and change his luck?"

Oh boy, will it never end?

Downtown Honolulu dispelled my last preconception of "island life." A major disappointment. I realized there would be no villages for adventure, no native girls running through lacy green ferns, bare bosomed in their grass skirts. The only *girls*, it turned out, were the ones selling photo opportunities along Hotel Street.

"Have your picture taken. Better yet, have your picture taken with me sitting on your lap. Show 'em back home you're not lonely here in the islands." The black hair, parted down the middle, fell to both sides and concealed most of her somewhat long, but attractive face. Like a model from a Greek urn, her nose blended into her forehead in an unbroken flow. Her light complexion was over-powered by the dark hair color she'd chosen, but my attention was distracted by her casual touching of my arm. Her sweet smile, eyes penetrating mine, urged me to follow her playful tugging in the direction of the "studio."

Boy, this little tomato really seems to have a thing for me. She can't keep her hands off.

Inside, guiding me with her two hands on my shoulders, this bubbling photographer sat me onto a chair and turned to prepare her camera. Holding the remote control in one hand, she settled into my lap and positioned her other hand, with its long tangerine-painted nails, lightly on the back of my neck. We faced the camera, she pressed her cheek against mine, and my head filled with the aroma of *passion woman.*

POP. The flash went off and she darted forward, adjusting the camera. Before I could get up from the chair she was back. Leaning over toward me, exposing a slight, but distinct cleavage. Her face was so close to mine I could smell her cinnamon gum. She rested her hand, her hand, IT WAS ON MY INNER THIGH. *Am I dreaming, or is she coming on to me?*

"What do you say we take one more picture? I'd rather be with you than out on that hot sidewalk, talking to those slugs. I don't often get a sailor-boy as cute as you in here." Her seductive smile mesmerized me. Not waiting for my response, she sat down on one of my knees while she repositioned her hand a bit higher. I was beginning to get real wiggly.

"How...how much is another picture? I may not have enough money."

"How much do you have?"

"Well, there's the other picture then this one. I only have, like 5 dollars."

POP. The flash went off again. I couldn't stand it anymore. I wondered how I was going to be able to get up and walk out without having to bend over to conceal my obvious excitement. I flashed back to junior high school, hanging out around the exit of the girls gym, attempting to hide inopportune "woodies."

She walked toward the entrance and separated the black curtains an inch or so as she spoke. "I need the five dollars now." A sliver of bright, tropical, sunlight pierced the drab interior of the "studio." She peeked out to the sidewalk, scouting the action.

"The pictures will be ready in two hours." She turned, "Have fun tonight with your little friends." I was grateful for my white hat and carried it low in front of me. *Is this why they call our cap a cover?*

"Come by on your next liberty and we'll put together another session. Bye Sweetie. Two hours." She gave me a slow wink, a sweet smile, and left her hand an extra moment after patting my cheek.

Without missing a beat, she began pitching a young sailor passing on the sidewalk. "Hey Cutie, how about sending home a picture of yourself in those sexy whites?"

For the next several weeks different shipmates shared photographs of *my* photographer girl on *their* laps. Some had hotter stories about their studio experience than mine. It seemed the more pictures one agreed to, the more forward Miss Smarty Pants became.

"Spit, I swear to you. I spent twenty bucks. Here, look at this 'portfolio' I ended-up with. During this one," Red Putney flipped toward the back of the pack of prints and pointed, "she actually had her hand *on it*."

Can you believe that?

GETTIN' INKED

The actual tattooing area was partially curtained off, about three feet up from the floor, to allow some privacy for those being "inked." One of our deck force guys was getting a ship's screw tattooed on his buttocks. His other cheek showed a colorful, completed screw.

I had strolled up Hotel Street, the seedy part of Honolulu sailors frequented, hoping to find a friendly face. After passing a tattoo parlor, Arnie Randrup opened the door and called from inside, "Hey Spittle, come on in here and see this." I was happy to see his familiar smile. Several other guys from the radar shack stood around watching the victim being worked on.

Arnie laughed, "He's going to have signs put on each of his hips, 'Twin Screws-Keep Clear' just like the boards we hang on the stern of the ship in port." Everybody snickered and jostled around.

The whole place gave me the feeling of a musty attic that needed a good cleaning out. The walls were covered with bizarre offerings. Some were faded sketches, others peeling photographs of past commissions. From their condition and style I figured some had been up since WWI. One photo showed two hands with individual letters on each finger. When the fingers intertwined, the letters spelled out "SCREW YOU."

Pretty funny. But Mom would have a fit.

Another showed a hand with a small fouled anchor above the "V" formed by the thumb and index finger. I liked that one, but the wiser Arnie advised giving a lot of thought to getting something in a spot so conspicuous. There were snakes winding from the eyes of skulls, spiders, girls names with roses and scrolls, American flags worked into each military service's logo, and bull-dog faces wearing dough-boy helmets. All with caption references to fighting and other macho interests.

The artist stopped working on his "butt art" piece and lit a smoke. "Check these out," he pulled some photographs from a drawer in the little stand beside him that held the needle machine with the various colored inks and extended them toward me. The top one caused my face to become uncomfortably warm. I could see why these were kept under wraps.

"That barber pole will make you a real hit with the ladies." *My gawd! This is a close-up shot of a penis with the red and white barber pole stripes swirled around it.* The next photo showed a penis with a fly tattooed on its head.

I don't think so.

"Barber pole took five sessions. Very challenging. Nobody seems to be able to stay hard long enough to finish the project in one sitting. Maybe you could manage it, eh Mate?" He exhaled an explosive laugh. Smoke charged from his nose and out past his stained teeth.

The radar crew joined in the ribbing. The next photo caught me completely off guard. At first glance I wasn't sure what I was looking at. Again, the picture was taken close-up, to catch the details of the tattoo--a multi-colored butterfly--SPREAD ACROSS A WOMAN'S INNER THIGHS. Shaved and alien, the bizarre sight moved my stomach to roll over. This was past the limit, even for a guy trying to quickly leap into manhood. I raised my gaze, and everyone in the shop was looking to see my reaction. A big smile on each face. They had obviously seen the photos earlier.

"Well Mate, what's it going to be? Did you see the picture there on the wall behind you, of the spider? Done that one on a Marine's forehead. I heard later he was discharged because of it. There's the hard-ass Corps for ya." I prayed the attention would move away from me.

"I don't have enough money this trip. I had pictures taken. I'll catch ya next time."

In unison the radar crew flipped out wallets from waistbands of their bell-bottomed trousers and began digging. Bills were extended in a chorus of hands. Followed by more grins.

I'm being sucked out by a riptide. Better gather my wits fast before they tie me into that chair with Mr. Needles working his ink business on me. I returned my attention to the wall exhibits.

Then I saw it. In a hula skirt, a long-haired native girl danced with her arms extended and hips swaying. Her stance captured the rhythmic movement of the island dance as well as an action photograph could. If I got this , it would announce I'd been "overseas"--Hawaii. Instant recognition whenever my shirt was off.

"I'll take this one. Up here on my shoulder," I patted my arm on the target area, pulled my jumper over my head, and stepped inside the work area. A cheer went up and every spectator applauded.

A few finishing strokes and "twin screws" pulled up his trousers. I plunked myself down on the stool where the sailor had been resting a knee, and took over the spot-light. My position had me facing the gallery of onlookers. The artist squinted through the curling smoke that rose from a cigarette dangling between his purple lips, and pushed my skivvy shirt sleeve up to my neck to expose the work area. Satisfied he could accommodate my skinny arm, he rose and searched through a file drawer whose contents looked to have no order or organization.

Finally he located a small, transparent sheet and brought it back to the work space. Across the entire cartoon, he shook black powder from a salt shaker. Then rubbed the powder into every crevice, removed his cigarette, raised the sheet perpendicular to his mouth, and blew the excess powder off toward a trash can already filled with beer bottles and bloodied paper napkins. Taking up a straight razor, he deftly exposed the business end and proceeded to dry shave the peach fuzz off my scrawny teenage arm. Taking a large, nearly empty, petroleum jelly jar, he spun the big lid, gathered three fingers of salve from the side and bottom, and proceeded to work it into the target area. Carefully he rolled on the cartoon across my arm, then peeled it away to reveal a dot-to-dot outline of my dancer.

I raised from the chair when the initial punctures began as the needle machine buzzed at a rate near the whine of a dentist's drill. Again and again the artist dipped into blue ink and permanently outlined the dancer into my flesh. I resigned myself to settle into the discomfort.

Can't cry. Can't even complain. But it hurts too damn much to smile.

The needle darted in and out to the buzz of the vibrating device. The process was interrupted by the frequent wiping away of small droplets of blood that arose on my skin following the penetrations. This he accomplished with a paper napkin pulled from a shiny metal dispenser, like the ones on a cafe counter. Soon my arm was numb from the pain.

With their caps pushed to the backs of their heads, the spectators leaned forward, gawking across the curtained barricade separating them from the young sailor being initiated into the ancient order of mariners. It must have resembled a Norman Rockwell painting.

The tattoo man stopped for another smoke break. He relaxed back into his chair, twisted the top from, and emptied what was left of a half pint of Four Roses he'd pulled from the dirty picture drawer. Discarding the whisky bottle with a well-aimed pitch, he replaced the single needle with a double and began shading in greens and reds, bringing the scene on my shoulder to life.

Finished. One last wipe-off.

I don't think I'll be doing this again. I've got to begin choosing my company more carefully.

A clean napkin became the bandage to cover his artwork, transparent tape holding it in place. Another round of applause from my shipmates. *Now I can't help but smile. I am the man.*

"Nothin' to it," I blustered, "which one of you guys is next?"

GOIN' TO THE SOUTH SEAS

For more than 13 months the OZBOURN alternated between assignments out of Pearl Harbor, Hawaii and mainland San Diego. San Diego allowed visits home nearly every weekend. Hawaii was like a vacation.

I had been to Personnelman's School and became a third class petty officer--finally, a crow sewn onto my slick sleeve.

Working in the ship's office had turned out to be a good assignment. I enjoyed the people and had gotten a handle on my job. I was rapidly becoming a "short timer," with my enlistment expiring in less than a year.

Harris opened, then logged each piece of official incoming mail, hurrying along, just catching the "subject" and "sender" lines. He stopped to read a particular paper that caught his interest. I was on the stool by the door when he turned, holding up the CINCPAC directive.

"Boys, we is leavin' for Christmas Island in ten days. Look here, the OZBOURN is directed to accompany the U.S.S. NORTON SOUND AY 11 on a special mission to the South Pacific."

Corothers broke out the Atlas and began searching for Christmas Island, finally locating the tiny speck approximately in longitudinal line with the Hawaiian Islands and lying south of the equator.

Thomas Solomon Blessings, the radarman, was standing beside me at the half opened door, just outside in the mid-ship's passageway. Earlier he'd been sharing his disappointment. "Some people think their word is like a biscuit, made to be broken." He was lamenting a promised standby letting him down the previous evening by 'no-showing' to take his watch. Interrupted by Harris' hot scoop, he asked through the doorway, "When are we leavin'?"

"Ten days," someone inside answered.

In a half hour every enlisted man on the ship knew of the OZBOURN's upcoming deployment. Unfortunately the Commanding Officer had been left out of the underground communication loop--not a good thing. The letter was resting, unseen, in the Executive Officer's stateroom incoming basket, which was the routing procedure for incoming mail.

Later that day Harris was summoned to the wardroom. Slipping back into the ship's office afterwards, he shared his dressing-down: "The Old Man tore me a new ass-hole. Between him and the Exec, they couldn't chew enough off my butt. Skipper yelled that he was to be the FIRST to know, not the last. 'AND ON HIS SHIP.' Damn, that man was pissed. Soon as he'd stop yellin' to take a breath, XO would start--they tag-teamed me. Who the hell let the word get out anyway? It's not like I yelled it for everybody. I just opened the mail and there it was. SHIT."

Harris was deeply wounded. The poor guy. Each of us had unthinkingly told others the news. It seemed a natural progression.

Commander Ousey, the XO, appeared at the office door, stepped in and closed both halves behind him. We all rose in the cramped space and awaited the explosion. Before he spoke, the door opened and Jimmy Gargas started in, stopped, exhaled an, "Oh, oh," as he took in the scene. He began to ease the door closed, but XO interrupted his retreat with, "Come in here and lock that door." XO was noticeably pacing his words, wrestling to maintain control of his irritation as his head rhythmically bobbed, out of sync with his speaking pattern. Harris had squeezed against the rear bulkhead, almost as if he were hiding behind Corothers who was standing before him. "From now on, whenever an *interesting* piece of correspondence is opened, log it and bring it directly to me. Place it into my hand. Into my hand. Got it? HARRIS, COME OUT FROM BEHIND THAT MAN--I WANT TO SEE YOUR FACE." The red on XO's neck was raising upward. "If I am not aboard, take it directly to the captain. Put it into *his* hand. Wherever he is, find him. AND, DO NOT DISCUSS THE CONTENTS WITH ANYONE. The captain will inform the crew of the deployment of this ship when *he* feels the time is appropriate. Is that understood?"

Each of us softly answered, "Yes, Sir," no one wanting his individual volume to bring attention to himself.

Commander Ousey turned and over his shoulder directed, "Carry on," as he unlocked the door and left, shaking his head and muttering.

The NORTON SOUND, a seaplane tender, was to launch the largest missile ever fired from a ship at sea--the 5 1/2 ton, 50-foot Viking rocket. The launch was to take place on the equator with the OZBOURN helping track the missile.

But first there would be the dreaded ceremony initiating all of us crossing the equator for the first time. We heard plenty about that celebration during the upcoming days. Having to run the gamut between a double line of crewmen swinging their shillelaghs all over your body sounded frightening. We watched men sewing three-foot lengths of canvas around a swab handle, removing it, and stuffing the cavity with wet toilet paper, preparing their individual shillelaghs for the event. I couldn't believe they meant business, but Chief Brown, the Doc, assured me, with a knowing smile, there was no way out.

The daily work routine began changing before we had been a week into our mission. With no correspondence arriving, the volume of work in the ship's office reduced considerably. This was fine for the first few days. Everything got caught up. Big projects waiting on the back burner were tackled and completed. But after two weeks of relative inactivity, some of us became bored with the lack of responsibilities and looked for something to relieve the monotony.

I amazed myself by offering, "Let's paint the office." It surprised me because I really meant it. This was a first for me, strictly contrary to my long standing non-work ethic. I was prepared to do the job alone if I got no takers. I've always found something psychologically satisfying about painting. One can analyze the task, begin, and at any time during the process, easily calculate the remaining parts. I never shared that with anyone, it could have come back to haunt me.

Harris seemed the only one who didn't relish the change of pace offered by the painting project. "I have other fish to fry. I'm leavin' after we requisition the painting supplies." The rest of us put on our worst work clothes and, joining Harris, went below and forward to the paint locker.

Boulanger's "worst work clothes" were pressed, clean, and nearly new. He wore the only shoes among us that showed no signs of previous painting experience. Boulie refused to enter the paint locker with us and later wondered aloud, "Why do they call that seaman down in the paint locker, 'Sixty-Six?' How does he breathe with all those fumes in that disgusting hole? I couldn't live like that."

Harris, being the longest onboard and knowing the personal profile of every crew member, bantered, "Route 66, Boulanger," he mispronounced his name again. "The boy's from Oatman, Arizona, where US 66 goes right through his little town. He'll show you the T-shirt to prove it. Ever heard of Route 66 back in Beantown, 'Baker-man'?"

"Well, certainly. We're not barbarians back there in the 'Cradle of Democracy.'"

"Sixty-Six" wore clothing that showed more paint than fabric, he reminded me of an artist's palette with muted colors. We were outfitted with brushes, tarps, rags and several buckets of light gray regulation U.S. Navy paint.

Back in the office we started spreading paint. I stretched to reach an almost inaccessible area behind the file cabinets when my brush bumped into something. On my tiptoes I grasped in my hand and eased out....four service records. We recognized the names as men who had reenlisted months ago. When a new service record is created for an individual's reenlistment, the old one is closed-out and forwarded to Chief of Naval Personnel. While it was a routine house-keeping chore and its completion had no effect upon the person reenlisting, closing them out did take some work. Someone had chosen an alternative to the official procedure. More painting produced more old service records, until a total of eleven were piled on the paint cloth covering one of the desks. Again, Harris, the longest onboard, was senior man. It would be his ultimate responsibility to insure closing those records and forwarding them.

When Harris returned to the office we pointed out our finds. He let out a war-hoop. Feigning anger, he pushed Boulinger into a chair with such force it crashed into the back bulkhead with an explosive sound that caused Boulie's eyes to pop like two eggs sunny side. Harris withdrew his web belt from his trousers and began whaling it about the excited yeoman striker's body.

"You turd licker, I'm gonna break your knee caps."

It was clear to most of us in the crowded work space that Harris was not seriously putting the belt to Boulinger. Every time Boulie would try to get up from the chair, he'd be tossed back and the cursing and whacking became more intense. I was bent over, laughing uncontrollably. Bob Howie was hooping and hollering and dodging the attack. Harris turned and, with his foot, forced my legs out from under me. Knocking me to the deck, he began kicking me, using the sides of his shoes, pulling the punches and avoiding my sensitive parts, as he had with Boulie and his belt. He continued, alternating between Boulinger and me. "You dead-beat jerk-offs. I'll keep you from making rate as long as I'm on this ship. I'll take your marks so low you'll all retire as seaman, if you're not kicked out first with administrative discharges for shirking duty."

He left Boulie for a moment and turned the belt on me. Boulie saw his chance and struggled over the two of us to get outside. Safe, with the bottom of the Dutch door closed between them, the still wide-eyed victim confronted his attacker. "You are a mad man; you ARE a mad man...." He ducked and disappeared as a chair flew toward the door. That just heightened our laughter.

The ship's office donnybrook created a diversion which left the topic of hidden, unclosed service jackets to rest. No one in his right mind would mention those records to Harris and risk opening that hornet's nest. The man was out of control. And we loved it. With that experience I realized I would gladly reenlist if I knew I could always work with this nut.

I hadn't had so much fun since camping with the Boy Scouts when we "pantsed" Herbie Ziskraut and squirted catsup on his wee-wee.

NEPTUNUS REX ONBOARD

Why was my commanding officer telling me about his mother? He didn't send for me just to reminisce over his family. *You don't suppose...*

"My mother is dead. Died when I was 38 years old. It happened at the worst possible time. I was Assistant Gunnery Officer on the YORKTOWN and right in the middle of the Battle of the Coral Sea. Naturally, I couldn't come home, but worse than that, I didn't get to be with her before she died. Since then I've thought of a hundred things I wish I had said to her. I've cried over that, Spittle, and one day you may too. Now it's too late for *me*--my mother's gone.".

"Sir, is my mom okay?"

"Yes, Spittle, your mom is okay."

Then what gives here? I guess I just stand at attention and wait like a dummy until he gets around to his point.

The skipper wasn't going to drop the other shoe, not just yet.

"I have children of my own so I know how a parent feels. We worry about our children, especially when they are far away from us." The captain picked up a handwritten paper from the desk before him and continued speaking as he glanced at it. "Your mother is very concerned about you. You have not written her in some time." He placed his steel rimmed glasses low on his nose and secured each temple, one at a time. His eyes searched the paper. "She indicates here that she can not be sure you are even alive when you don't answer her letters."

Holy crap. My mother wrote a letter to the old man? I don't believe this. It's the worst thing that could happen. Nobody wants the CO to know who he is. Unseen, not thought of--like Ensign Pulver in the play "Mr. Roberts." Keep a low profile.

"Your mother's letter arrived some time ago. I have waited for this discussion since there was no hurry. We won't have mail service for weeks.

Turning in his chair, he focused his eyes upon mine and demanded, "Why is it you don't write your mother?"

"Well, Sir, I just don't have anything much to say. We're out here with nothing going on to talk about. I've told her that if anything ever happened to me, the Navy would let her know right away. She doesn't have to wonder if I'm all right. She'd know right away."

"That must be very comforting to her, Spittle.

"See here, Spittle. Our mothers are happy with *any* correspondence from us. She tells me she mails you a newspaper once a week, cookies regularly, news from home, but she doesn't even know if you get them."

He pulled himself erect in his chair and leaned slightly forward toward me. "Sailor, write your mother. Tell her you miss her. Tell her you love her. Tell her how much you appreciate all she's done to get you to this point in your life. Tell her how you liked the damn cookies. Tell her what you had for lunch. Talk about the weather. But *write* her.

"Does that seem too much, Spittle? To write your *mother?*"

"No, Sir."

"At Request Mast tomorrow morning you will show me a letter you have written to your mother. Do not seal it. I will read it and determine if you have applied yourself sufficiently to the task. You will continue to write her every week you're away from home and bring the sealed envelope here." He pointed to a top basket on his desk. "Into my in-basket. I will mail it.

"I do not want another letter from Mother concerning this problem. Because it is no longer a problem. Understood?"

I have never heard of anything this crazy. Of course, how would you know? Who would ever admit to it? I sure as hell won't be telling anybody.

I'd forgotten, with my anxiety in the captain's cabin, not to lock my knees while standing at attention. My legs were shaking. I wiped perspiration from my forehead with the back of my hand and promised to, "Get right on it, Sir."

Dear Mom, you have just screwed me up big-time. Oh boy.

Longitude 160W
steaming southward at the Equator
May 12, 1950

Waiting in the chow line, Boulanger, standing just ahead of me, turned and pointed up toward the second forward 5-inch mount. There, standing atop the mount in nothing but his skivvies, was our Executive Officer, Commander Ousey. Training what resembled a massive pair of binoculars across the horizon, he demonstrated a business-like manner except for his incongruous outfit. Even *he* wasn't excused from the equator crossing initiation activities.

"He's searching for Neptunus Rex so the ship can be prepared when the Royal Party arrives." Davis, the Master at Arms, laughed as he motioned three more men down the narrow ladder toward the serving line on the mess deck.

XO is taking it right along with the rest of us Pollywogs. This is not a good sign for my safety later on today.

During lunch I spent an anxious 20 minutes pushing food around my tray. The long dreaded *festivities* would begin after noon chow.

1300. OZBOURN boarded by His Majesty,
Neptunus Rex, the Royal Scribe,
Davy Jones, the Queen,
Royal Princess and Royal Babies.

"NOW HEAR THIS. ALL POLLYWOGS, BARE A HAND AND MUSTER ON THE MAIN DECK, STARBOARD SIDE, AFT OF THE MID-SHIPS PASSAGEWAY. HIS MAJESTY AND THE ROYAL ENTOURAGE WILL NOT BE KEPT WAITING. WARNING: IT IS PARTICULARLY DANGEROUS FOR LANDLUBBERS TO FLIRT WITH THE ROYAL PRINCESS, OR WORSE STILL, WITH THE QUEEN. THE ROYAL BABIES WILL NOT BE TEASED."

Laughing nervously, about thirty-five of us gathered to await, first, our turn with the "Royal Barber." Two crewmen moved toward our group with a charged fire hose, its white linen bulging with the saltwater payload. The nozzle man pushed the brass valve lever forward, and both men muscled the direction of the water force back and forth over us, knocking legs out from under those in front and forcing us all backwards.

Once thoroughly drenched, each initiate had enough hair quickly sheared to guarantee the need for a complete buzz later.

"Move it down, Scum." Wham--wham, shillelaghs screamed out across my buttocks from each side of the aisle as I proceeded forward, toward the King.

Neptunus Rex sat majesticly upon his make-shift throne. Each Pollywog approached the robed regal and stood at attention while the Royal Scribe read the charges:

```
CHARGE I:    In that you have hitherto
willfully and maliciously failed to show
reverence  and allegiance to our Royal
Person, and are therein and thereby a vile
landlubber and pollywog.
```

CHARGE II: Questioned the fact as to whether the parents of Honorable Shell Backs were married.

CHARGE III: Did join a secret league which is planning to upset the reign of His Majesty, and by habit does use Irish language against His Majesty and Royal Shell backs.

CHARGE IV: Does say he is a big shot from Inglewood, California, who joined the Navy to avoid working for a living, whereas his sole ambition is to become a beach-comber, and by habit does sleep with his shoes on, thereby creating a perturbing odor to issue forth and cause undue suffering to many Shell Backs.

CHARGE V: Imitating a human being.

Wham--Wham. Two more shillelagh whacks to my butt and upper legs. The crowned Neptunus Rex, wearing a beard made from a swab, scowled at me and lowered his three-pronged trident toward my chest.

"Our vigilance is ever wakeful. Our vengeance is just and sure. Kneel before the Royal Baby and show your respect by kissing her." He motioned his head in the direction of the Boatswain who sat, diapered, his huge belly protruding, with what looked like engine grease smeared all over his hairy navel.

Once kneeling, I was motioned forward by "the baby," who grabbed my head and forced me, face first, into the mess to kiss his stomach. The Boatswain then moved my head in a circular motion, holding it into him, until I fought for air, thus insuring a good covering of goop about my face.

Gasping, I attempted a joke, "You know Boats, I don't have shots for this."

"Move on, Scum. There's more treats waiting for ya down the line."

Past the other members of the Royal Family. Wham--Wham--Wham. "Bow down to the Queen you landlubber." Wham--Wham.

After bending at the waist to each member of the Royal Entourage and receiving more whacks for my trouble, I was pushed through the gambit of waiting Shell Backs, shillelaghs wailing. Once through the line, we collapsed, fully initiated and free to witness the discomfort of those still behind us.

The worst beating of my life. But I'm a Shell Back now.

I ached all over, especially in the black and blue areas where the shillelaghs had done their work. But all I cared about was a hot shower to try to remove the Boatswain's belly-grease.

Anchored 200 yards off the palm-crowded island sitting low in the sea, I marveled at the scene composed of darker and lighter shades of blues and greens, right out of a Michener novel. We were not allowed to go ashore on Christmas Island for the announced softball game and picnic just yet, some morning reshuffling was taking place among the inhabitants. A string of long, native canoes moved away from the larger island, each carrying a full load of passengers. To satisfy my curiosity, I hurried to the bridge for a look through the powerful glasses.

"Hey, Horn Toad," a signalman, reclining deep back into the flag-bag, greeted me. "They're movin' all the squaws off the island; can you believe that shit? Looks like softball and potato salad will have to make do for today. Back to spankin' your monkey."

Finally, we boarded motor whaleboats and were delivered onto a splintered, weathered jetty. Immediately we fanned out to explore--my first *real* tropical island. Simple structures served as homes, with palm frond roofs, sides open half way down from the top, wide doorways with no sign of doors to close. Seating was on woven palm mats that covered the floor.

A mother wearing a printed wrap around skirt, the top-half of her body exposed, sat on the stoop of a hut. She directed a large, full breast into her baby's eager mouth and gazed up at me matter-of-factly. I turned away, feeling I had violated her privacy, although I doubt any discomfort was felt by her--just doing what comes naturally in her little niche of the world, surrounded by hundreds of miles of shimmering blue water.

Older women, men, and inquisitive, laughing children--but no women my age. These folks had visits from sailors before, probably Australian, but sailors. They knew the drill: sailors and young women meant trouble.

Flies droned their nuisance, swarming about piles of drying copra, the product of coconut harvesting. We were told by the white, island overseer that the copra would be used by Palmolive Pete Company for manufacturing soap. It was the only evidence of income producing activity I saw in the isolated little community.

Giant crabs did the side step across sparkling sugar-white beaches. Radically curved coconut palms had established themselves wherever nature had felt the urge. Dark brown boys, some almost black, followed me wherever I ventured, volunteering to climb up to the swaying, tree-top fruit. Using only their bare feet and hands, they scurried up and sent fresh, green coconuts thumping into the sand below. After gathering several, the boys expertly shucked them, exposing the brown, hard nut. Guarded chops with a machete opened the shell, offering its clear milk. Once the cool, sweet milk was gone, the nuts were broken apart and the snowy coconut meat pulled out in delicious chunks.

It was a wonderful interlude for us "civilized" visitors, but the thought of living the simple island life--without my car, movies, roller skating or cheeseburgers--months on end, held no allure. I was a man of action, and the Polynesian tempo was much too slow, despite the tempting promises of Paul Gauguin's lovelies.

Two days after the softball game, the Norton Sound launched her rocket and history recorded another milestone in Naval missilery. None of us dreamed we were witnessing a progression, there in the South Pacific, that would lead to Mars exploration and Neil Armstrong walking on the moon.

With our mission accomplished, it was time to hoist the Homeward Bound Pennant. The old timers liked joking, "We're making homeward turns towards our loved ones *and our dependents.*"

There is always a special excitement aboard a Naval vessel when the wrap-up part of a cruise arrives and one begins preparing for the return to home port. I sure could feel it. I was ready for San Diego, California.

I wrote my mom a letter.

WHERE IN THE HELL IS KOREA?

The Korean mess began June 25, 1950, when North Koreans swept down across the 38th parallel that separated them from independent South Korea. The United States became a major player through the coordinated "Police Action" of the United Nations.

Fifty-four thousand Americans were killed in Korea in three years of fighting. Winters on the Korean Peninsula were bitter. All personnel in the field lived with this constant discomfort. Frost bite was a constant threat among ground troops and often resulted in amputation of effected extremities.

The sobering fact was we were not there just to drive back the North Koreans. The Communist Chinese had entered the action in support of their North Korean Communist allies. They arrived with materials and a near unlimited source of fighting men.

Hermosa Beach, California, was at its finest. It was still hours before mid-day, but the June sun had already heated things up, making it uncomfortable to walk on the sand with bare feet.

"Hey you guys. Look at this." Arlene, waving a newspaper high above her head, ran toward our group sitting around the large blanket. She fought to catch her breath; "North Korea invaded South Korea. My dad says we're goin' to war." She handed us the torn-off newspaper page. We spread it out and crowded around.

The *Los Angeles Times* front page showed a map with bold, curving arrows, printed in red and black, showing troop movements down from the north toward places with unpronounceable names, identified by small icons of explosions. It was clear no one in our group of childhood friends knew a thing about this Korea place--not the geography, history, or culture. But I was going to learn, beginning the next Monday morning.

Only a few months remained in my enlistment, in October it would expire. I was excited because I was being considered for an August "early discharge" to attend college. My ducks were all in line. I was just waiting for the go-ahead from Chief of Naval Personnel. The weekend at the ocean, with cute girls, was like a preview of many more soon to come. I could be out of the Navy in a matter of weeks, with my beach time no longer interrupted by long periods away from home.

I caught 2 hours sleep after returning to the ship in San Diego harbor late Sunday night. Although I was groggy at quarters the next morning, my division officer held my full attention while he announced we would be getting underway for San Francisco Bay Area, before 1200.

I pleaded out loud, almost a prayer, "Hold it. I can't leave. I have plans for next weekend --at home."

My ship's office pal, Tom Corothers, who'd been aboard all weekend with the duty, understood what was coming down. He knowingly smiled toward me and cackled, "Surprise, surprise, Needle Dick. You're goin' to Korea."

Now I'll see where the hell Korea is.

I didn't know it then, but I wouldn't feel my toes in the Hermosa Beach sand for the better part of the next year. Forget my early discharge. Forget beginning college in September. President Truman was to extend all enlistments "one year or the duration of hostilities, whichever comes first."

After a couple of weeks in the Vallejo Naval Ship Yard we were ready for action. I called my father in Alameda and told him about leaving for Korea and that I'd be seeing him in a day or two. I had seen my mother earlier, while home in Inglewood, so that would have to serve as our good-by. Before the ship got underway the rumors began: The Chinese and North Koreans were long time allies; the Russians were tight with both of them. This was going to be a big, long, nasty war that the Commies had no intention of loosing.

At Port Chicago we rendezvoused with an ammunition ship that was being loaded. In 1944 there had been an explosion here that took 320 sailors, two ammunition ships, and the entire waterfront. We couldn't leave the place soon enough to suit me, but first our own magazines were filled with ammo.

In a couple of days the two ships would be sailing, in tandem with the OZBOURN following the slower vessel, beneath Golden Gate Bridge, heading East, Far East. But not before I had a chance to visit my father.

Dad was worked-up, reliving some of his youth through my situation. He had been in W.W.I, first in the British Merchants and later in the U.S. Army. He recycled the story of jumping ship in Panama and enlisting, with the incentive of promised U.S. citizenship. His briefing,

132

preparing me for *my war,* had me ready to "cover my ass and do nothing stupid, like volunteer--for anything."

The atmosphere of hurried preparations fed on itself. Dad sent my mother a plane ticket. We sailed before she arrived.

OZBOURN escorted the U.S.S. MT. KATMAI AE-16, with her explosive cargo--you can't fight a war without bullets. We were among the first U.S. naval vessels to depart for the Far East from Continental United States since the North Koreans had jumped off.

While underway, all talk revolved around our first liberty in Japan. If you could believe those who had been there, "Every night is like New Year's Eve. There's the local hospitality, dance halls, plenty of women, cold beer, steak and eggs with French fries, hot baths and massages." *Can there be a place like this?*

The testimonials continued, "Japanese liberty ranks up there with Havana, Cuba, Subic Bay in the Philippines, and Panama. The best damn liberty anywhere in the world."

Experienced sailors advised the rest of us to start saving our greenbacks from every payday, "Don't leave any money on the books. Draw everything, every payday. Have as many green dollars as possible when you hit the beach in Japan." They could be used for a higher rate of exchange than the government script we would be paid once there. "But be careful; don't flash cash around town. It's all under the table--not quite legal." General MacArthur, who was directing the occupation forces in Japan since the W.W.II surrender, would stand for no nonsense from military personnel in their relations with Japanese civilians. The rumor was he had incarcerated money black-marketers and directed public hangings of rapists.

During the long voyage across the Pacific, some of us were inducted into the Ancient and Sacred Order of the Golden Dragon. On July 29, 1950, when our two ships crossed the International Date Line, there were no highjinks associated with this mariner's rite--completely different than we "Pollywogs" had been subjected to on the OZBOURN's Equator crossing the previous May. Perhaps the seriousness of our mission and the high tension of the times discouraged any ceremonial rowdiness.

On August 6, while most of us slept below, OZBOURN anchored in the large natural harbor of Yokosuka, Japan. Only five years earlier the Japanese had formally surrendered, signing off the official papers on the deck of the battleship MISSOURI (The Mighty

Mo) in this very place. We were reliving history, proud U.S. victorious history.

In the morning, topside, my nostrils filled with a pungency that I would recognize wherever I was in Japan during the next year: The aroma of honey buckets and smoke from charcoal used for home heating and most cooking. The honey bucket gases rose from sewage sludge being transported continuously by "night soil" men to the outlying vegetable gardens for fertilizing. We smelled it out at sea before entering port. I'd never seen turnips and melons back home the size these Japanese gardens produced. But we were warned not to eat them because of the health hazards of fertilizing with human waste.

The second assault on my senses was visual. I joined several shipmates standing at the rail, looking out through the early morning haze that shrouded the view beyond nearby Tokyo. The conical majesty of snow-capped Mount Fuji commanded our attention. Its size dominated the panorama, even out far in the distance. I felt a kinship with the ancient who worshiped its majesty. What a beginning for my Orient adventure.

Reality. "There will be no liberty." Lieutenant Remmen didn't seem upset announcing the bad news at quarters, probably because the officers would get over one way or another--always some *business* to attend to. Jimmy Lipman, the Quartermaster Striker, complained to no one in particular, "If I don't do more than run water through this sharogie of mine, I'm scared it will atrophy."

"Really James. Really!" YN3 Richard Boulanger screwed up his face while raising his nose in disgust and, using his well enunciated English, expressed distaste over the "gutter language." Two guys in the back rank demonstrated their feelings toward the conversation by jointly reaching forward and goosing Boulie. He jumped three feet ahead, his cap tumbling off. Beginning to reach down and retrieve it, he thought better and turned around facing us--then bent over.

Japan liberty would have to wait. We soon got underway. Our mission was to get the KATMAI's destructive cargo into the hands of the United Nation Forces in Korea. Sasebo, Japan, the jumping off spot, was a day's sail. Exercise for Jimmy Lipman's sharogie would have to wait.

Sasebo, on the southernmost Japanese island of Kyushu, is one of the closest militarily viable ports to Korea. While not fully operative for the coming buildup, all of that would soon change. Passing through the submarine nets and into the harbor, our responsibility for the well

134

being of the KATMAI was terminated here. We were to join Task Force 77 in support of United Nations Forces.

But first, we were granted liberty.

Australian sailors, in their distinctive white "Donald Duck" hats, filled several tables at the enlisted men's club located a short walk off the quay. The place wasn't much, but we were away from the ship and ready for some fun after weeks underway. The beer would have been better if colder, but no one complained. Burgers were on the grill. As the club began to fill with boisterous men intent on recreation, the noise level escalated, the profanity gained momentum, and you had to yell to be heard around your table.

Suddenly the air was split by a challenging insult hurled toward the boys from Down Under. "FUCK THE QUEEN."

Oh, shit. That ought to get it. Where the hell can I run?

The shout from the middle of our very large group caused every white Donald Duck hat to turn toward the general source. The conversations in the hall tapered off--all eyes were on the Aussies. A lone Aussie shot back, "We're Australians, mate. Save that shit for the Brits."

The anonymous big mouth from the American group followed up, "WHO CARES? YOU'RE ALL LIMIES. FUCK YOU TOO."

The Aussies rose in unison. The hall filled with the scraping noise of a couple of dozen chairs as they were pushed back from the tables. Dragging along their chairs, they advanced toward us.

"Here we go, Frankie Boy. Let's see some of your L.A. Roy Rough Butt style." The cheery voice from Al Pugh at my elbow sounded as if he enjoyed the idea of getting a chair wrapped around his head. A few Aussies in the point position of their wedge of approaching combatants threw their chairs forward into our group, and broke into a run in the direction of the still hidden trouble maker--who was now silent. I'd seen enough John Wayne films to know what *I* needed to do. There wasn't time to run for the door. I hit the deck and took refuge under the table, sitting in the center beneath it with my knees pulled up tight against my chin. I'd worry later how all this would leave my clean dress whites.

At 137 pounds soaking wet, I hadn't been in a fight since the fourth grade. This mob scene was terrifying me. But many of the combatants were obviously enjoying blowing off steam, trying to land at least one punch before the Shore Patrol stormed in, blowing their whistles and swinging their night sticks. At the first sound of a head being split by a *billy* I thought I would lose my lunch. The two shore patrolmen were more intent on breaking up the turmoil than taking anyone away. That suited me; the last thing I wanted was to return to the ship.

Many of us non-participants were edging our way toward the exit, trying to be gone by the time SP reinforcements arrived. We less valiant tussled each other to squeeze through the doors, then ran toward the gate and the waiting line of pedicabs.

Nothing was going to spoil my first afternoon ashore in Japan. I couldn't wait to test the expert advice I'd been getting for the past month.

For starters, that hot bath and massage business sounded about right.

GOOD LIBERTY

"Town" was an unpaved street. It stood half a mile up a slight, but steady grade from the Enlisted Men's Club. The few small shops lining the "thoroughfare" carried only the basics for locals and simple souvenir fans and figures for interested visitors.

As if he was competing, my sinewy muscled driver maneuvered the three-wheeled pedicab around pedestrians and between other rickshaws. I waved a five-dollar bill past his perspiration glistening right shoulder and motioned toward the shops asking, "*Yen Yen.*"

The pedicab maneuvered a wobbly 180 and came to a stop a few doors back. The driver quickly dismounted. Panting, he pointed to a shop doorway, "*Yen.*"

Inside, I was immediately aware of the hard-packed dirt floor. Empty of customers and servers, only a scant display of merchandise, a variety of small lacquered items all unrecognizable to me, stood carefully arranged on shelves made from unfinished wood. A woman wearing a gun-metal gray *kimono* with a subtle pattern entered from the rear of the shop. A wide, maroon and black silk *obi* wrapped around her waist. Wooden "clacker" sandals were barely visible beneath the impressive ensemble. She bowed repeatedly as she shuffled toward me. The measured lighting finally allowed me to view her face. With a slight grasp of my forearm she guided me toward a simple six-foot square platform near where I had been standing, then sat down beside me.

More nodding, bending at the waist, and smiling ever so courteously. Her appearance changed the ordinary atmosphere of the shop. Not so much her beauty, because hers was a plain face that commanded no particular notice. But the costume suggested an Oriental venture. Speaking Japanese, she attempted to communicate something. Of course I couldn't understand. I dug the five dollars from my jumper pocket and held it toward her. "*Yen?*"

"*Hai. Hai.*" She left toward the back of the shop, returned with more bowing, and extended two 1000-*yen* notes. The official exchange rate was 360 *yen* to one script dollar. Greenbacks commanded a higher, though officially unauthorized, exchange. I had scored a 200 *yen* bonus

137

in my first black market endeavor. That would satisfy my rickshaw driver's fare.

"I look forward to your return." A little English phrase she had probably learned in school.

"So, you like to practice your English."

"English, yes." She lowered her head somewhat, self-conscious.

"Say something else," I smiled.

"What say?"

Getting poetic, I suggested, "Say whatever's in your heart."

"I like you very much." *Oh brother.*

Resuming her seat, she urged me beside her, nodding. Her smile exposed a sparkling yellow-gold cap enclosing one of her front teeth. With gestures, she spoke again in Japanese. I gathered she wanted some of the *yen* back in exchange for something offered in the back of the shop. But I had other sight-seeing plans and said good-bye. Half way out I turned, thinking I had better get more *yen* while I had a ready source. She took my second five, returning with another two thousand-yen notes. Beaming an even bigger smile, she followed me through the shop, continuing her suggestions in Japanese as I moved out the door.

I climbed back into the rear of the pedicab. My new loquacious acquaintance exchanged some pleasantries with the driver, who pointed to the shop and pantomimed a dead person by crossing his arms over his chest. He rolled back his eyes, then closed the lids. I translated all of this to mean the items for sale in the store were purchased for one's home, to honor deceased family members. The shop lady smiled and nodded vigorously, exposing two additional gold caps I hadn't noticed earlier. *Strange combination of activities, all in one small establishment.*

Pushing the bike in a half circle, his body leaning far out over the handle bars, the driver used short steps and strained in an effort at running, then jumped onto the seat. My "downtown" exploration continued until, coming from our rear, another rickshaw came along side. In the back sat Big Willie from the ship's deck force. Both his arms were spread wide across the top of the seat back. One hand held his white hat, exposing a shaved ebony head. The cigar jutting from the side of his smiling mouth completed the picture of a man who knew what he was about. Alone, his bulk filled the open pedicab. There wasn't room beside him for another full-sized man. *The friendly giant* was a welcome sight.

Willie shouted, "Follow me, Spittle, if you want some action. I got the scoop." I tapped my man on his back and motioned him to join the other hard pumping driver straining up the hill.

In tandem, we pulled up before a large, stand alone, wooden structure overlooking the town. I raised my eyes above the roof and read the big letters over the entrance. In English writing that could be seen from downtown was "TAKARAZUKA." Willie pointed to the sign laughing, "The taxi-dance-hall, my man." Paying his driver, Willie patted his back several times, congratulated him, "*Joto. Joto.*" Then handed out a generous tip. With his powerful arm firm around my shoulders, he escorted me up the wooden steps.

"If you don't have fun here tonight, Frankie, you're brain dead."

We joined a short line of white hats waiting to purchase tickets. One dance, one ticket--the equivalent of about a dime. Inside, the place was just beginning to fill with customers.

At the far end of the large dance floor, musicians energetically produced the familiar sounds of *Indian Summer*. Thirty ladies sat around the perimeter of the room, dressed in white party dresses. Their jet-black hair, dark-brown almond eyes, olive skin, and flat noses gave them a similar appearance, as if they were all relatives from one large family. Most were short and slight in stature. Their builds reminded me of boys masquerading in *dress-up*, except their mannerisms were quite feminine and "cute." I strolled before them, feeling somewhat uneasy in the role of "Rent a Chic." *Should I request to examine her molars?*

As I passed, each stopped her conversation and smiled, or giggled, behind a cupped hand. It was like a candy store, all those sweet, appealing darlings.

You pays your ticket and takes your pick. What a place.

I chose a bubbly little thing. She stood and indicated a ticket was required in advance. After placing it into her small clutch bag, she raised her arms into the dancing position. I stepped in comfortably. We eased off, slow dancing to *Sleepy Lagoon.*.

Her head was chest-high to me. As she looked up smiling, I asked her name. "Imiko." She asked in Pidgin, "You name, please?"

"Frank."

"*Ah so, Frank-san. Frank-san. Hai. Hai.*"

We glided off in the direction of the bandstand. A hand-made sign, resting against the base drum, introduced, "Johnny and His Filipino Boys." They wore tuxedos in a variety of fits and misfits, but produced some pretty good sounds. The trumpet man reached for Harry James' notes, to the delight of all the homesick swabbies. Once around the floor, the next revolution past Johnny's boys disclosed, on closer examination, that each wore black tennis shoes, with white soles, to complement his tux. Even the leader sported the same interesting combination.

The number ended and *Beer Barrel Polka* struck up immediately. Every woman in the hall squealed. Those seated began looking about anxiously. These girls wanted to dance the polka--bad.

Another ticket torn off, Imiko and "Frank-san" jumped into a fast moving, ground-covering twirling run, my partner leading the way with gusto. The hall was large with plenty of room to spin around and travel.

"I'm having fun." I hollered across to Willie sitting at a table, between two ladies.

Halfway through the number, when it was apparent they would not be invited onto the floor, many of the seated girls rose and danced with each other, laughing and having a wonderful old time. I was swept along in their excitement.

A cold beer and a chance to catch our breath seemed like a good idea, I was working up a sweat. Taking Imiko's arm, I motioned an unspoken request to join me at a table. Before she sat, she made it clear that I must surrender one ticket for each number played--whether dancing, or just sitting together.

"No problem," I gestured with my hand toward a seat. Like a big spender, I tore off another ticket, placing the remaining string onto the table. A waiter in black trousers, white shirt and black bow tie brought the largest bottle of beer I'd ever been served--Japanese Asahi. My lady asked for, what turned out to be, a lemon drink.

She was so innocently pleasant, I couldn't help but enjoy the time we were having. As the band began each new number, she removed a ticket from the table and beamed a smile.

I guess this is what all the past month's enthusiasm on the ship has been about. Good liberty.

In typical boy-girl fashion, I explored the chances of seeing Imiko sometime when she wasn't working. Thinking about maybe a picnic, or perhaps she'd show me around her little part of the country--whatever folks did in this alien place that would take me away from shipboard routine. Again, with some language difficulty, I pieced together that she was not allowed to see patrons outside the dance hall. She convinced me this was a fast rule--no exceptions.

The waiter brought peanuts, still in their shells. Imiko opened one, removed a red-skinned nut, motioned me forward, and discharged

140

the nut into my mouth, retaining the red skin between her fingers. We both laughed.

I held her hand, but attempts at kissing were politely rebuffed. Again, not allowed by management. Nobody was makin' any time with these ladies, but everyone looked happy.

A few more spins around the hall to *I'm Beginning To See The Light*. Then, *The Breeze and I*. More peanuts, more beers, another lemon soda, and it was time for me to head back. Cinderella liberty--return to the ship by midnight. I promised to return my first chance. Maybe the next night.

We stood and she extended her hand. I took it in mine and shook it, as I supposed a gentleman would--firmly, but respecting her daintiness. Imiko bowed and I said, without any reservation, "I had a real nice time." I meant it more than she could know.

So this was what a prom is like.

The pedicab reduced speed, approaching the gate after the downhill-derby ride through town. From the other side of the fence I could hear the din of hundreds of conversations, men waiting for motor whale boats to deliver them out to anchored ships. The jetty was long, narrow, and crowded with sailors. The over-flow formed a huge semi-circle at the land end. As is the way with crowds, the mass slowly eased its way forward, onto the docking area, like oozing molasses.

People on the water end of the jetty, unable to withstand the human surge pressing them, peeled off in twos and threes into the drink. One man resurfaced hollering , "No bottom at six," and began a crawl stroke through the inky coldness toward the shoreline, the wharf too crowded to allow helping him up. New replacements advanced to the terminal positions--like bowling pins set up to await the next strike ball. All attempts to create some manner of crowd control were ignored.

Of course many of us waiting there had enjoyed more than our share of Asahi beers. One nitwit held a fireworks device he'd bought in town, which he lit, sending balls of white explosives discharging from its end. The first went into the sky in a beautiful bright arc. Everyone "ooooed".

Next everyone "Eeeeooooed!" Without warning, a gorilla had leaped from his cage. The staggering inebriate lowered his arm, sending the next fireball hurling into the chest of a sailor standing across from him, just eight feet away. Several more discharges shot across ducking heads of nearby hysteric sailors as they screamed and dove for the ground.

Nervous potential targets jumped onto the pyrotechnic wizard, knocking him to his butt. Others rushed in to take away his remaining toys. He grumbled and fussed until a burly First Class Carpenter's Mate, with a gold-on-blue "SP" arm band, cuffed his hands behind him.

Yeah, this was gettin' pretty close to the promised "New Year's Eve" craziness of Japan.

BIRD-DOG STATION

The weather turned "brass monkey" cold as winter took charge. At times the surface of the sea iced over. Dark woolen watch caps and gloves came out of seabags for the first time since they were issued in boot camp. I had never owned a pair of long-johns, but I wrote home asking Mom to mail several pair along with some wool socks. She had a little trouble finding the underwear in Southern California, but her supply system outperformed the Navy's in getting the warm clothes to me.

Week after week the OZBOURN cruised within the task force, off the Korean peninsula, steaming above and below the 38th parallel dividing the two combating nations. When we weren't on station in the circular screen of destroyers, protecting the carriers within the formation's nucleus, we were directed to leave our position and bombard shore targets. With the crew at General Quarters, we shelled ammunition depots, shore defenses, rail or bridge opportunities, fuel storage farms, and enemy troop concentrations.

At General Quarters every crew member had a battle station. No one was working in the laundry, the mailman left his sorting to man a gun mount, the yeoman deserted his typewriter, climbing ladders to his station on the bridge, and the barber joined his Damage Control Party.

Only a galley crew remained at its regular task during General Quarters, since the duration was usually unpredictable. The Navy always feeds its sailors. The rumor was the galley laced our chow with potassium nitrate--saltpeter. My dad's wartime experiences bore that out. He swore the government used "niter" in preparing military food, hoping to calm young servicemen's libidos and insisted that during the First World War some of his pals were writing letters home to their wives beginning, "Dear Friend ...." Supposedly, the regular adding of this pacifier lessened the risk of an efficient crew becoming an uncontrollable, sex-mad gang.

In 1950 the United Nations Forces were tasked with maintaining a Naval blockade of North Korea. Any vessel our ships encountered above the 38th Parallel, not responding properly to the challenge to

143

identify itself as friendly, was sunk by a destroyer ordered out from the formation.

These were usually fishing boats, but with no way of knowing if they were guilty of placing the free floating mines we regularly encountered, our job was to sink them. We sighted mines frequently. The destroyer CHANDLER had been badly damaged in an earlier mine contact. They presented a serious hazard, and violated the Geneva Convention--dirty pool.

From my GQ station on the bridge I could observe each of these encounters with enemy vessels. Often there would be families aboard the smaller boats--women and children. In such cases a verbal warning would be delivered by an on-board-interpreter, to return to port and not revisit those waters, or risk being sunk.

In other situations a round from one of our five-inch guns would be directed in the path of the suspect vessel, off his bow. The sight of the round erupting in the water nearby usually encouraged the civilian crew to abandon. Sometimes a second round, placed close enough for them to hear its whistling scream come in over their heads, was required to convince the occupants to leave the boat. By the time we were firing repeated salvos toward the target, any lagging crew members realized we meant business and would be scurrying away to the safety of shore in a boat, floatation device, or simply executing an excited breast stroke.

In attempting to reach the target, it was not uncommon to expend fifty rounds of 5-inch ammo and an additional thirty rounds of illumination projectiles if in the dark of night. With that kind of accuracy, the safest place might have been aboard the target.

From my vantage point as the Captain's telephone talker I could view all of the action. My battle station assignment meant I must be near enough to him to hear and be heard. As we took part in these engagements, I considered the expense of delivering just one round of ammunition. I speculated, from my position on the bridge, the logic of putting a boat into the water to approach the enemy vessel's master with a proposition.

"Your pilot house is constructed from pine; our destroyer's is enclosed in 1/2 inch steel. Here is a certified check for $1000, yours if you will voluntarily scuttle this vessel--in return for saving us all a lot of energy and waste."

They'd have their lives and a $1000 grub-stake. We'd conserve ammo, and a potential mine-layer would be disposed of.

Carrier task force planes, returning from sorties into the interior of the two Koreas, sometimes had to ditch into the sea. They might have been hit by enemy fire or their aircraft suffered some malfunction. The pilots knew if they could get as far as the coast, destroyers were regularly stationed offshore to rescue them. In the scheme of the action plan, when performing in this capacity we were referred to as "Bird Dogs." Because of uncertain water depths when rescuing a pilot forced to ditch close to the shoreline, we would usually launch a motor whale boat. When called to man their stations, the Plane Crash Detail aboard the destroyer mustered at the ship's armory to be issued weapons and ammo. Then, positioned in the boat, they were lowered to the water from the boatdeck where the craft had been suspended by davits. The race toward the downed flier then began. Hypothermia and the pilot's potential physical injuries demanded urgency.

On one such mission, enemy troops on the shore had spotted the downed plane and its struggling pilot, floating 500 yards off the beach in the middle of an enemy mine field. They launched *their* boat and were proceeding toward the desperate flier as our crew scrambled to get the rescue boat lowered and race for the victim. Beside the concern for the pilot, there was the possibility of the boat crew engaging the enemy and perhaps suffering loss of life or being taken prisoner. They had to arrive before the enemy boat, speeding toward the common prize. Orbiting planes from the Task Force directed the team toward their downed comrade. We who remained aboard could only watch the contest from the deck, helpless to shoot at the enemy boat, as the pilot was in the line of fire. I counted the downed man lucky our marksmen didn't fire *anywhere* near his sector.

This time the good guys won. The shivering pilot was plucked from the water and brought back toward our vessel. Now the enemy boat was hauling ass toward shore, fearing we would fire upon them when we had a clear shot. It would have been rewarding, but we couldn't risk the safety of our Landing Force Party and their prize. Another good "sharp-shooters" decision.

Safely onboard, we all slapped the backs of our shipmates from the boat crew. They had performed the dangerous rescue without a hitch. Ike Voles, the laundryman who worked across the passageway from my office, shared with me his feelings traveling in the boat.

"I was scared shitless. I had that M1 ready the whole damn ride. I wasn't going to let those guys take me prisoner. No way. I've heard the stories."

Ike and the other crew members in their motor whale boat that long cold day, received Letters of Commendation with Combat Distinguishing Devices. The Boat Officer, Lieutenant Junior Grade John Moriarty, was awarded The Bronze Star.

Will I ever be able to perform in a way to merit such an award? I wanted some "fruit salad" on *my* chest.

The following day a grateful pilot, now fit for duty in his clean, dry flight suit, shook hands with the ship's captain and nearby crew members. It was time to return to his carrier, USS VALLEY FORGE (CV 45). Our destroyer had taken an underway position parallel to the USS CHARRA (KA 58) for ammunition replenishment. Maintaining a comparable speed with the ammo ship, a seaman from our deck force put the rifle to his shoulder and carefully aimed. He fired the metal projectile, with line attached, that carried the 150 feet of rolling green water separating our two vessels.

As intended, the weighted metal leader, carrying its line, passed safely over the CHARRA as deck hands there scrambled to retrieve the line, then running with it, pulled the following heavier high line aboard. Secured, everything was in place. Our crewmen helped the smiling blond warrior into the boatswain's chair suspended by a pulley from the high-line. He would take the same trip later in the day, when the VALLEY FORGE took on ammo from the CHARRA. Tucking his cap inside his jacket for safe keeping, he waved good-bye to us. It was a special moment for me and I knew for him too. We both realized that 24 hours earlier he was a coin flip from death, now he was back in the game.

Steaming along beside us, the deck hands on the CHARRA ran with the pull line as our two men, holding the pilot ready, released their grip. He swung out in a great arc and was gone. I figured if he could land on a carrier's flight-deck at night, he could sure as hell face the excitement of this little joy-ride.

Rising seas made it difficult for the ships' helmsmen to maintain a constant distance between the two vessels. The two ships momentarily eased slightly toward each other. The traveler was not quite half way to his destination, suspended from the high-line, secure in his harness. His journey was interrupted as all eyes locked onto the isolated image dangling above the water. The high-line slackened, and as if he hadn't already spent enough time in that threatening sea, the aviator received his second dunking--in as many days.

"DON'T PAY-OUT ANY MORE LINE." screamed the Chief Boatswain's Mate in charge.

I watched, open mouthed, as the line and its cargo splashed and jumped on the surface. The passenger disappeared from sight.

Just as quickly, the ships steadied course. The high-line regained tension. Our hero sprung into the air, bounced wildly as he reached his apex and, with his smile still beaming, signaled he was okay by waving a free arm forward, back, and around like a rodeo rider fanning his bronco.

The crew members manning each end of the line waved their white hats, jumped and cheered wildly.

It was either chicken or feathers when it came to relieving the boredom of everyday living, underway for long periods. But on some days, you couldn't beat Navy life for offering plenty of excitement.

"YOU COME MY HOUSE"

Looking down I saw a pretty Japanese girl, dressed atypically in Western clothing resembling a college sophomore wearing a lemon colored sweater, dark blue skirt, and white bobby sox. I supposed she wanted to avoid attention from others on the street, because she kept her face expressionless and her eyes straight ahead as she coaxed, walking and softly repeating the invitation.

The foot traffic heading toward "downtown" Sasebo was heavy. My closest friend, Merrill Hansen the ship's barber, was on my left as we merged into the flow. I had soon sensed her slide up close to my right side.

"You come my house, okay?" She spoke in a whisper, "Please-ah, you come my house." The words pleaded, but the manner was simply one of courtesy and respect. A very odd combination to my young, Western ear.

An idea surfaced. "How about a hot bath and massage?" I looked at her, smiling.

She immediately brightened up, dropping her serious pose. *"Hai, hai. Joto, joto."* In Pidgin English, "Bahs, bahs." You come my house."

Turning to Merrill, I teased, "Catch you later, Pal, looks like I got myself a date. I'm getting a 'bahs'."

He saluted with a wink and peeled-off into the crowd. Watching his back for a few moments as he merged in with the herd, I caught sight of a lady gliding up alongside him. I imagined her playing out *my* earlier house invitation scenario.

My new companion hailed a passing rickshaw driver. She fired off rapid directions in Japanese and we were gone. Sitting in the rear of the pedicab, I introduced myself and learned her name was Toruko. Ten minutes later the two of us stood in a residential area several blocks from the main thoroughfare, facing a bank of attached single-story units. Toruko led me to a small sheltered porch and doorway. Before entering we paused to remove our shoes.

"Please-ah, please-ah," she bowed extending her arm toward a wooden door she had opened, insisting I enter first. Inside she motioned for me to wait and began to call out in Japanese, undoubtedly announcing her return--with company. Motioning me to remain, she left to another part of the house, returning in a moment and ushered me through an open sliding *shoji* screen into a bare, but pleasant room. It lacked decorative color and contained no western furniture--apparently life here took place upon the *tatami* mats that covered the floor.

"You want beer-ah? Saki? Steakie, eggo, french-fry?"

"You left out the hot bath and massage," I laughed. *I'd better watch my manners. I'm a guest in someone's home.*

"Hai, hai, I make bahs." She turned to leave.

"That beer with steak and eggs sounds good too," I gushed.

Ever so delicately, Toruko turned and with lowered eyes managed to explain that Mama-san would require 800 *yen* to purchase the groceries. Her manner suggested discomfort at having to mention money.

"Not a problem." I removed a 1000 *yen* note from my wallet. "I don't want to cause your mother any bother, going to the store."

But it was Grandmother, not Mother, that would be recruited to fetch the provisions.

Toruko's limited English allowed little meaningful conversation, but we were enjoying ourselves with a minimum of awkwardness. She produced a deck of cards from a hinge-topped box on the floor against the wall. Kneeling, we sat facing each other as she demonstrated a game. While my "bahs" was being drawn, we played several hands before I recognized the game was "Fish." The lesson completed, we began playing in earnest. Each time one of us told the other "Go fish," she in Japanese, me in English, we both had a good laugh.

After checking the bath again, Toruko returned and announced, "Bahs ready." She took my hand and led down a short hallway where she stopped midway to slide a *shoji* screen, revealing a small dressing area adjacent to a steaming sunken tub. Toruko began to pull her sweater over her head, indicating I should do the same with my jumper. She continued to strip, down to her practical, plain white cotton panties, which remained in place. She urged me on, though I showed some reluctance to remove *all* of my clothing, not knowing exactly how completely I should strip. She indicated *everything* was to come off.

Her perky, small breasts commanded my attention as she directed me toward the bathtub. *My gawd, the "great Japanese liberty" stories, they're all true!*

In that setting, so foreign, my heart was pounding. I considered our remoteness from the Western world, both geographical and cultural.

Away from my own familiar home turf, thousands of miles on the opposite side of the Pacific. I felt carried along in a dream.

The concrete lined depression in the floor measured about three and a half feet square, another three and a half feet deep, I saw it allowed me to be upright if my knees bent. I moved to enter the tub and was stopped by a quickly extended arm across my chest and an excited, "*Neh, neh.*"

We were standing on the concrete surface that surrounded the bath. Toruko dipped a wooden bucket into the heated water and gently poured its contents over my shoulders. I screamed--it felt scalding. She giggled and drew another bucketful. Soaking me, she applied soap with a sliver piece that smelled reminiscent of iodine. As a mother giving her youngster a Saturday night scrub-down, she maneuvered a football-sized loofah over my body. She averted her eyes and discretely handed me a knife-cut bar of soap to wash the areas she felt too personal. Then it was her turn to prepare for the tub, rinsing and soaping herself . More buckets of clear water over our bodies, the soapy water moving toward a floor drain and gathering into a churning vortex. We were now washed and ready to bathe. I was allowed to enter the water.

It was hot, but I was able to slowly ease in. The earlier rinses had helped condition me. Toruko followed behind me into the bath, guiding me forward onto a stool she submerged. I continued into the water until it caressed my chin. All tension, along with my strength, began draining from my body. Then it began--the "sagee."

There was no one, anywhere in the world, more content than I at that moment. No amount of money, power, or position could have created an environment better than I was experiencing in that little room, secluded in her world--*my* lady. Her deft fingers, thumbs, and palms mashed my muscles, probed deep into my shoulders and neck as I reclined, submerged in the fiery cauldron. Sitting upright, my physical position wouldn't have been possible in the more shallow, Western style tub.

After half an hour of oriental adventure, we left the water and she briskly toweled me, then herself. I put on my skivvy shorts and shirt. Facing me, Toruko placed her hands on my shoulders and turned me away. From the corner of my eye I saw her reach for a small white wrap, then, in a moment, replace it on a wall peg with her damp panties. She indicated I should not dress any further--the massage was not complete. I teased her about the need for the bra she was putting on, considering her junior cup size. We both laughed good naturedly.

Back in our original room, she motioned me to lie, face down, upon the clean towel she had placed over the floor matting. Then began an introduction--me to my body. I had thought after inhabiting my "temple" all those years, I was familiar with it. I was to become much more aware of its distinct parts--from the top of my head and my temples, down my back, my legs, feet and toes, my arms, hands and fingers. All were manipulated by hands surprisingly strong for such a small person. She finally rose to a standing position and slowly, precisely, walked her barefoot little self up, then down my spine several times, balancing in tight-rope walker fashion--administering the final touches to the most enjoyable physical experience of my young life.

As I relaxed in the fantasy, she stealthily disappeared, returning, dressed in a traditional long *kimono* wrapped about her body and held by an *obi* at her waist. She carried my folded uniform in her hands and a man's cotton *yukata* across her arm. I took the whites from her and set them down. Taking both her hands in mine, I told her she looked fantastic. I gave her hands a little squeeze and shake. I created my moves as things proceeded. It was all so new to me. She squeezed back and smiled pleasantly.

I slipped into the light gray *yukata* as she held it up. She wrapped a long, plain slate blue *obi* around me. I mentally pinched myself. Never had this much attention been paid just to me. Then she was off, I supposed to arrange our food.

Back in a few moments, balancing a bottle of Asahi beer, a teapot and two cups upon a tray, she asked if I cared for tea. From the bamboo-handled ceramic pot she poured steaming tea into a small cup and extended the tray. I chose the beer. Toruko set down the tray, took the handleless teacup for herself and invited me to bring my drink and accompany her to another part of the house.

At the far end of a hall she slid an exterior partition to reveal what I recognized from photos, a miniature garden with raked sand and half a dozen rocks, several too heavy to be lifted by one person, arranged in a manner inviting a serene feeling of peace and tranquillity.

Drops of rain began pelting the sand, creating little alien indentations in the swirls of raked designs. Secluded, the small area was enclosed on all four sides. We sat on mats under the protection of a covered porch, enjoying our drinks, feeling the effect of the scene. My nose caught little whiffs of smoke from our teriyaki steaks, grilling somewhere unseen, I supposed on a hibachi. The smell reminded me of Sunday barbecues in Uncle Harry's backyard.

151

The delightful sepia portrait of interior melded with the outdoors was accompanied by the intensifying tattoo of the sudden, summer squall.

Despite the generous number of rooms, the overall size of the dwelling, though not large, was compact and orderly. In a partially exposed closet I had glimpsed piles of colorful quilted bedding waiting to be spread about for evening sleeping arrangements. These wouldn't require dedicated rooms, but would use the same spaces that had been enjoyed during daytime activities. The entire home was delightfully simple, organized, and designed in a way to create a feeling of unity with its occupants.

An invisible accomplice had prepared steak, eggs, and French fries. Making several trips, Toruko brought dishes of food into the room, placing them on a large, low table. I noticed, with some uneasiness, two sets of chop sticks, but no knives or forks. I settled in, sitting up to the table on a large, thin floor pillow, and watched in awe as Toruko picked up an entire steak. Holding the steak with her chop sticks, using just one hand, she aggressively wrestled off a bite, never touching the meat with her fingers.

I made a couple of attempts, each time losing my shaky grip. I watched the steak do half gainers back onto the plate while my empty chopsticks crossed each other in my hand. Toruko giggled uncontrollably, her hand covering her mouth. Rising, she went to the sliding screen and, opening it a few inches, spoke to someone nearby, alert to our needs. Several minutes passed before the murmur of a Japanese voice called from the other side of the screen. A knife and fork arrived, procured from where, I did not know.

The meal was excellent, although I was surprised when two of my requests could not be met. While there was salt, coarse, in a small cut-glass receptacle and applied by using one's thumb and forefinger, pepper was not available. Nor was there bread for the toast I usually had with eggs. Bread, I learned, was not part of a traditional Japanese diet. Toruko finished her entire meal, including the eggs "sunny-side," which she maneuvered, the yoke unbroken, into her mouth balancing it on her chop sticks.

After our feast Toruko brought a stereoscope from a nearby closet. More searching produced a box of worn, copper tinted, stereographs, side-by-side photos of general subjects, locations about the Japanese Islands. My grandmother had one of those when I was growing up, and I'd always enjoyed the three dimensional novelty. Toruko didn't seem to tire of adjusting the slide for focusing the view, as we worked our way through the antiquated collection, passing the device back and forth.

Rain rustled against the wall outside. I hadn't dressed for the change in weather. The thought of walking back to town, through the muddy unpaved alleys, to find a pedicab for my return to the docking area, dampened my spirits. Toruko sensed my thoughts, indicating I was not to worry--she would arrange everything. A cup of hot tea and half an hour later, the voice from an unseen messenger announced to Toruka the arrival of my pedicab. It had been summoned by Grandmother, who had once again walked into town, but this time rode back with the rickshaw driver.

How different that day had been from the teenage boy-girl experiences back home in the States. I hoped for a chance to see and thank Grandmother before I left, but I knew from the day's experience that probably would not happen.

I grew pensive thinking of the end of this special day. Toruko, the lovely creature, had gifted me with her time and had anticipated my every wish. The day had flowed as if we shared some sort of relationship, but I realized we were strangers until she invited me home that afternoon. She had been so creative, generous, and entertaining. Could I approach the idea of paying her something without insulting her? I wanted to be as courteous as she and perform in a way acceptable within her culture. But families in war-torn Japan had to survive. A new thought made me uncomfortable. This family might well have lost someone in the fighting, killed by someone wearing my uniform.

Surely she anticipated something for her efforts, though she made no suggestion. I folded two one-thousand *yen* notes and placed them halfway beneath the teapot. As I approached her, she looked up into my eyes. It was time to say good-by. Toruko glided silently forward, continuing her eyes turned up to mine. I took her gently into my arms. In some inexplicable way I felt her diminutive body demanded a softness on my part.

She fit so comfortably against me. A long, soft kiss, a warm lingering embrace--neither of us initiated separating.

The rickshaw will just have to wait.

153

WHEN MY BUNK AND I PARTED COMPANY

Outside the pilot house, silhouetted forms of port and starboard lookouts resembled alien beings. Wearing foul-weather masks, their faces were protected from freezing, with only openings for vision and breathing. Ice had formed on the sea water and I was glad for the long-johns my mother had sent me.

The United Nations "police action" against North Korea had been underway for several months. The bridge of the USS OZBOURN DD846 was occupied by watch standers. At 0230 during my mid-watch, all of us were trying to accommodate the bone-chilling, Korean winter night. To ease monotony, I'd sneak occasional looks into the hooded radar repeater. Glowing green blips formed a mile-wide circle of seventeen destroyers. The "tin cans" encircled the carriers, cruisers, and a battle wagon, creating the circumference of our formation. If every man on every ship in Fast Carrier Task Force 77 felt the extreme fatigue I experienced, I wondered how the whole configuration held together.

My destroyer, the OZBOURN, sailed "darken ship" in the Yellow Sea, off the west coast of Korea, with no exposed topside lighting. In all exterior areas the smoking lamp was out.

The Force Commander had set Condition Baker days ago for all his vessels. This required certain adjustments to the ship's routine and steaming conditions. Watertight hatches remained secured until opened to allow passage. To maintain darken ship integrity, each time a hatch to the weather decks was undogged and opened, all visible interior lights automatically went out, to return only when the hatch was secured.

The entire crew stood watches four hours on and eight hours off for twenty-four hours, seven days a week. To the uninitiated, eight hours off watch before returning sounds adequate to ensure rest. Adequate, until one realizes sailors must also report each morning to their working areas to commence routine ship's work. On any given night I stood a watch, 8 P.M. to midnight, midnight to 4 A.M., midwatch, the worst, or 4 A.M. to 8 A.M.

The problem of finding opportunities to get into my bunk for some rest was compounded by daily general quarters drills, where all hands manned their battle stations for approximately one hour during sunrise and another hour during sunset. Sleeping time, splintered into small segments by all these demands, meant a greatly reduced portion of sleep during a 24-hour period, compared to that of a normal working schedule.

The Officer Of The Deck "had the con." The Commanding Officer was resting in his underway cabin, directly aft of the pilot house. If called by the OOD, the CO would answer, speaking up into the highly polished, brass sound tube that flanged out over his reclining head. Brass was always polished brighter in officer's country and never brighter than in areas where the captain lived or frequented.

On watch with the OOD, cloaked in the charcoal gray created by the absence of light, were the helmsman at the wheel, lee-helmsman on the annunciator, Junior Officer Of The Deck and a messenger. A quartermaster stationed himself near the oceanographic chart board. A boatswain's mate, keeping the ship's log, stayed within reach of the loud speaker mike, the bank of hand held phones and brightly colored levers for sounding alarms. All these devices were mounted against the after bulkhead of the pilothouse.

In a semi-daze from fatigue and the prevailing absence of attention-getting activity, I completed this sleep-deprived group on the bridge--the nodding-off telephone talker. My sound-powered telephone circuit could be very busy at times. It reached the engine room, Combat Information Center and port and starboard lookouts, but there was very little voice traffic coming up to or going out from the bridge at this early hour.

Suddenly everyone in the darkness started to the clatter of someone collapsing. The exhausted messenger, Seaman First Class Marian "Tiny" Burntree, had fallen asleep in a standing position. His dead weight slammed onto an empty metal trash can which then went banging against the annunciator and ricocheted off the adjacent bulkhead. In falling, his dislodged battle helmet added to the cacophony as it skipped and clanged across the steel deck.

"Gawd damn it, you can be shot for sleeping on watch in wartime; who the hell was that?" roared the OOD into the darkness. No one but Tiny, and I, standing near him, knew who had fallen. But everyone recognized the cause of the ruckus. The OOD's outburst was mostly a knee-jerk reaction to the split tension. Technically, Tiny's performance could be interpreted as a serious offense.

Tiny Burntree was an especially large man--the kind that would be summoned when heavy lifting was required in his Deck Force section. Once, when his Division Chief Petty Officer commented, "Tiny, you're sure a big sombitch," he joked, "Chief, you gotta be to get into the Klan." His size defied anyone to comment on his frightening facial expression--which he delighted in twisting into the most grotesque presentation he could create. He had a reputation for grabbing smaller men (with his bulk that could be almost any crew member) and, laughing, place them into a headlock. But to this teasing he added a little enhancement. Their heads would be turned around until the victim ended up with his nose buried deep into the big boy's sweaty arm pit. Here the victim would dance in their awkward, almost up-side-down, position until Tiny tired of the amusement.

Naturally, everyone hoped they wouldn't be chosen and those who were hated it. But if you made a big thing out of it, you'd be grabbed again soon. There was a long line of frustrated crew members waiting for some kind of "get-back-time." Floyd Rizzer was familiar with the armpit exercise. He'd been there a few too many times. He liked to say, behind Tiny's back, "He has a face that would frighten a buzzard off a gut truck."

Whenever Floyd saw Tiny about the ship, he would turn around and rush off in the opposite direction. Tonight, although Floyd could not have seen who had fallen because of the darkness, he knew Tiny was in the pilot house. He couldn't resist the opportunity and in his distinctive squeaky voice whispered, loud enough for everyone to hear, "Sounded like Burntree's fat ass bouncing off the deck."

Oh help, I hope the big fella doesn't think I said that.

We all felt like a good laugh, with the shock from the high tension created by the OOD's outburst, and then Rizzer's comment. Except we didn't want to see anyone stand before a firing squad. Even that red-neck bully.

Each person there had experienced the same unconscious submission to fatigue. That included the OOD himself. The difference was that he and the JOOD generally sat in the two large "underway" chairs, when the routine permitted. The chairs were situated on opposite sides of the pilot house and reserved for the Commanding Officer, when he was present. Should anyone sitting there fall asleep, the darkness would keep his secret. Unless he snored or failed to respond when spoken to.

My earphones brought me back to life, "Bridge, Combat Information Center, I have a bogie bearing 290 at 27 miles, heading 145 and closing. Closest point of approach, 4 miles."

I relayed the message of an unidentified aircraft being picked up on our radar to the OOD. It was understood that the bogie would be challenged by Big Dog, the Force Commander, and undoubtedly identified as friendly, since there had been no enemy air contacts to date in this war.

Tiny scrambled to retrieve his helmet and right the trash can. I heard him mumble thankfulness for the darkness. It allowed him anonymity, concealing his discomfort and probably a flushed face. He swore under his breath that Rizzer, the little light weight, would get his later.

That was the end of it. No more was said. The OOD busied himself with the routine bogie information. It was as though we had all agreed to pretend the Burntree incident just hadn't happened.

Moving about a bit to increase my circulation, I tried to drag my body systems up to the alertness level the watch and the OOD demanded. And stay awake!

Could a guy really be shot for sleeping on watch in war time? I was new at this "war" business and I didn't want to be the first one on the ship to find out.

COLD, COLD EVERYWHERE

On liberty back in Japan it was too cold to remove any clothing for the enjoyable bathing ritual. Winter R and R liberty activities were different from the possibilities in warmer summer months. We swabbies wore our wool peacoats and dark blue, wool flat hats. Civilians bundled-up in layers of heavy, mismatched, clothing. Since the war had ended for Japan, the civilian population was eager for any hand-me-downs. Fashion and color coordination took a back seat to utility.

Inside the local establishments and private homes of Sasebo, it was a constant challenge to keep warm in the absence of Western-style space heating.

We visited my favorite *ryokan* for some long-missed female company, enjoyed lobster and a few beers. Dennis and I were allowed to share the company of the young women working in this small, traditional inn where they took rest breaks in a little retreat area. These were not prostitutes, simply female employees of the six-room inn and restaurant. Individuals in the group of about six were constantly getting up and down, remaining alert and available for serving food about the inn, or performing different hotel services. But the demands were sporadic with few visitors. A parade of lovelies, breaking from their chores, entered and left the room through bamboo framed sliding *shoji* screens. Their laughter and teasing showed they enjoyed the novelty of young male foreigners as much as we welcomed their numbers, at times two and three-to-one odds. In the middle of all of this, I wasn't thinking much about the girls back home, nor was I lonely being far away. Being with these vivacious, bubbly darlings was fun and I was soon caught up in their carefree gaiety--like being allowed into a slumber-party.

They sat under a large quilted covering. Beneath its center, a toasty *hibachi,* containing several glowing pieces of charcoal, radiated warmth. I supposed they knew what they were doing. The small amount of fuel probably discouraged excess carbon dioxide. We visitors sat beside them, and stretched our legs out before us. Our little group formed a spoked wheel pattern on the *tatami* mats that covered the entire floor area. I wondered if I would ever become accustomed to sitting for long periods on the floor without a backrest.

I sat with three chattering girls and Dennis Hickman, all of us doing our best to ward off the late October cold that had taken control of Southern Japan. Heat from coals in the hibachi forced me to withdraw my feet a few inches at a time, then ease them back again, alternating a warming-cooling motion.

We drank hot tea, then ate our lobsters along with large bottles of beer. Unlike New England types, these lobsters were small creatures with tails about the size of their bodies, and were served-up without claws. They were cooked, then cut length wise, without being cleaned. Their insides remained when they were served. We delicately ate around the brownish-gray.

When finished, Dennis sang "Happy Birthday"--I was twenty-one that month. He tried to get the girls to sing along, but they really didn't get what was happening. Finally, one face registered a "light going on." She spoke to the others, they laughed, and began singing what I guessed was *their* "Happy Birthday."

We were both enjoying ourselves. It was good to be "home" after the lengthy deployment. Mama-san always welcomed me as if I were her own off-spring. My friends called this "Frank's Place" because here, I was the fair-haired boy. On an earlier liberty I had returned an antique table clock that some radiomen from my ship had "borrowed" during a rowdy evening weeks earlier. I brought it directly into the kitchen, where Papa-san could usually be found cooking. He turned from a sizzling wok and stood round-eyed when he recognized his missing heirloom. I presented it, with a little speech in Japanese I'd memorized, apologizing for my fellow-American's behavior. Not a demonstrative man, particularly in the situation of occupying forces controlling his defeated country, he still made his gratitude understood. He summoned Mama-san and spoke rapid Japanese. She bowed toward him. She bowed toward me. He bowed toward me. Both repeated *arigato* half-a-dozen times.

From that day on, I could do no wrong in their *ryokan*.

Dennis had grown up in the desert heat of Bisbee, Arizona. This cowboy type had a particularly hard time with cold weather.

"Hot *Saki*, my sweet, before I start trembling again. It's so damn cold you could hang meat in this place. You understand, 'hang meat'?" Dennis laughed in my direction, enjoying the amused cavalier phrasing in which he had framed his request, that had fortunately gone over the heads of the girls.

Shizuko, the round faced young lady snuggled beside him, smiled and nodded, "First you dance." She wiggled out from under the puffy quilt and placed a record, one of several Westerns Dennis had brought with us, onto an antique turn-table. A few cranks on the side handle wound the spring-stored power. She positioned the needle and sound leaped through the disc shaped device that held it above the record. *Ah, the simple things.*

A brassy tune energized the circle of reclining ladies. They swayed their arms, hummed, and bounced in place to the beat. Dennis struggled from beneath the warm covering while the girl sitting at my elbow hooked her arm under mine and helped me up. The four of us danced to Eddy Arnold singing Dennis' favorite, "Slippin' Around." We were in our stockinged feet, as shoes were not worn when entering Japanese dwellings. In an exaggerated style, Dennis rocked his partner to a Texas two-step while I tried to imitate his lead. All the ladies applauded us when the music ended and the needle clicked repeatedly, waiting to be lifted.

I continued to hold my animated partner and impulsively kissed her, to the delight of her friends who howled and chattered in rapid Japanese. Her face flushed as she lowered her smiling eyes. I wasn't feeling so cold any more. *Damn, I love the Japanese ladies' eyes, small mouths and glowing complexions.*

Our two partners bowed several times as they backed from the room to execute Dennis' saki request. After the screen closed I heard more tittering on the opposite side.

All the Japanese bowing, unusual as it was to me, never seemed condescending. It was simply a tradition of courtesy they had all grown up with, as a young person from my culture might use the terms Sir or Ma'am.

The ladies returned with a tray of two little cups and a small, vase-shaped, ceramic container--all fired in white ceramic, decorated in blue leaves and delicate branches. One young lady knelt before the tray held by the other and, with ceremony, filled each cup with steaming *saki*. She held the cup in two hands, politely remaining in a head-bowed position until I accepted the rice wine. I glanced into the small cup. When heated the otherwise clear liquid took on a milky hint.

Will I dislike it heated as much as I do drinking it cold? I took a sip. *It's even worse hot.*

Soon the *saki* loosened Dennis' tongue. With great animation he addressed everyone around the little circle of foot warmers. He paused

160

to look into each face with that grin I'd seen him successfully employ with ladies. His secret weapon, it never failed to capture them.

He described the family's cats in his southern Arizona desert home. His Japanese speaking audience listened as if they understood every word.

"Back where I come from we keep a lot of cats, cause they make good mousers. At feedin' time you can't put their food out on the ground, desert critters will eat it before the poor kitties get their chance."

One of the girls seemed to understand some of what he was saying and rapidly translated every few sentences into Japanese for the others, who giggled behind hands cupped over their mouths.

"My daddy had come out West from Oklahoma to work in the mines. He knew a lot of tricks. One was to put the cat's food up on the edge of our flat roofed house. Ya'll should have seen those cats lined up in front of the house at supper time, meowing like crazy, eyes glued to the roof and their tails sticking straight into the air. Daddy would walk down the line, grab each cat by his tail and sling him, stiff arm, over his head. Right up onto the roof. They'd always land on their feet and head straight for their bowls."

The hot *saki* and the close room made me woozy. It was still only mid-afternoon, most of my liberty time was ahead of me. I suggested we get some air and stretch our legs. We said our good-byes and promised to return soon. Mama-san led us to our shoes. She'd placed them inside the entrance where they wouldn't get too cold. As Dennis brought his boots to the bench, Mama-san placed her hand on my forearm and led me several steps away. She stood on her toes to whisper into my ear. "Fugimo-san make good *oksa.*"

"Hey, Mama-san, don't get crazy. If the Navy wanted me to have a wife they'd have issued me one. Now Dennis here..."

The pleasant lady playfully pushed me toward my shoes, bowed, and returned to her guests.

When off duty, Dennis wore armadillo skin western boots, when he could get away with it. Their toes were so pointed, he bragged they could kick the eyes out of a snake. It had taken some persuading from Mama-san to get him to part with them, even for the short time we were to be inside. He slipped them on and we headed out the door. Gray sky urged buttoning our peacoats all the way to the top. I pulled my woolen flat-hat down tighter as I walked into the chill of the wind.

"Why did you tell that story about your Daddy's cats?"

"Ah, I don't know. They seemed to like it though"

"Well they liked you tellin' it, that's for sure."

161

"Hey, they did, didn't they?"

I teased, "Maybe we should go back."

"Keep movin' ahead, Kissing Bandit, we got other fish to fry."

He laughed, his breath piercing the cold in silky-white spurts. We quickened our step toward the main drag. The cold weather seemed to govern the odors so prevalent in Summer. But the wind off the water carried in the harbor smell of diesel and seaweed.

Since the beginning of the war, when we arrived in Sasebo, hundreds of entrepreneurs had come down from the north to provide the visiting United Nation's Forces amusements, food, drink, merchandise, and entertainment. They staked their claims for a share of the Yankee dollars, Australian pounds, and Indian rupees. Other monies came to them from sailors off ships that flew a rainbow of flags representing nations making efforts, though sometimes only token, toward the South Korean cause.

Down the dirt street, there were no sidewalks, these sailors of diverse nationalities were now flowing along before us. We filed in and became part of the wave. There weren't any cars to worry about. All our attention was being commanded by propositions from jostling rickshaw drivers for rides to the pearl farm, money exchangers offering special "black market" deals, and offers for "the best short-time girls in Japan." One enterprising pimp handed out printed cards.

Lucky Bar.
NUMBER ONE HOUSE OF PROSTITUTION.
We offer you nice girls.
They'll be give you love and happy.
Present card for complimentary peanut.

Recently opened shops offered quality binoculars and cameras at affordable prices. Noritaki china sets, eight place settings, were thirteen dollars. Novelties in glass and wood gave everyone an opportunity to purchase something to take back home. Hand made toys, many animated, were the most popular. Sales people every few yards squatted before two or three of them, wound and moving about on a board. I picked up a frisky toy-dog. The speed of his legs accelerated when they left the table. On his under-side I recognized the colorful label of a discarded beer can. Each of the entertaining little creatures I examined revealed Coors or Budweiser beer cans that had been fashioned into the bodies which housed the wind-up movements.

After I examined everything, I was struck by the ingenuity and craftsmanship--particularly the optical equipment. *And these people lost the war?*

I chose a lumbering brown bear, paid 300 *yen* and was handed a plain brown box with lettering that announced "Lovely Walking Bear."

I hope it will give my Mom "Love and Happy."

Dennis and I waved down an empty pedicab and pointed the driver in the direction of the familiar large building, the dance hall, high up the hill.

I followed as Dennis leaped into the back, "Takarazuka, partner," he said to the driver. "My illegitimate son here, and I, are goin' to do a little polkaing."

We whirled the night away with the taxi dancers. Despite the "no smooching" rule in the dance hall, dancing could still be a good way to keep our blood flowing. We circled the large floor to the beat of "The Pennsylvania Polka," then stood waiting for the next tune. The girls never tired of their favorite dance-step.

A wonderful way to fight off the cold.

A FOLK HERO FOR THE LITTLE PEOPLE

ALL SCRAPPERS, ALL SCRAPPERS, THIS IS BIG DOG. AT MY COMMAND COME RIGHT TO COURSE 070 AND MAKE PREPARATIONS FOR FLIGHT OPS.

Everyone on the bridge could hear the crackling of the radio speaker. It was easier to remain awake and alert during the daylight watches when there was more voice communication traffic coming into and going out from the ship. It held our attention.

BIG DOG, BIG DOG, THIS IS SCRAPPER 9. I HAVE VISUAL CONTACT WITH A MINE BEARING 127 AT 150 YARDS. REQUEST PERMISSION TO BREAK FORMATION AND DISPATCH WITH 20 MILLIMETER FIRE.

Another destroyer in the screen that encircled the Task Force was reporting a mine sighting to the Task Force Commander. These free floating mines were not uncommon north of the 38th parallel off the coast of Korea. The destroyer CHANDLER had struck one several weeks earlier and sustained serious damage. Eliminating mines was routine. Our vessel alone sank six while assigned there.

I forced myself to concentrate on the flow of activity and keep an eye on the captain, who usually had the con during those daylight working hours. Daylight also meant that everyone could be more easily observed, insuring our best behavior.

During daytime steaming, it is not uncommon for all the officers to leave the pilot house into the fresh air on the adjacent open bridge. One officer might speak with a lonely lookout, reminding him he was still part of the real world by repeating an admonition to keep alert for mines, aircraft and other vessels. A second might watch light-signals being sent or study the signalman adroitly selecting colored flags from the flag-bag to hoist high up the yardarm to communicate from our ship to others. Another might search with binoculars for anything of possible interest. Like all of us, they wanted a little diversion. Sometimes I suspected they were just seeking some privacy to enjoy a little officer scuttlebutt.

We kept our eyes on them.

When these brief intermissions occurred, we enlisted men were alone in the pilot house, but denied complete privacy because of the

164

surrounding port holes. We'd exhale and relax a bit. I could pull one ear piece of the sound-powered phone off of my ear and onto my cheek to get some relief from the numbing pressure.

Logic would dictate during these respites, since social conversation among the enlisted watch standers in the pilot house was forbidden, one might express a quick observation or voice a complaint in a quiet way. Keeping a low profile, we would kid around, enjoying the change of pace. We were always ribbing each other, and you had better develop a thick skin. On that morning watch, Tom Corothers laughed and offered that I had my nose so far up the Skipper's butt if he turned around fast he'd break it off. It was sophomoric behavior performed by youngsters who, if they hadn't been in the Navy, would still be in high school. Most of us were teenagers and susceptible to innate urges for mischief.

These occasions of being left alone, while frequent, were brief in duration. They were always interrupted by one of the officers re-entering the pilot house. Everyone automatically snapped back into a military mode.

A rated quartermaster manned the helm when our ship entered or left port, received fuel or stores while underway, transferred personnel by high line between vessels, or was in any situation that required experienced steering skills to maintain a heading or change course smartly. At all other times a seaman stood the helmsman watches. Often on my watch cycle that would be Elwood McCory. It was Elwood McCory who placed his ceramic dog turd, always carried by him, somewhere to demand your attention. You'd see it on the pillow of your bunk, on a seat you were about to relax into, or next to the chow tray you had left unattended for a moment.

Historically, in any military unit, a light hearted rebelliousness exists. When properly functioning, this form of esprit de corps binds the lower ranks. It is acknowledged by the establishment as relatively harmless considering the overall potential benefits to morale. Elwood was deep in the middle of this philosophy. But one of his pranks was not so harmless.

The wheel of the 2200 ton destroyer was a twenty-four- inch brass disk, trimmed around its circumference with polished mahogany. At its center was a fist-sized, closed end, brass hexagon nut.

The nut secured the wheel.

The nut was only hand tight.

The nut *could* be removed.

Seaman First Class Elwood McCory, the duty helmsman, removed the nut.

The task force was steaming in formation, doing 18 knots.

The first time I saw him do this I went into such a state I thought I would explode trying to contain myself, which, of course, was his intent. What if he dropped the nut? Someone would hear it strike the metal deck. What if the wheel came off? What if we received an order from the Task Force Commander for an immediate change of course? There could be twenty or more huge vessels in the formation, all executing the course change in unison. Imagine the radar picture, with the USS OZBOURN abandoned by the circle of other destroyers changing direction.

I fantasized over the possibility of a collision. What if we rammed one of the carriers? If McCory had been seen by anyone other than his small audience of buddies, his head would have rolled, and of course ours also.

I thought of the court martial charges. *"Did willfully and negligently place in harm's way ..."* or *"Seaman Spittle, being aware through his direct observation of the severity of the act, did knowingly and without regard for the safety ..."* Those found guilty would go to the Naval Prison at Portsmouth, behind bars for years, subsisting on piss and punk. The prisoner would become old and skinny from a diet that was only varied by the full ration every third day that Naval Regs required.

But after a while, when the absence of officers allowed, removing the hex nut on the wheel had become a break from the mind numbing tedium. During one boring watch OZ steamed alone, away from the task force. A mess cook brought a sample of the noon meal from the enlisted mess to the Officer Of The Deck, as was Naval custom, to insure a monitoring of the quality of the crew's rations. The OOD was eating from the tray and facing aft, as the tray was resting on the chart board. His back was to the helmsman. The JOOD was off the bridge, in the nearby radar shack. Elwood stood at the helm exhibiting just a hint of his crooked smile. Silently he caught my attention with a slight jerk of his head. I watched as he eased his body close against the wheel. With his right hand concealed before him, he removed the hex nut and slid it into his jacket pocket.

The next event left us standing about still, gaping and immobile. The boy from Macon, Georgia, had truly gone *Asiatic*.

His puckish air, transmitted by a devilish facial expression, released a surge of titillating shock within each of us whose position permitted us to observe him. Elwood McCory, with both hands on the wheel, slowly eased himself backwards, pulling the wheel with him. He actually shifted the wheel, discernibly sliding it along its spindle, the large threaded bolt that held it in position. For those few seconds my heart stopped and I gulped in disbelief. He pushed the wheel back into position.

His behavior created something of a folk hero for us "little people." It scored a twisted win in the ongoing game of unrated, lowlife seamen against our experienced, established military superiors. We wanted to applaud his spunk, but instead sent silent facial accolades.

In our teenage estimation, he showed the most adventurous, but foolhardy spirit. That brand of shenanigans could lead to time in the jail house, or the nut house. The United States Navy maintained accommodations, steel barred or with padded bulkheads, for all of her Elwood Mc Corys.

In this instance the line that restrained outrageous behavior had been crossed. Since the line was never clearly marked, *experienced* players knew to remain safely back from it while poking a stick into the cage of authority.

But those "acting the jackass," as my mother would say, always pushed the envelope. That morning in the pilot house Elwood found his moment of fame.

MY VIEW FROM THE OPEN BRIDGE

When I was 20 years old, I compared each new experience to those I'd seen shown across the screens of darkened movie-theaters. The more traumatic an experience, the more intensely I'd process it through my "Hollywood filter." Korea had me working overtime.

The OZBOURN was anchored in the mine-swept channel of Wonsan Harbor, North Korea. Our two U.S. destroyers sat in the natural shelter, the harbor large and open for hundreds to thousands of yards in every direction from our positions. But we weren't there seeking shelter. Our mission was bombarding shore targets.

The noon chow line had been shifted from its customary formation, port side along the main deck, into the cramped interior passageway because occasional small-arms fire from shore splashed near the vessel and occasionally pinged off the ship's exterior.

Sitting at a mess table, I admired my tray of chicken breast, mashed potatoes and white country gravy. As usual, a good Sunday lunch. But the relaxed atmosphere that weekends usually promised was shattered when a no-nonsense voice boomed from the ship's loud-speakers.

"NOW GENERAL QUARTERS, GENERAL QUARTERS. ALL HANDS MAN YOUR BATTLE STATIONS. THIS IS NOT A DRILL. THIS IS NOT A DRILL."

No, we don't drill during chow times. This is real.

The general alarm, an excitement producing BONG, BONG, BONG, BONG, repeated for thirty unnerving seconds. Each bong ratcheted my adrenaline up another notch. In less than a minute I was on the bridge wearing earphones and helmet, receiving "manned and ready" messages from my stations.

Then Satan began rolling his movie projector. The scream of an incoming projectile pierced through the brisk mid-day air and my throat constricted. Had I been forced to speak, I'm sure my voice would have squeaked. It felt as if squeezing fingers were clamped around my neck. The unmistakable roar, with accompanying explosion, immobilized me. As a Captain's talker on the bridge, I'd been close to the firing of our ship's large guns, both in practice and in anger. The two forward twin five-inch mounts were immediately below my GQ station.

But this sounded just like a freight-train barreling past my face. Instinctively I understood. Like the universally recognizable metallic double-clacking of a shot-gun round being chambered. You hear it, you get it. Even if it's your first time.

I tried to force the dream-like moment into focus. I looked across to Dennis, another bridge talker, five feet away. He was looking toward me, and we mentally connected. Terrorized, certainly in shock, we burst out laughing. The situation was unbelievable. Someone was trying to kill us. The shell had over shot the open bridge by what felt like inches.

In the military scheme of things, this was the ultimate. To prepare for this, during the past two years I had drilled, trained, enjoyed three *hots*, a cot, and a monthly paycheck.

Will I perform properly? What to do? What not to do? God, don't let me screw this up.

Despite my fear, I found some comfort. If I could just deliver as I had during the endless daily drills, I'd do the job exactly right.

My mind flashed to John Wayne, everyone's hero. His performance in *Sands of Iwo Jima* was a model for every young warrior. But inside our ship's pilot house another personality was playing out a drama, and it wasn't John Wayne. I watched through the porthole as a well-tailored, very excited, mature man looked out of place in the midst of young, dungaree-clad crew members rushing around him, executing their tasks with practiced precision.

I knew this man had lived world-war-two up close, and survived. In his crisp pressed khakis, the uniform worked as John Wayne. But "Duke" would have run out toward the action, swinging, and this character "hit the deck" like a blanket. Dennis checked to see if I was watching.

Our seasoned Commodore had wedged himself between the steaming chair and the pilot house bulkhead. The Commander of the Destroyer Division hollered out to our skipper, "Charlie. Charlie. Get us underway. CHARLIE?"

I realized that this man knew what the hell to do when someone was shooting at him. He understood you're no good to anyone with your head blown off.

But Captain Charles Akers had his plate full for the moment. The Commodore, the only onboard officer superior to him, would have to hold on. There was his anchored vessel with 360 of his sailors, all in harm's way, to whom he would devote his primary attention. He'd answer his superior after discharging several higher priority tasks.

A second round screamed over and exploded behind me. It cleared my oversized talker's helmet first, then Dennis', and hit the water on the starboard side. Dennis' shoulders flew up so quickly he must have wrenched his neck spinning around toward the direction of the explosion. The burst of sea water sent a downpour over both of us. We hustled to take our cue from the Commodore--it's okay to try to do your job with one hand, while you held onto your ass with the other. We ran around to the protection of the starboard side of the pilot house, away from the source of fire coming at us from the coast, but still close enough to respond to the skipper.

My eyes burned, a smoky chemical stung them and filled my nostrils, searing the inside of my nose. It was hard to catch a breath. And my insides shook uncontrollably. The last time I'd lived anything like this kind of trauma was back home when, as a small boy, I watched my dog Gerry bite at the rolling tire of a feed-truck passing before our house. I called out, but the truck had his full attention. He put his head too far under the tread, and my childhood pal was gone. Until Wonsan, that had been the worst.

"Tell the engine room, 'standby to answer all bells'." Our Captain didn't want his ship lying-to when enemy gunners finally found their range. I alerted the engine room.

Dennis and I had followed the Captain onto the forward section of the open bridge. We stood near each other, alert for voice traffic on our lines and ready to respond should he direct a communication to any station on our circuits.

Poor Mom. We regret to inform you... Oh God.

"Captain, Chief Pharmacist Mate Brown reports two crew-members have been treated for shrapnel wounds--both still fit for duty." Dennis relayed the message in the Skipper's direction.

Shit, we've been hit. The laughing episode was far behind us now.

There'll be no leaving here to go to the head. I just can't think about that.

With the entire crew at General Quarters, there was no one on the forecastle to raise the anchor. But the vessel could not remain stationary while hostile gunners held us within their sights. The ship struggled to move, dragging the massive anchor along the harbor's bottom. After steaming, encumbered, for several hundred yards, we still remained in danger. Directly ahead, splashes sent a tell-tale message. The Commies were getting their firing range and bearing adjusted.

"Captain, Mid-ship's Damage Control reports a hit at frame 130. A round went into the wardroom. Fragmentation holes in several water-tight doors."

"Very well." The more things heated up, the cooler the Skipper became.

More explosions. Fragments from a near miss shattered a signal searchlight. Glass blew over everyone on the port wing of the bridge.

"Captain, CIC reports the Mark 56 director has been hit and is out of commission."

"Very well. I want reports from all Damage Control Parties. Direct all stations to report casualties."

The CO fixed his sight several feet before him upon a shocked sailor with one side of his face crimson wet. Something else to deal with.

"Get a medic up here, we have a man with a head wound."

I was busy sending and reporting messages when the Skipper completely broke from character and climbed atop the forward radar repeater on the open bridge. This was the exact area the two rounds had passed only moments earlier. In the excitement and confusion of battle he resembled a lightning rod--higher than the things around him and out forward, alone. Repeatedly he yelled down in the direction of the gun mount below. Finally, a Chief raised his helmeted head up toward the bridge.

The Captain screamed down, "GET A PARTY TO THE FORECASTLE AND SLIP THE ANCHOR CHAIN."

The chief stared back, unsure of the order. "SLIP THE ANCHOR, SIR?"

"AFFIRMATIVE. SLIP THE ANCHOR, CHIEF. AND BARE A HAND."

Soon a group of men near the gun mount scrambled forward toward the anchor chain stretching across the forecastle. They spread out and each examined a section of exposed chain, searching for the link that allowed its parting. One man yelled for the attention of the others. He had found the detachable Kentner shackle. The Chief pointed to a heavy hammer resting in its storage place on the bulkhead. The largest man from the group stepped out, took the handle in his two hands, and swung at the forelock pin in the shackle. Then again. The third try the chain parted. A deafening rumble vibrated the ship as 60 fathoms of U.S. Government anchor chain joined the port anchor at the bottom of the channel.

The Captain jumped down from his high profile position, hurried to the open hatch of the pilot house adjacent to the chart table and directed the Chief Quartermaster.

"Get a good fix, and log our bearings Chief. Someone will be back here for that anchor."

"Aye, aye, Captain." The Chief Quartermaster grabbed his writing pad and raced toward the port-side gyro repeater. He'd served long enough to recognize the consequences of losing valuable government property.

We were underway, making turns through the channel. But OZBOURN's guns were silent.

"Ask Combat Information Center why we are not firing." The Skipper tackled the next item on his mental priority list.

"CIC reports they have no targets, Captain."

The Captain yanked a hand phone from the pilot-house bulkhead and yelled into the mouth-piece.

"Begin firing immediately. Let's provoke some flashes from them. Then we'll have targets."

In moments the two forward five-inch mounts fired simultaneous salvos, fifty-five pound projectiles with a range of nearly ten miles. I stood on the open bridge, just above the guns. The rapid concussions blew my helmet and ear-phones off my head. The helmet bounced toward the far railing. My ear-phones dangled from their transmitter chestplate.

Chin-straps, we need chin-straps for these damn talker's helmets.

Dennis held his helmet to his head with both hands. Firing continued in rapid succession, jolting my entire body. Directly below, bouncing around the deck, empty brass clanged, discharged from the five-inch turrets. Shock-waves made it difficult to stand without being blown against the bulkhead or opposite rail. The pungent smell of burned powder wrapped the entire bridge. I thought of the gun crews, enclosed in their mounts, right at the source of the noise, smoke, and concussions.

We fired toward shore as we hurried from our anchorage and soon were in a position out of the enemy's firing range. Finally, secured from General Quarters, I followed Dennis down the ladder leading off the bridge. He laughed over his shoulder, "Spit, I've got to change my skivvies before we go finish chow."

An hour earlier, when I manned my General Quarters battle station, I had felt the usual controlled urgency. Several times each day, since entering North Korean waters, we'd gone to General Quarters. The drills had become routine. But not on this day.

During that fraction of an hour in Wonsan Harbor, each young crew member made a quantum leap into manhood. I knew I'd never be the same again. I'd crossed from innocence to the ranks of the knowing. Now I was part of the fraternity.

And I had something for my next letter to my mother.

⚓ ⚓ ⚓

Not many hours later, back home in the States, loved ones of OZBOURN crew members were in for a serious shake-up when they read in their morning newspapers an erroneous report of the USS OZBOURN being *sunk* in North Korean waters.

THE LUCKY STRIKE "BROWN" MARKET

.   Mao Tse-tung's Red Army drove retreating Chiang Kai-shek and his loyal Nationalists off China's mainland and onto the relative safety of Formosa. One hundred miles of water separated the two old combatants and offered a respite from fighting that both of them coveted--for the moment. Mao had no intention of ceding Formosa to Chiang, and Chiang had every intention of returning to, and regaining control of, Mainland China.

The rest of the world wanted the two of them apart, with neither crossing the water and stirring up more trouble on the international scene. Mainland China supported a Communist government. The United States defended the Nationalist's position on Formosa and sent a naval contingent to demonstrate that resolve. U.S. Naval Task Force 72 patrolled the Straits of Formosa. The U.S.S. OZBOURN made up part of that small unit of several ships and land-based aircraft.

Until the end of the Second World War, for fifty years the Japanese occupied the large island. Their defeat returned the territory, with its Chinese inhabitants, to mainland China's control and "Formosa" became "Taiwan." The natives of Taiwan spoke little English, but those who had lived there during the occupation spoke Japanese as well as Chinese.

In November, 1950, Keelung, Formosa, became our operational port.

Charged fire hoses stretched out, ready to soak "bum boats" and their occupants who risked approaching our tied-up vessel. There were always crew members relaxing on the main deck. Snipes came topside from the firerooms and enginerooms for fresh air and relief from the heat. Down in the bum boats natives held up merchandise for prospective customers on deck to examine. Souvenirs and Canadian Club Whiskey offered for greenbacks or U.S. cigarettes. But security required an open perimeter about the vessel. A watch stander hosed down those who ignored shouted orders to stay away.

Tom Corothers jumped a hose and threw open the bottom half of the Dutch door of the ship's office. It crashed against the file cabinets, startling all of us. He filled the doorway, beaming an enormous smile. We watched, waiting for him to do some damn-fool thing.

"Boys and girls, I've just come from visiting my friends in the radio shack.

"There is, as we speak, sitting on the desk of this vessel's Executive Officer, a message from BuPers. I've just delivered it."

He reached into his dungaree shirt pocket and slowly withdrew one of his Tampa Nugget cigars and extended it toward me.

Come on, you nit-wit. Drop the other shoe.

"Frankie, my boy. It seems the Chief of the Bureau of Naval Personnel, in one of his less lucid moments, has deemed you worthy of advancement to Petty Officer Second Class."

I leapt out of my seat, looked all around at the faces of guys I had come to love over the past two years, and cheered wildly. I put on a smile bigger than Corothers'.

I'll write Mom this afternoon. This ought to make her proud of her Jackass. I felt rewarded for all my studying, preparing for the fleet service-wide exams we'd taken months earlier.

Gus Gustafson, visiting from the engine room, pumped my hand.

"Let's go over and celebrate--on you," he gushed.

The phone on the rear bulkhead buzzed, interrupting the excitement. I reached for it and blurted out, "Yeah."

"Who is this?" the voice on the other end growled.

"Spittle. What do ya want?"

"This is the Executive Officer, Spittle. A second class petty officer should know how to answer the telephone. Let's try it again."

"Aye-Aye, Sir. Ship's Office, petty officer Spittle, Sir."

"That's better. Come aft to my stateroom."

Lieutenant Commander Barr Palmer had been pulled away from his civilian business, called up to active duty for the Korean "conflict." He'd just reported aboard from the states to relieve our old Exec, Commander Ousey.

"Gotta go boys. The new XO's got a bug up his ass and I'm in the middle of getting my butt chewed out." I grabbed my white hat, gathered up the pile of things from the basket for XO's signature and a legal pad.

Knocking softly at his cabin doorway, I waited. Commander Palmer directed me to come in. I placed the correspondence into his in-basket and sat down on the edge of his bunk. This was the manner I'd always assumed with our old XO.

But this was a new XO. "Do not sit on that bunk unless you're invited to. Spittle, your military courtesies are getting rusty out here. Just because we allow a little facial hair doesn't mean I'll stand by while my sailors' behavior goes to hell in a handcart. I'm not going to remind you again how to conduct yourself. Get with it, if you want to keep that new crow."

"Yes, Sir." I stood at attention beside his desk. *Another officer who actually thinks "they" run the ship. When I finally get my Exec whipped into shape, they transfer him and I get this hard ass. It's going to take a little time to educate this one.*

He held the list of crew members who had been advanced in rate. Extending it toward me, he directed, "Announce these names over the loudspeaker. I'll be listening. Your manner had better be 'by the book'."

I returned to the midships passageway, pulled down the bullhorn from against the bulkhead next to the ship's office door, hit the switch, and began "by the book."

"Now hear this. Now hear this. BuPers announced the following named men have been advanced in rate." I read down the alphabetical listing. I knew how exciting the moment was for each man whose name I called. When I got to my own name, my chest puffed up.

I read out, "Spittle, Frank H., to Personnelman Second Class."
I like it. I like it a lot.

After I read the last name, I heard the sounds of whooping and congratulations coming from all directions on the vessel as individuals were smacked on the back and cigars were lit.

Gus greeted me as I walked back into the office. "Well, what do ya say, Second Class? Ya ready for some liberty?"

"Can't make it over today, Gus. This Formosa business is just too damn expensive for me. Beers, dancing, rickshaws, everything costs two and three times Japanese prices. And I'm not going to borrow five-for-seven anymore. I get paid and it's gone before I can buy toothpaste. I'll be staying aboard for awhile."

My $117 a month take-home wasn't lasting the pay period, especially when I'd join crap games on paydays. Every two weeks we played on blankets spread out in the berthing compartments.

"Frank-san, you need a lesson from Doctor Gustafson." He pointed to an empty chair. "Sit down here son and listen up. What do you pay for a pack of sea-store cigarettes? Seven cents, right? Now that's seventy cents a carton. Okay, do the numbers. You go to the ship's store and buy two cartons of Lucky Strike cigarettes. I know you smoke Old Gold, but they don't sell as well on the beach. Asians like the word "Lucky."

"My snipe brothers are taking a carton of cigarettes into Keelung and selling it, in any bar, for ten dollars. Two cartons equals twenty dollars, less the dollar forty you paid up front, and you're left with eighteen dollars and sixty cents.

"Come to think of it, you shouldn't try to buy both cartons the same day. In fact they may not even give 'em to you. The disbursing officer is starting to lean on the Ship's Servicemen to ration them out, since even non-smokers are buying all they can get."

I had some reservations. "The brass have been yappin' a lot lately about the black-market business and how they'll put our ass in a sling if we deal with that stuff. I don't know, Gus."

The last thing I needed was to foul up my chances for a transfer. I had decided that two years on my destroyer, bouncing around the ocean like a ping-pong ball, were enough to earn me a shot at duty aboard something larger. I had requested a transfer to a heavy cruiser, and my chances were good since it involved another ship within the command, Cruisers-Destroyers, Pacific Fleet--CruDesPac.

"No sweat, this deal's so clean it squeaks. Here's the drill, Frankie. Secure one carton of cigarettes to each leg with adhesive tape. Your bell-bottomed tailor-mades will hide 'em, no problem. We go to the bar first thing, and you have liberty money."

I was weakening. Gus made it sound too easy.

Later that afternoon, in our dress blues and smelling of Old Spice after-shave and butch wax on my crew-cut, the two of us led the rest of the liberty party scrambling down the gangway. Gus hailed the first pedicab in the long line of rickshaws waiting on the dock paralleling the ship. We settled into the back and the driver began pumping.

"Take us to a bar in town where we can sell some cigarettes."

We headed out from the docking area toward Keelung--and the action. Sitting in the rickshaw, with the added height of the rear seat, I could see down into the water at a different angle. My view was closer to the pilings than when I stood on the dock.

Twenty-five feet from us, floating face down in the water near the rocky edge, rested what looked like a new-born baby. She bobbed as the swells washed across, tumbling her lifeless little body.

"Is that what I think it is? Holy shit. It's a dead baby. What do ya figure...?" Riding along I was feeling a lot of mixed signals--here was the baby, me, us, all the disinterested activity carrying on around us.

Gus tried to explain the mentality. "In this part of the world, anything they don't want anymore they heave into the water--the ocean, a river, a lake. It's always been that way. We can't do anything about it. Don't let it throw you."

I'd have to go with Gus' advice. In our travels we were constantly running up against cultural differences, this was another one. But it handed me a strong jolt.

We'd left the docking area and were headed down a narrow two-lane road. Half a dozen scenarios placing that baby into the water flashed through my thoughts. But something happening nearby grabbed my attention. Large brown Army trucks, with olive drab canvas covering their loads, whizzed past us. Driven by uniformed Chinese Nationalists, they were heading in the direction we'd come from. Each time one passed, the wind it dragged behind made our rig wobble and jerk uncontrollably to the right, then left, before our driver regained control.

Continuing to peddle toward town, the struggling man, his muscular calves bulging, turned toward us and proposed, in broken English, to buy my cigarettes. I wanted ten dollars a carton, he argued for half as much.

"Forget it, Jack. Just take us to the bar."

From his position on the bike seat, the agitated driver used grasping motions, reaching around and grabbing at the cartons taped to my legs. I took hold of his hand and we wrestled a bit while again he veered the pedicab, moving in one direction, then the other. The traffic continued to whiz by, now speeding in both directions. The jackass kept turning his head and body around, trying to free a carton from my leg. I don't know what he thought he was going to do if he succeeded in pulling one off my leg, but he was determined to close some sort of deal for those smokes.

Gus yelled and pushed on the man's shoulders to force him to face forward. No way. Greed completely possessed this guy and safe driving wasn't on his mind. We were still far from town. I became fed up with him, and though probably crazy to continue, determined to ride it out .

We traveled further off course, toward the oncoming traffic. Gus yelled louder, the driver turned the pedicab abruptly to the right. A second later his front wheel hit the row of stones lining the side of the road and the bike bounced violently, lurching us forward in our rear seat. In shock, we watched the driver catapult over the top of his handlebars, tumbling ass-over-tea-kettle, ending in a heap on the soft shoulder of the road.

The sight snapped us out of our downer mood. We began to laugh and hoot, our heads back, caught up in hysteria. This was the culmination of speeding traffic threatening our lives, the earlier unnerving experience of seeing a discarded human life, the baby, and finally, the acrobatics of our annoying driver, airborne over the front of the bike. We were helpless to move from the back of the cab. I couldn't coordinate my legs to step out. Gus and I carried on this way for several minutes. The driver turned his head slowly, nearly hidden by the thick grass, and emitted a stream of low moans.

My stomach ached from laughing. I had to get out of the cab and try to gain some relief from the wacky moment. I eased myself down slowly, continuing to laugh, held in the grip of the scene. Tears flowed down Gus' face as he shook and bounced up and down, wailing, his arms wrapped tight around himself.

Bent over, I eased out of the cab, still holding my sides and carrying on, out of control. The stress had broken, but its release only prolonged the hilarity. Slowly I moved backwards, away from the cab, toward the side of the road.

Suddenly I lost my footing. One leg went out from under me. My head and chest pummeled against the earth. I gathered my bearings and discovered my right leg deep into a slit-trench designed to carry away sewage--the effluent came up my leg and poured into my sea-boot. My left leg remained at street level, straining my crotch until I thought it would rip to my navel. My left knee was jammed against my face. The position must have resembled an athlete in mid-air, clearing a high hurdle.

Gus' laughter gained in volume and enthusiasm as my misfortune compounded the situation. I looked over my shoulder, watching him still sitting in the cab.

"Gus, I'm stuck in a shit-hole here. Come over and give me a hand."

By now the driver had pulled himself together enough to get onto his hands and knees, then struggle upright. Gus slid down to the pavement to help.

179

The driver approached, looking apprehensive, undoubtedly feeling some liability for the mess. And rightly so. But for his damn foolishness, we'd still be on our way into town, safe--and clean.

ALL MUCKED UP

Gus and the groggy driver each took an arm and lifted me from the trench. Where there wasn't sewage, mud was smeared--over the front, back, and both sides of my uniform. My once shiny leather liberty boots could never pass another inspection. Gus fought to contain his laughing.

I exploded with frustration. Using my index finger I drilled into the driver's chest, leaning my face down into his.

"Take us some place I can get cleaned up. Now. Fast. MOVE IT." He knew I meant business.

Gus quieted down, sensing my agitation. He jumped back into the cab first, hugged the far side, and held up one hand to discourage me from getting too close. The driver peddled us away, forgetting, for the moment, the cigarettes still taped to my legs.

On the outskirts of town he turned up a residential street and after passing several doors, stopped. Jumping off the bike seat, he hurried to my side and offered both hands to assist me down.

I waited. "Where are we? I'm not up for any more of your shenanigans, Pal."

The driver spoke in Chinese and encouraged us toward a dwelling. We remained in the pedicab. He left us and went to the door. His knock brought an immediate response. Three young ladies struggled through the opening, each trying to be the first outside to greet the day's early customers. The driver indicated through pantomimed hip gyrations that these smiling commodities were ours for the taking.

Oh, swell. This clown almost gets us killed on the road. I look like a creature from the swamp, and smell worse. And he thinks he's off the hook by introducing us to his little screwing machines.

Now it was my turn to pantomime. I stepped out of the cab, the ladies drew back, their smiles dropped. With me standing upright, they were able to observe my total appearance, and probably caught a whiff of me. In unison they retreated up the steps toward the door. From that safer distance they witnessed the vilest demonstration of language that required no translating. My anger had boiled over.

The driver urged me back into the cab. Gus looked at the ladies, exaggerated a shrug, and raised both hands, palms up. We peddled off as the working girls waved from the front stoop, chattering after us in Chinese. More distraught each moment, I harangued the driver as he pumped determinedly toward what I hoped was relief from my messed-up situation.

Gathering speed down a short hill, one rear wheel raised as we careened around a corner without slowing down. The driver stood erect on the pedals and put his weight down on the brake. The pedicab slid to a stop, and without speaking he hurried off his seat and ran through the closest door that faced the dirt street. Seconds later he reappeared with a woman, pointed toward the two of us in the rickshaw's back seat, and jabbered what sounded like a series of commands. The lady motioned us toward her doorway, but stopped me just inside. My clothes were to come off before proceeding further. I set my boots by the front entry and removed the soiled pants and jumper. She held a small quilt for me to wrap myself in, then indicated the socks should also come off.

I didn't want my dress blues washed, for fear they might shrink, but one lower leg demanded special attention. She hung them onto a line near the warmth of a stove occupying one wall of the single-room arrangement. Into a chipped enamel pan of warm water, without the help of soap, she emerged the soiled leg, worked it about, and squeezed it within a piece of old towel material, smoothing it out. With new water into the pan, she kneaded and rinsed my socks, wrung them out tightly and hung them beside my uniform to dry on the line.

Moving about as if she performed the routine regularly, she went from the hanging uniform to a steaming kettle and prepared a pot of tea, bringing three cups and the china pot to the bench arrangement where Gus and I sat leaning against the wall. After pouring steaming cups for Gus and me, she prepared a third for our driver, whom I figured must be her husband, or a relative, for her to put up with his stream of orders. With only skivvies and the quilt around my shoulders, I must have presented an interesting picture. The two cartons of cigarettes, protected by the heavy sealed wrappings peculiar to sea stores, were still taped to each of my legs.

Knife in hand, she inspected the damage to my drying blues. Where mud had dried, she scraped it. After she removed all she could, she used a brush to whisk at what remained. Hot water and a rag brought my tailor-made pants back to a reasonable appearance. I showed her how to arrange the pieces inside-out so the seams were all inverted--regulation style, and she finished the job by ironing, steaming the hot iron over a damp piece of cloth protecting the material. The smell of the iron's heat upon the damp cotton reminded me of my mom ironing at home.

In the meantime, between sips of his hot tea, our nemesis had taken my boots and, manipulating a stick, scraped at the muck. He brushed them and used the same hot water and rag procedure for the finishing touches, then brought them over to the warm stove. I could get them shined in town, and soon be back into the liberty game.

Bowing slightly, the lady of the house extended the fresh trousers toward me, and I eagerly slid my legs into them. They felt warm from the pressing and while not one hundred percent in appearance, nor odor, they were passable. I pushed my wallet into the rear pocket, money and liberty card into a front pocket, and was beginning to feel whole again. I gave the host some *yuan* to fetch a couple of beers while we waited for the lady to finish my jumper. With the driver gone, I forced a few bills onto my reticent savior, indicating with a finger pressed against my lips that it would be our secret.

I hoped their simple little home had some kind of decent bathroom. Some of the facilities we'd seen in Formosa were frightening. I asked our hostess, in Japanese, the location of the head.

"Benjo doko?"

She guided me through a back door into a small adjacent bathroom. The Spartan space consisted of four walls and a hole in the center of the floor. There was a white ceramic edge around the floor opening, as was customary in nicer arrangements. These were Asian toilets. One squatted rather than sat. No flushing water, as in the West. I hung the quilt over the door handle and unbuttoned my thirteen buttons. Positioning myself over the hole, I inserted my thumbs into the top of each side of my pants and I pushed them down toward my ankles. Regulation uniforms don't have a pocket in the rear for one's wallet. I had forgotten I was wearing my liberty tailor-mades.

My wallet flipped out from the trousers, bounced on the porcelain rim and, as I watched in horror, tumbled into the darkness of the hole.

I won't live out this day. I have never been made so crazy. I've got to get that wallet.

Back in the other room the driver and his lady chatted over tea, celebrating the completion of their chores--they thought. I brought him into the *benjo* with Gus following, smiling like the Cheshire Cat. I supposed by this time the driver was figuring he also was having a bad day. After surveying the situation, he left and returned with a flashlight and the lady of the house. The four of us formed a circle around the hole and peered down into the blackness. I had peeked down into neighborhood out-house toilets as a boy, I knew what to expect, privy makeup and stench being universal.

There, illuminated by the flashlight's weak orange beam, rested my wallet, several feet below in the midst of a gagging mess.

The driver barked more directions at poor mama-san. She left and returned with two sticks of wood, each about three feet long. Gus held the flashlight while I managed the sticks. After several disappointing attempts to bring the wallet part way up, and lose it each time, the rickshaw man took over and brought it up on his first try. I supposed using chop sticks gave him a special knack for that sort of thing.

Once again the lady went to work. She gingerly picked the wallet up from the floor, taking it inside where she wiped it, emptied and ironed the contents. The wallet and things from inside were arranged near the stove.

Gus popped open the two remaining beers. I took a swig. It was disappointingly lukewarm. Somehow it fit the entire scene.

Raising his bottle toward me, Gus smiled. "My friend, watching you today has been like witnessing a monkey make love to a football."

We clinked our bottles and tilted them up.

OWENS, ONE--DELANEY, ZERO

Everything not lashed down fell to the deck, or overboard, in those first few hours after the winds began. OZBOURN was underway, dispatched from Keelung to search for survivors of a downed Navy patrol plane in the Straits of Formosa. In the officer's wardroom stewards mates arranged cherry wood fiddle-boards on the dining table to contain each officer's spilled food during the heavy seas. In the galley, cooks for the crew went crazy. Large institutional kettles secured to the deck sloshed their brew, up and over the sides, leaving the compact work space awash in cream-of-chicken-rice soup. Scullery personnel would have a tough time cleaning up. Finally the Chief Cook surrendered--no more liquids.

In the passageway outside the after head, I stopped to BS with Delaney. He steadied himself with one hand as he tested the batteries of the bulkhead mounted battle lantern listed on his checklist.

"Frankie Boy, old Red's feelin' a little shitty." Brian "Red" Delaney talked of the unfamiliar feeling in his head and gut, questioning if it was to be his first experience with sea-sickness? "Back in '42, when I was a coxswain on a Coast Guard cutter operating out of Astoria, Oregon, we performed Search and Rescue Ops. The weather gets pretty nasty up by the Washington border, winds and water always battering the ship--it came with the job. But this storm, man, this is a monster. I've never seen anything like it."

He pulled off his knit watch cap and ran his fingers through his carrot-topped bush several times. "Something's been running through my mind ever since we left Keelung. You know, wherever Coast Guardsmen struggled out on Search and Rescue, there'd be the old turn of the century admonition, 'You have to go out. Nothing says you have to come back.' It's posted on bulkheads of stations, usually framed next to the picture of the president.

"I think it's a premonition." He pulled on his cap, turned, and slowly walked away toward the next lantern as he muttered and shook his head.

I tried to rationalize my concerns. *But things are different now. This isn't the Coast Guard, isn't the Pacific Northwest. And there's a new war going on. This storm can't last forever.*

"Snipes" came up from the forward engine room and swore the dial of the inclinometer registered exaggerated rolls of 80 degrees. That magnitude would put the vessel practically on her side. But more factual engineers toned down the reports to "over 40 degrees."

"That's better?" In the reduced light of the Sonar Shack heads turned toward Red Delaney, his clipboard checklist tucked under his arm. "How bad is bad? 40 degrees? 80 degrees? A destroyer could go tits-up in seas this heavy. I've read about it happening in hurricanes during the Second World War."

First Class Boatswain's Mate Owens, the sage of the deck force, had come down looking for a hot cup of coffee, but the sonar pot was secured. The day before it spilled over in a heavy roll. Hot coffee scalded the neck and shoulders of the unfortunate sailor sitting beside it, confining him to his rack under Doc Brown's direct supervision. Chief Corpsman Brown ordered the coffee maker "out for good," then proceeded to check all other compartments on the vessel for unsafe Joe-pots.

Owens, with his oversized front teeth spaced apart in the center, presented quite a picture. A two-inch band of curly, salt and pepper fuzz circled the sides and back of his freckled bald head. You never saw him without the white handmade lanyard around his neck, securing the shiny silver boatswain's pipe resting in his front dungaree pocket. It all somehow came together to give him a legitimacy--the consummate boatswain. A man whose experience one could trust. Tested, reliable, he told it straight. Korea was his second war and he had completed two tours in the "tin-can" Navy of 390 foot destroyers.

Everyone, except the sonar operator who sat before his pinging green scope, looked in the direction of "Boats" as he began to set the record straight. "What we're seein' here is a typhoon, not a hurricane." He glanced toward Delaney, who appeared too busy planning his rebuttal to catch the gibe. "You know what it costs to put one of these destroyers into the water? Millions. Do you think, after all these years, Naval Architects would design a ship that comes apart in hundred-mile-an-hour winds? Come on, typhoon Clara isn't uncommon. Every year they come up. Just Mother Nature flexin' her muscles."

Red Delaney shot right back. "That's all fine as long as we stay headed-up into the force and don't fall-off for some reason. But let us go "beam-to" and no little pissy-ass Navy Architect in Bath Maine, or anywhere else, could save our *cojones.*

Slight built Jimmy Gargas, yeoman striker from the ship's office, got into the exchange. "If you want a thrill, go aft to the machine shop when this baby starts actin' like a buckin' bronco. When water disappears from under the fantail and those twin screws whirl with nothing to bite into--we're talkin' major vibration. Rockin' and rollin'."

Owens nodded, "Cavitation." Giving the technical term for Jimmy's description.

From his rack outside the wire-mesh faced sonar work-space, a resting crewman shared with others in the berthing compartment, "Brian Delaney says the problem with these heavy rolls, we could take water into the boiler rooms and extinguish the boilers. It's when you lose power you're in deep shit. If the skipper can't keep this can headed-up, if she turns sideways on us, we've all bought the farm."

A voice of another man who hadn't seen Red Delaney inside, carried on. "Don't talk to me about that Clam-Digger, Delaney. He don't know his ass from a hole in the ground. Maybe that's the way it worked in his Shallow Water Navy, but this ain't the Coast Guard. This here's a 2200 ton combatant vessel, designed to do just what it's doin'--head straight into the storm and ride it out." A couple of his shipmates caught his attention, signaling Delaney's unobserved presence on the other side of the wire separation. The speaker's jaw slackened as he squinted, searching about the dim interior of the sonar shack. When he discovered Delaney glaring back at him, he forced a half-smile that contrasted with the discomfort shown in his eyes.

"Just kiddin' around, Red. Didn't mean nothin' by it. Red, DON'T COME OUT HERE."

Everyone but Delaney laughed.

A new voice broke the tension. "I don't give a shit, the next time I'm tossed out of my bunk by one of these rolls, you won't find me anywhere below the main deck where I'm not ordered to go. I want a quick escape route."

Delaney argued, "You can say what you want, but OZ is just bouncing around out here. We can't even look for the downed patrol plane and its crew. We're too busy fightin' to keep *ourselves* afloat. Seen the electric wipers up on the bridge's port hole glass? Can't open a peek through the sheets of water flyin' against them. We can't even see where the hell we're goin'. Half the time the lookouts are starin' straight into a wall of green water when we're at the bottom of a wave trough. It's spooky as hell out there."

Someone in the group moaned, "Lost at sea. Nobody knows what happened to 'em."

I saw Owens flinch his disapproval. He didn't appear to like the direction the comments were taking.

A man still wet from being topside removed his foul weather jacket. "Do you think, if those guys were still alive out here in this nightmare, we'd be able to find 'em--let alone rescue 'em? Wind driving rain in horizontal sheets, waves crashing over the bow, and surf washing the length of the ship--shit, you take your life in your hands even stepping out onto the weather decks. We'll be lucky if someone finds *us*, never mind finding those fly-boys."

"Listen..." Red Delaney hardly got his mouth in gear when Owens locked him into the strength of his narrowed green eyes and forcefully whispered.

"Knock it off, Brian. Our job is to keep the kids on this ship from bein' so scared they can't perform their duties. We're gonna make it."

I recognized the end of *that* conversation.

For three days the ship shuddered as it plowed through mountains of waves and fell deep into the bottomless troughs. Finally, the disappointing directive from the Task Force Commander ordered OZBOURN to break off the search for the crew of the downed plane. I felt guilty having been so concerned over my own safety while we were the only chance the downed flyers had of getting out of their mess. But we had done all we could.

What a business.

LOST STEERING--FOUND HONG KONG

The duty helmsman moved the wheel slightly starboard to correct course. The ship did not respond. He concentrated his attention on the gyro compass mounted before him and put the wheel farther right. Still no change in course.

In a voice loud enough to insure the OOD hearing him, but a tone that showed no sign of his anxiety, the helmsman announced, "Lost steering. We have lost steering."

The ship's wheel, positioned in the center of the pilot house, steered the vessel--at least that's the result when it was turned by the helmsman and the ship's heading responded. In truth, the wheel activated a servo-mechanism whose motor produced the energy to move the large, heavy rudders. The helmsman on the bridge could never physically accomplish that.

The OOD and JOOD rushed to opposite sides of the helmsman. The OOD directed him to demonstrate the problem. All three stared at the gyro compass.

"Shit." The OOD turned toward the telephone talker. "Tell After-Steering to engage emergency manual steering." He spun around and crossed the pilot house toward the sound tube near the chart table. Leaning toward the tube, he swallowed, cleared his throat, then forced himself to measure the words. "Captain? Captain, we have lost steering." He held his breath.

Directly below the pilot house, the Old Man's tiny sea cabin, where he stole moments of rest away from the bridge, accommodated little more than a bunk and a sink. The flanged end of the polished brass sound tube terminated directly above the head of his bed. In a groggy voice the skipper ordered, "Repeat that." The second report confirmed he'd heard it right. He grabbed his cap and pulled it down tight. Racing out into the rain and wind still pulling on his jacket, he paused just long enough to set one dog on the closed hatch behind him and strode, two steps at a time, up the short ladder onto the bridge. He was in the pilot house in seconds, his jacket still unzipped and his khaki shirt rain-soaked down its front. With both hands he pulled down his cap more tightly, as if to begin serious business, and stood on his toes, peering over the helmsman's shoulder. The softly lit gyro compass told the story. The system for moving the rudders had indeed failed. OZBOURN had lost the ability to steer from her bridge.

A message cracked into the talker's earphones. "Bridge, After Steering. You'd better get some more muscle down here. I'm fighting this son-of-a-bitch and it's lookin' to whop me."

The watch stander in the bowels of the after part of the vessel, busy following the course directions from the bridge and manually positioning the rudders, was acknowledged with a smart "Bridge, aye." Then, using the man's exact wording, the bridge talker relayed the message to the Captain.

Without replying, the CO moved directly to the loudspeaker. He reached out toward the toggle switch, paused, then withdrew his hand. Appearing to reorganize his thoughts, he turned toward the duty Boatswain's Mate standing at the ship's log. "Request LT. Remmen to call the bridge immediately." In seconds one of the hand-held phones mounted in the bank across the after bulkhead, buzzed. The Captain jerked it up to his ear. "We've lost steering, Armond. After-steering is having a time holding course. Assess the overall problem and get right back to me. I'll wait here for your evaluation."

No one understood better than a Chief Engineer, that aboard any combatant vessel *he* brought the weapon system to its target. Armond Remmen found a great deal of satisfaction knowing he was *the man*, and his manner reflected it. A "mustang" who came up through the enlisted ranks, he possessed a talent that served him well through his years in underway engineering departments. He took pride in his experience and his knowledge of every gear, lever, valve, and motor aboard the vessel. But he had to report, after consulting with his Chief Petty Officers, that this time he was unable to perform his mechanical magic. The problem could not be repaired with the limited parts and capabilities onboard the destroyer.

The Captain, mindful of his responsibility to maintain the psychological well being of his sailors, and realizing the crew would soon be aware of the situation, pulled down the mike of the public address system.

"This is the Captain speaking..." Throughout the vessel people came to a stop and listened. One didn't often hear the Skipper's voice. This had to be important.

Red Delaney waited for the Old Man to announce, "Prepare to abandon ship." But the Skipper, in his calm, authoritative voice, simply apprised the crew of the situation and reminded them that with existing backup systems in place everything was under control.

190

Delaney almost looked as if he felt disappointed.

Safety dictated that the time remaining to get the ship's steering repaired was measured in days. U.S. facilities were too far away. International maritime custom dictated much of what took place in the next few days.

The good news was, during the evening following the loss of steering, the force of the typhoon relaxed, most of its anger spent. Crew members not on watch enjoyed the luxury of a restful sleep.

The obvious geographic opportunity for repairs was Hong Kong, China. Under ordinary circumstances the British would have happily obliged their American friend and ally. But China had sent "volunteers" to fight alongside the North Koreans. U.S. forces were killing Chinese troops. The U.S. Navy, patrolling the Straits of Formosa, was a daily irritant to the Communist Chinese Government, who didn't want any part in aiding an "enemy" vessel to return to the line.

The British Crown Colony of Hong Kong was experiencing its own diplomatic problems with mainland China. England's participation in the "Korean Conflict" heightened concerns over negotiating a renewal of their historic territorial lease of the island. The new issue that had the Queen's Governor General tossing at night was whether the lease would even be allowed to run its remaining fifty years.

After extended U.S. communications with the British, emphasizing the risk to crew members sailing under dangerous conditions, an invitation was reluctantly extended for a *brief* visit--only long enough to accomplish the needed repairs.

Steaming in calm seas, at 0700 on November 11, 1950, the OZBOURN entered Hong Kong's bustling harbor. The water teemed with sampans that showed no concern for right-of-way as they maneuvered across our course. The ship's horn, so loud it was traditionally used only when safety dictated, emitted frequent short blasts--the first nautical rule-of-the-road being "avoid collision."

Fishing and transporting commerce brought a livelihood to the boat people, who, each day and night, lived out their entire lives upon the water. Some of the boats were one-man contraptions, guided by a helmsman standing high on the after section, pushing and pulling a long tiller for propulsion. On larger boats children scampered about the decks while women tended smoking cook-fires. Drying laundry flew like pennants.

On the OZBOURN all hands wore the uniform of the day, undress blues, and stood in ranks, lined up smartly at quarters. Each sailor's anticipation, and the excitement of surrounding vessel traffic, reached a crescendo when British fighter planes made a series of passes over the ship. My limited military experience didn't allow me to bring much meaning to the show. But seasoned officers nearby questioned the planes' low altitude--certainly not the performance of a welcoming committee.

The Plan Of The Day announced liberty for the starboard section would begin soon after mooring. We were all lined up waiting when the word was passed. "Now hear this. Liberty, liberty for the starboard section. Liberty expires onboard at 2400."

The Engineer jumped up and scurried toward the bow of the liberty boat as it approached the dock. He squeezed past seated sailors, then grasped at a piling using the boat hook to steady the motor whaleboat. When the last of our liberty party scrambled up onto the heavy timbers, he let go. The Coxswain stood aft at the tiller, waiting for him to return to his position behind the engine, then struck the bell and they shoved off.

On the dock boisterous activity surrounded me in a swarm. One side was crowded with merchandise displayed on the wooden surface. Vendors had staked out little pieces of frontage and arranged their detailed, intricately carved ivory and cherry wood, tooled leather photo albums, jade pieces and flashlights. Flashlights seemed to provide an industry for anyone with no other source of support. My experience with them at home only dealt with the two-cell standard unit and the long, multi-celled professional model used by police and other emergency personnel. But Hong Kong brought the industry into its own with miniature models requiring special little batteries and tiny bulbs, larger pen-light sizes, and hefty models fronted with impressive reflectors, all very cheap. Each of us ended up with several to compare back on the ship.

The sellers squatted behind their displays, elbows on their knees. Between puffs, each held the end of the burning cigarette close by his mouth. They smoked and waited, spring loaded and ready for action.

The noise they created moved like a wave through the spectator's bleacher at a football game. As I passed each arrangement the owner excitedly encouraged me, in pidgin, to "Take a look. Take a look." He'd quiet down when I moved on to the next, as his neighbor started to pitch and the wave progressed until I'd gone down the entire row of makeshift "shops." Although I glanced at all the offerings, I kept moving toward my destination, downtown. I figured I could pick up those things anytime. After I'd gotten the big picture, I'd have a better idea how to spend my limited dollars.

With the last display behind me, a very courteous young Chinese man approached holding a felt-lined tray with a multicolored assortment of cut gems. The hinged lid opened against his chest. Treasure pieces glittered and caught my attention as he selected individual stones and offered them for my inspection.

"Thirty dollars Hong Kong? That's about five dollars US. That fits my budget." I pointed and he removed different pieces. From the corner of my eye I sensed a blur of movement. With a startling bang the tray and its contents went flying straight into the air. Stones came down, bouncing like hail in every direction. Some fell through spaces separating the dock's planking as others tumbled over the side.

Two British sailors wearing Donald Duck caps and white uniforms with distinctive blue collars, were bombarding the young gemologist with shouts that attracted the attention of everyone on the dock. "You slanty-eyed little bastard, we've warned you about selling this glass shit here."

Down on his hands and knees, scrambling about to retrieve what he could, the man jammed stones into his trouser pockets while the two angry Brits alternated between booting him in the seat of his pants and kicking individual pieces of his precious merchandise, one by one, into the water. Native observers excitedly jabbered amongst themselves as they watched the shiny pieces splash into the bay-water below. They looked as though they were considering a jump to salvage one or two for themselves.

The scene took the wind out of me. Not just startled, I had never seen a fellow human being dealt with so callously. The incongruity of white foreigners treating a native so disgracefully, *in his own country,* shocked me. Hardly off the boat, I'd witnessed a first hand lesson of the attitude the British held toward the Chinese--something less than human. What sort of offense could this man have committed? These two Limies appeared to be on liberty, just as I, not in some official capacity.

Leaving his partner to dispatch the pathetic Chinese, the shorter of the two Brits came over to me. "Well, mate, it looks like it was Her Majesty's Royal Navy to the rescue. You didn't buy any of that trash, did ya?"

"No, but I had my eye on a piece. What the hell's the problem here anyway?" The tone must have hinted at my discomfort.

Appearing surprised, he shot back, "You wanted one? What color did you want?" He glanced about the dock at the few remaining pieces.

"I was looking at an...Alexandrite the guy said it was. A purple one."

He called out to his friend, several yards away, "Archie, find this here Yank a purple one." The taller sailor bent several times to examine stones still lying about, tossing each over the side when it didn't satisfy him. The vendor continued retrieving, but nervously kept him in his sight.

Archie found one to his liking, and brought it to us. "This what Wally says you're lookin' for, mate?" He extended a beautiful emerald-cut piece toward me. I took it between my thumb and forefinger, turning it in the sunlight.

"This is great. But I want to pay the man for it." I removed a few wadded bills from my jumper pocket. "I don't have any Hong Kong yet, just these."

The one called Wally looked over the bills in my hand, sorting through the wrinkled ball. "Let's see here. This will do just fine for the Chinaman." He removed one of my US dollar bills, turned, and walked toward the Chinese, extending the bill before him.

Showing mixed emotions, the fellow seemed afraid to come close enough, but his eyes telegraphed his desire for the money. He said something I couldn't hear, accepted the bill, and resumed picking up more jewels.

But Wally and Arch had had enough, and both began kicking the man, driving him off the dock, barking singular Chinese words after him. Together they sauntered back toward me. The shorter extended his hand. "I'm Wallace Poundstone, and this here bloke is my mate, Archibald Wainwright."

I shook his hand, feeling a little more settled. "Frank Spittle."

Smiling up into my face as he pumped my hand he gushed, "Spittle. Sounds English to me." Turning, "Doesn't it Arch?"

Archibald nodded, flashing a smile that exposed two brown caries in the front of his mouth. I shook hands with Arch. "Pleased to meet ya, Archie. Both my parents *were* born in England, so I guess you pegged me right."

Wally explained that the gem-stones were "crap." British sailors wouldn't have anything to do with them. They couldn't believe the Chinese fellow had the nerve to show his face around after earlier being ordered to keep off the dock.

194

Archie, whom I'd determined was the mental light-weight of the twosome, jerked his thumb back over his shoulder. "I'm going to fetch a rickshaw." In a moment he was back, sitting in the rear of a high, wood spoked, two-wheeled apparatus, being pulled by a barefooted, mature man dressed in black shorts and a ragged top. I had never seen this type of rickshaw, only those built from bicycle parts. The older Hong Kong model carried only one passenger. The runner in front leaned into a cross-bar before him, attached to two rails going back to the cab area. Behind Wally and his man, a string of similar black rickshaws, all empty, formed a waiting line. Each of the runners wore a wide brimmed woven reed hat tied beneath his chin. They seemed darker skinned than the vendors I'd passed earlier, probably dirty from running day and night about the city.

Looking down from his perch, Archie announced, "Move lively now, lads. My dick's atingling."

I had to laugh. This tall, narrow-faced fellow, with the angry red pimple on his right temple and smaller ones splattered about his head and neck, had business on his mind that would not wait.

"Frank, we're off to Wan Chai section. You'd like it there. Fine spirits, good food, and the loveliest birds you'll find in China. Refined, mind you, not the grimy, back alley whores." He exaggerated a sneer up towards Archie. "Diddle with them and you'll go back to your ship with a dose of the pox. Why don't you come along with us? You being a fellow Brit and all. Eh, Arch?" He called up to Archie who was anxiously bouncing up and down in his seat, rarin' to go. "We'll show our visitor some sights along the way."

The boys were beginning to appear a little more human. Their proposal made sense. "Let's go to Wan Chai."

I ONLY CAME TO DANCE

I didn't know where I was headed in the confusing city. Wally and I climbed into separate rickshaws waiting in line behind Archie. The disappointed remaining runners hurled abuse upon our rickshaw boys. We rode half a mile through the bustle, down a canyon of high commercial buildings. I caught my breath as we were passed closely by double decker red buses and black and white checker striped British taxis. The lead man abruptly turned and trotted into a lane lined with market stalls. Foot traffic crowded along like a stream of molasses past the produce stands, making it impossible for the rickshaws to proceed. Wally called a halt, motioned to me he would pay the runners, and the three of us took off on foot.

Twenty paces into the lane it was as if we'd turned the page of a picture-storybook. Colorful mounds of fresh fruit and vegetables were arranged along each side, engulfing us.

Stacked cages of chickens and ducks, added barnyard sounds to the clamor. Fish splashed in metal tubs resting on the ground. Archie directed my attention away from the lively fish by pointing toward my foot. I looked down at the clay alleyway, hard and smooth, compacted by thousands of passing feet. Beside my foot, snakes twisted around each other in half a dozen cages. I jumped away, nearly knocking over a surprised shopper.

"Tell me these are pets," I exclaimed, still reeling from the shock.

"No such luck," laughed Wally. "One of those twisters will grace someone's plate tonight."

"Ugh. I don't think so."

Nothing phased Archie. "Actually they're quite good. It's monkey brains I can't develop a taste for."

Ready-to-eat hot food vied for the attention of hungry shoppers wanting a break from the vendors' haggling. Steaming offerings, unfamiliar to me, emitted their pungent, alien aromas. My senses were on overload. Bowls and chopsticks were set out. A customer took a bowl, *perhaps last used by a leper*, extended it toward the bubbling pot or sizzling wok that interested him, and delights were served-up.

A man expertly moving chopsticks in his right hand, held a bowl under his chin and in a steady rhythm packed in steaming mouthsfull of food. After a whirlwind ingestion, the empty bowl and sticks were left upon the counter. The attendant rinsed them in a bucket of cold water, leaving swirling bits of rice and other small leftovers for the next cleanup. Set out to dry, they awaited another customer. The iffy sanitation in this outdoor cafeteria threatened everyone with hepatitis-in-a-bowl. But no one was discouraged.

Twenty minutes of fighting our way through native shoppers discharged us into a changed scene. Neon lights on each side of a less crowded street blinked invitations in a combination of Chinese characters and English letters. Pedestrians walked on sidewalks, rather than down the street's paved center. In front of a brightly lit jewelry store an East Indian, well over six feet tall, stood at parade-rest, guarding the glitter. He held a threatening shotgun that was huge, even beside his impressive form. It made me consider the value of my stone from the dock where there had been no guards. Not just his height clenched my attention, but the picture he presented in his loose white outfit and matching spotless turban. With his feet apart, aqua blue eyes focused straight ahead, and right hand pressed smartly into the small of his back, he was ramrod military in manner. But certainly not a trooper in his person and dress. A full beard complimented his handsome dark face and its large features. I found it difficult not to stare.

Arch saw my interest. "They're always Indian. He's not afraid to use that cannon either. He won't move and he won't talk to you, unless of course...well, then it's too late."

Ahead of us a sprinkling of dim red lights adorned doorways. Away from the market area, in this more orderly atmosphere, my new friends knew exactly which red light they were seeking. Trumpet music, loud and mellow, flowed out to the sidewalk from an establishment several doors ahead. Archie led the way into a smoke filled barroom where nicely dressed hookers outnumbered three-to-one the half-dozen drinking patrons, all sailors. A handful of these aggressive barracudas rushed toward Archie, our point-man. It was a feeding frenzy. As professionals, these tootsies sensed his desperate condition. With each of his arms about the waist of a boisterous, painted working-girl, he headed toward the rear stairs, past the bar. The three of them, all laughing at something Arch had suggested, disappeared into a room opening off the second floor balcony. Archie kicked the door closed behind them. Wally and I dropped into seats at the first empty table.

The remaining ladies retired to neutral corners when they saw Wally was more interested in getting the attention of a waiter.

"They stock all the British ales here. I'm having a Guinness Stout myself," he announced while glancing about.

I was cautious. "I don't like the flat stuff. You know, no bubbles." I'd had foreign ales and beers and hadn't liked many of them. "I want something wheat colored, effervescent, and cold. Can we get that here?"

"I suppose that means you wouldn't want lemonade in it either. You're not much of a Limey after all, Frank. What you'll want is a lager. If you wanted lemonade in it you'd order a shandy."

The waiter quietly approached the table and stood at Wally's side. "Two pints. A Guinness Dark, and a lager for my Yank cousin here. Bring the bottles and open them at the table." The waiter nodded and left.

"And no glasses." Wally called after him.

I pulled a pack of Old Golds from my sock and put one into my mouth as I dug in my jumper pocket for the Zippo. Wally removed a box from an inner pocket and set it before me. "Here, have a *real* cigarette. None of *that* horse shit."

I recognized "Players" from the picture of the smoking sailor on the cover, wearing a beard and an old time large blue flat hat. I laughed, "Guess these'll kill me as fast as my own. Thanks."

I lit both of our Players. "I'm getting hungry. Where do we get something to eat?"

"He'll bring things with the ale."

The waiter balanced a small tray holding quartered cheese sandwiches and a bowl of pistachios with one hand, and the fingers of his other hand curled around the necks of two unopened bottles. As he took an opener from his pocket, Wally instructed me.

"Around here you can't be too careful. If they don't try to slip you a 'Mickey,' you'll get sick anyway just imbibing from a glass, or drinking the water, or even rubbing up against one of the little yellow creatures.

"What a shit-hole this Hong Kong is. I can't wait to be rotated back to Britain, or at least somewhere in the Med. Ever since the Japs sank the Repulse, our battleship here during the war, we've kept a strong military presence and the tours of duty are longer.

"I tell you, all these Chinkies are trouble. They'll rob you blind, maybe even kill you if they think they can get away with it. Our British trained Chinese police officers, you've seen them on every block in their olive drab uniforms with black Sam Browne belts, they're the only thing that keeps the lid on here."

"What about Archie, alone upstairs? Is he safe?"

"I'd say no, but he lets his Johnnywop do his thinkin'. Someday he'll get his bloody throat slit. He wouldn't be the first British seaman to be buggered in this bag of farts. I leave my buttons closed around these trollops."

"Then what are we doing here?" He was sending mixed signals--he didn't like it, he liked it.

"This is it, Mate. You either stay on the ship or you come here. I tease the chippies, dance, take some nourishment," he passed his hand over the pistachios, "and get a little pissed. Sometimes more than a *little*, and I have to be carried back." He took a long swallow of his thick dark brew.

A woman rested against the bar and watched us from across the room. She leaned back, her arms stretched out on the polished mahogany. Wally beckoned her over. "Come on Wormey, trot it on over."

She eased herself off the stool, ran her hands down each side of her hips to straighten her dress, and slithered our way. As the anointed one, there was no need to hurry. Her arrival at the table signaled the need for another, to round-out a foursome. By some generally understood arrangement, a second perky trick quickly approached. They were each dressed in high collared, long, printed silky dresses that came to within six inches of the floor and showed bare brown legs through the slits cutting deep up the sides. They both waited to be invited to sit. They looked like poster girls for Hookers Bazaar.

The latecomer sat herself on the side edge of her chair and leaned her head toward my ear. Her shiny black hair dusted over my cheek and neck and gave me a shiver. I liked her musky perfumed smell as she spoke in a whisper, allowing her lips to graze my ear as she formed each word.

"You want fuckie me? I the best. Come on. You fuckie me. okay?" She half rose, gently pulling my arm.

A little uncomfortable with the directness of her proposal, I took my cue from Wally's earlier advice. "I just came to dance. Would you like to dance?"

"We dance in bed. Come on." Standing now, and using a bit more force, she continued urging me in the direction of the back stairs. She relaxed her hold when the waiter returned.

Wormey, forming one word at a time, informed Wally, "We want whiskey."

"And whiskey you shall have, my pets. BUT NO BLOODY TEA." He left no doubt with the waiter, nor the ladies, that he would not tolerate any nonsense. "Real whiskey, poured from the bottle. Here at the table."

My little friend sat down again, sensing a new development. Wally explained the old B'Girl business. They got a cut from the drinks patrons bought them. And those drinks were usually tea, or some other colored liquid made to look like whiskey. Then he asked me, "How much money does she want?"

Not waiting for me to answer that I did not know, he looked toward my partner. "How much, fuckie?"

She looked into my face rather than toward him. "Thirty Hong Kong dollar."

"I only have U.S., and five dollars is too much."

"How much you have, Lover Boy?" Her hand moved up my inner thigh and began massaging the pack at my crotch. Her movements were hidden beneath the table, but Wally was aware.

"Enjoy this part, Mate. It's free and it won't last long."

I shifted a bit self-consciously. "The way it's headed right now, it won't have to last very long."

From the position and posture of the lady next to him I gathered the same thing was taking place under his side of the table.

Her sales technique was having its effect. I removed my wallet and opened it. She playfully pulled it from my grip and thumbed through the bills--nine dollars, a five and four ones.

"You cheapieskate. You have plenty money. Come on, we go dance in bed."

I reached across and retrieved my wallet, putting it back into my trouser pocket. Wally was right. The massage terminated. My partner sipped her "whiskey" and pouted.

From the juke box beside the front door, Jo Stafford began singing "You Belong To Me." I tried again. "How about that dance?"

"No dance. You cheapieskate." She stood up and stormed off, leaving her unfinished drink. I watched her hustle up the back stairs.

Wally and his date had finished their conversation and she didn't seem any happier with the results than *my* acquaintance.

I waved to the waiter. "Bring us another round."

Wally interceded, "Just the ales." He gestured toward the two glasses of brown liquid. "They're not having anything."

As the waiter approached with our order, I withdrew my wallet to pay. Inside rested four lonely dollar bills. No Lincoln.

"The little bitch snaked my five." I groaned with surprise. Wally's companion registered a blank, unknowing expression.

His quick reaction startled me. His chair shot back, banging against another table and shaking its contents. He was on his feet. "I'll take care of this." The anger he'd demonstrated earlier in the day on the pier showed again in his face.

I looked around the room. Everyone's eyes were on Wally. My instinct recognized the darkness of trouble and I gripped his forearm in a way that I hoped would convince him I was serious. "Forget it. It's not worth it. I'm ready to go back to the ship anyway. I'll just chalk it up to experience." He allowed me to ease him back into his chair, but his eyes glared at the upstairs balcony where she'd retreated.

To redirect his attention I laughed, "I can't wait to tell my old man back home. He wore that same British Navy uniform you're wearin' when he was our age. Always warned me about this kind of stuff--whiskey and fast women. His advice, 'Don't think with your dick.'

"He loves to be proven right. It'll make a nice gift for him. You know, the old 'I told you so' business."

Archie appeared at the top of the stairs holding the rail as if gaining his balance and began easing down, one deliberate step at a time. He wore his undershirt and carried his jumper and cap. He glided across the room toward us as if slow dancing in his untied shoes. His crooked smile and glossed over eyes gave him the appearance of a medicated mental patient.

Upon seeing he was headed for our table, the second unhappy female companion departed toward three singing British sailors who had staggered through the front entrance.

That left Wally, Goofey, and Cheapieskate to finish their beers, then make the Cinderella liberty midnight curfew.

201

BON APPETITE

I leaped from my bunk. "Horn" Davis was making his second trip through the berthing compartment since reveille. His shoes tap-danced against the metal steps as he jogged down the ladder from the messhall. The final wake-up round.

Horn shouted out as he descended, "This is it. I'm takin' names." It worked every time. Sleeping in, and having the Master at Arms report you, meant extra duty. I wasn't ready for that, not here in Hong Kong.

I managed to get some extra sleep after reveille sounded because I didn't care if I missed chow. My head felt as if it was coming off. All I wanted was Sick Call and a handful of APC's--the Navy's magic All Purpose Capsules. We joked that the Doc gave you APC's for clap, coughs, colds, moles, or sore assholes. The only skill required to become a hospital corpsman was the ability to shake the horse tablets from a huge APC plastic container. Diagnoses might vary, but treatment seemed consistent.

I took a breath and held it as I scrambled up the ladder, across the mess decks, and past steam tables being emptied from breakfast. One whiff would set off my stomach and I'd be a goner. Topside I stood a moment and took in the harbor air, filled with odors that defied identification. An initial glance about and I felt a jolting change in my normal shipboard surroundings. The scene momentarily confused me. Native Chinese had established little "shop" stations up and down the main deck. I approached the nearest man, sitting cross-legged, cleaning a dress blue jumper. Folded blue wool trousers and jumpers formed neat stacks on either side of him. With a bottle of transparent fluid in one hand he applied the contents to a rag in his other, and energetically scrubbed the white piping on the collar supported on his bare, brown thigh. The man managing the next station sat low on an eight inch stool. Several pair of black liberty shoes and sea boots were arranged against the bulkhead. One shoe was mounted on an upward positioned metal last. He nailed on an oversized, irregular shaped leather sole with such speed and marksmanship, I had to stop and admire his skill. A short-blade cutting device from his work box looked to have the razor sharpness craftsmen demand. With a flourish he expertly trimmed long slices off the leather and continued shaping the sole to its new home.

I'd never seen nationals allowed aboard to conduct their business, but later Old China Hands explained this was tradition in the Far East. However, none of the shopkeepers hustled me as those on the dock had the previous day. They simply smiled and offered their services with courtesy, probably not wanting to risk the on-site advantage they enjoyed over their competitors in town.

A long yellow tape marked off in black graduations hung around the tailor's neck. Several civilian coats and pairs of slacks, three bolts of material and dozens of swatches offered possibilities to prospective customers. He extended an Esquire magazine, opened to pictures of male models wearing the latest fashions. A dozen other dog-eared publications suggested styles he would recreate. He could deliver a finished suit the next day. A crew of tailors back in the shop would work all night. But he recommended returning for at least two fittings, if time allowed.

Neatly lettered price lists of merchandise were displayed on a board propped against a humming air intake. A tailored suit cost two hundred dollars HK, forty dollars US. The price seemed reasonable enough, although you couldn't have proven it by me. I'd never owned a suit or even a sport coat. Mostly officers, and lucky gamblers from the crew, were being fitted. The typical enlisted had better ways to spend his limited resources.

At the ship's office, beside the door in the midships passageway, "Chicken" Hansen stood with one bare foot on a piece of white paper while a Chinese craftsman knelt down and carefully outlined Chick's foot with a pencil.

"Frank, this guy'll make you a pair of shoes for eighteen dollars US. Look at these little leather pieces glued on the cardboard. Any color, any type leather, any style shoe. They measure you here, then bring the finished product back in two days. Five dollars now, the rest when you get 'em." Chick held a slick, color magazine and extended it toward me, pointing to a sporty pair of brown saddle shoes. "Pretty collegiate, huh? Wait till the Utah dollies in American Fork see these babies." The shoeman offered a variety of styles, displaying one of each, arranged around him on the deck. Several onlookers passed around a shoe cut down the middle like an apple, exposing the construction quality.

The Chief Boiler Technician, with his black billed tan cap resting on the back of his head, passed and joked to the busy Chinese,

"Hey, Joe. Aren't you afraid a one-legged man might steal these?" We chuckled, but the shoeman was too busy to respond.

Chick glanced up again from his magazine. "What do you think? Nice, heh?" He looked into my face. "Geese, you don't look so hot. Good liberty last night?"

"When it starts coming back to me I'll let you know." My temples still throbbed.

Across the passageway, outside the ship's laundry, Darrell and Ike rested on huge bags of dirty clothing, taking a break from the heat in their crowded workspace. Each labored over two of the largest bananas I'd ever seen. "This looks like a monkey convention" I laughed. "Did they have bananas at morning chow? Everyone's eating bananas."

"Nah," answered Ike, "a couple of women back on the fantail are selling them right off two big stalks."

Darrell tilted-up and emptied half his Coke, then wiped his mouth with the back of his hand. "They have bottles of Coke, too. Can you believe this floatin' geedunk stand?"

It *was* different. I poked my head into the office to check-in, then left to hunt down my own bananas and Coke. Heading aft, I approached a group of boisterous sailors leaning over the side, bantering with someone out of sight. I stopped to look over the shoulder of one of the spectators. Down toward the water, rigged scaffolding ran against the side of the ship, several stages each supported two or three young Chinese women. Large buckets of gray paint hung from lines secured to the main deck railing, each positioned near a willowy painter. Clothing covered as much of their bodies as was possible to still allow seeing and swinging a brush. Cloth material protected their hair. They wore long sleeves and white cotton gloves. Each breathed through a cloth mask large enough to cover her nose and mouth. It tied with strings behind her head like a surgical mask. Many natives throughout the Orient wore these gauze pads over their faces when out-of-doors. The ladies remained on task, not speaking to each other, and ignoring the fellas above.

I interrupted the supervising boatswain's mate who was pointing and shouting directions to his female crew. "Hey, Boats. Any of these little girls know how to type? Send 'em over to the office. What's the deal here, anyway?"

"We supply the paint and brushes, they paint the complete exterior of the ship, mast to waterline. But they're not allowed into interior compartments, so don't get any ideas, Romeo."

He looked around and began dispersing the crowd. "Okay you horntoads, break it up. Get your asses movin'. You heard what The Man said, 'Give her a clean sweepdown fore and aft'." He nudged a slow reacting seaman and pointed. "That's fore, the pointy end, up there. Turn-to, Goldbricker."

He pushed back his white hat and drew an index finger vertically across his wet forehead. "These gals are cute, ain't they? They'd rather work like hell movin' those brushes than earn ten times as much by popping their knees in some cat-house on the beach. You gotta respect that in this part of the world."

During our six days in port, I awoke each morning thinking I might die and feeling so horrible I hoped I would. I swore each time, I would not go over again. I was a ready candidate for AA's "Twelve Steps."

Corothers had never seen me so out of shape. "Frank, what is it with you? You come in here every morning sicker than ten tubs of shit. Look in a mirror, your eyes are like road maps. How can you go over again tonight?"

But I did go over, every opportunity. During the work day everyone around me discussed their plans for that evening. By liberty call I was feeling better and had forgotten about the morning's pain. I found a standby when I could. But they were in short supply, as everyone wanted to go over and cutup. Each morning I missed chow and barely made quarters. Two bananas and a Coke for late breakfast bought me a little more time to sleep in after reveille.

Lee Kee, the shoeman, measured feet each day, taking orders just outside my workspace door. After two days of saying good morning and exchanging smiles, we cut a deal for three dollars off a pair of sea boots, made to order. "You no speak nobody."

My liberty boots, sewage-damaged during the black-market cigarette caper back in Formosa, resembled skis. After completely drying, they curled up at the toes and never quite returned to inspection quality. I saved them for work.

For a lark, in downtown Hong Kong one afternoon, I composed a telegram to Pat, a gal I was sweet on back home in Inglewood. "Wish you were here" sort of thing. I'd never used telegrams. I thought it pretty sophisticated sending a "wire"--and from the Orient to boot.

Some memories I brought away from Hong Kong weren't so pleasant. In the Plan of the Day on the morning after my first liberty, I found something that has stayed with me since. In the notes section near the bottom of the sheet I read:

> All hands are reminded that after each meal they are to separate liquids and solids in the scullery area when dumping uneaten food from their chow trays. Garbage cans will be appropriately marked "SOLIDS ONLY." The Chinese painters are removing the solids from the ship. This is their compensation for the contract to paint the vessel. They are doing a good job for us and appreciate your consideration. Keep in mind, the food will be prepared ashore for human consumption.

Oh, man. God bless America.

AFTERNOON DELIGHT?

Aboard ship the boys were always on the lookout to try something different from the simple Formosa liberties. Times off the ship offered little in variety. When I learned there was train service from Keelung, north to the capital city of Taipei, I planned a Saturday liberty with Bob Howie, my Arkansas buddy in the ship's office. I didn't know of anyone from the ship who had taken this trip, and I didn't want to risk asking if we were allowed to go, and being told "no."

The ride was to be a couple of hours of bouncing around in the crowded, pre-war railroad stock. Air in the coach was stagnant and I wished someone familiar with the train would open a window, but it was cold outside. Passengers filled every spot on the rows of wooden bench seats that creaked with every movement of the car. Many were forced to crowd together in the aisle.

In our foreign uniforms, skin scrubbed and pink, we stood out amongst our shorter, darker fellow travelers.

A woman with a small baby slung onto her back stood five feet away, the top of her smock soaked from the infant's wet diaper. She balanced herself and held onto a massive, cloth wrapped package. The train bobbed, shifted and swayed. Each time it stopped, then jerked ahead again, she struggled to remain upright.

I stood and offered her my aisle seat. When I turned back I saw that an agile fellow had slipped behind my back and eased down into the vacated seat. The idea upset me. I took an assertive stance and motioned him from the seat with my thumb. He instantly responded, but his face registered confusion--why had I stood if I wanted the seat?

With hand motions I encouraged the woman, indicating the seat was for her and her child. She bowed slightly several times, seemed uncomfortable with the offer, and moved no closer toward me. I determined I would convince her to sit down if I remained standing. For the next ten minutes I guarded the vacant seat. By then the whole passenger carload of people was wondering what in the world this Western "Sailorman" was up to. She remained standing the entire trip.

Outside the crammed, noisy Taipei central depot, we found ourselves in the center of an ant colony of activity. There was a total absence of "big noses"--a name Orientals used among themselves to

207

refer to Westerners. Not only did rickshaw boys form a circle around us, but passers-by stopped to observe the oddity of two young Westerners dropped into the middle of their remote capital. Smiling youngsters crowded about. Three or four Nationalist soldiers in their baggy khaki joined in. Even a uniformed policeman took a place among the curious as the drama unfolded. Anyone seeing the crowd that had formed, came to investigate.

Bob kept turning; he looked like he didn't feel comfortable with people behind him. He laughed toward me, over the heads of black hair, "We ought to sell tickets."

We hadn't thought out our itinerary, just getting there had been a challenge. Nor had I anticipated the total "foreign" atmosphere of the capital. No one we'd met on our excursion thus far had spoken English. No one came to the rescue with the welcome, "May I help you?" that sometimes surfaced in these situations.

I squatted to the dirt and felt the growing crowd close in around me for a better view. Taking a stick, I sketched a building in the dust, placing an American flag atop. One of the half-dozen rickshaw drivers seemed to understand I was interested in the U.S. Embassy. He ushered Bob toward his pedicab, smiling and nodding with enthusiasm. I followed, working my way through the crowd. Off we went. Our new friends waved encouragement, as if they really understood what was taking place.

A half-hour ride took us away from the city crowds to a small house, standing alone beside the unsurfaced street. The proud driver pointed toward an American flag. In the still air it hung limp against the pole standing before the very unpretentious little place. It was certainly not an embassy, perhaps a consulate or some government mission. Up on the porch, a dark screen restricted our view of the dim interior. I joked with Bob, as we stood at the screen and waited for an answer to our knock, that we probably would be invited in for a drink and maybe dinner. They'd welcome a chance to use their English again after being isolated from fellow Americans.

The screen door eased outward, forcing us to step aside. We hadn't heard him approach. A young Occidental, just a couple of years older than we, examined the two of us up and down with a look of curiosity. I wondered how long he had been within hearing distance of our joking comments. It was clear he hadn't seen the likes of *us* around his neighborhood.

"What the heck are *you guys* doing here?"

"Just need a little direction. Where is there a safe place to eat? Is there anything to see while we're here for the day?" I waited for an invitation to come inside.

"This area gets *zero* visitors. There is no tourism. Where the hell are you two *from*, anyway?"

We explained our ship, the torturous train ride, and our thirst for adventure.

"Well," he scratched at a two-day growth on his chin, "there's a hot springs spa that's kind of interesting. It might be a good place to relax for the afternoon, and it's not very far. You can get something to eat there. But don't let time get away from you. If you miss the last train at eight tonight there is no other way to get back to Keelung and your ship."

We liked his proposal. He came out from the house and the three of us walked down the porch steps. After directing the driver in Chinese, our new acquaintance turned, effected a lazy "civilian" salute toward the two of us, and we were off to the hot springs. We both watched him as he shuffled his way back up the steps. The place seemed an odd setting for conducting the business of the mighty United States' government.

I shook my head. "His assignment doesn't look like good duty to me."

Bob stared back toward the little house, "You got that right."

The driver positioned himself upright, his butt off the bike seat for the strenuous pump up the switchbacks on the hill that brought us to the retreat. There trees and greenery surrounded a scattering of rustic buildings. Mineral vapors combined with piney scents to dominate the quiet, restful atmosphere. An antique brown motorcycle rested against a nearby tree. If anyone else was here they must have walked up the road.

A gray-haired woman came out the door of the closest structure and seemed surprised to see Western visitors. In a reserved manner, she invited us inside. We followed and inside the door were faced with a five-foot blue and white ceramic dragon, seated upright in the center of the small reception area. She spat out a series of commands toward a young man and woman standing idly nearby. They hurriedly departed while she motioned us down a quiet hall, stopped midway, and opened a door into a private room.

Four wood-backed chairs waited around a table, bare except for four tea cups and a vase in the center holding a single little white-petalled flower. Two pieces of threadbare furniture sat against separate walls. An unframed drawing of two long necked cranes, one holding a limp fish in his beak, rolled down one wall.

She looked directly into our faces and, as if promoting a snack order, questioned, "You want woman?"

Her gaze moved from Bob, to me, back to Bob. We were thinking only of food. She had caught us off guard. We pantomimed eating, then hoped she understood as she left us to sink down into the two large upholstered chairs and wait.

In minutes there was a knock on the door and, without invitation, our lady reentered with neither food nor drink. She inquired, as if for the first time, "You want woman?"

Bob and I slowly shook our heads, using exaggerated sideways motions, and renegotiated for eats. Twenty minutes passed before the timid young man we'd seen when arriving delivered plates of cubed tofu, which I had never eaten, dry cheese sandwich triangles and a pot of tea. After getting us settled at the table with our simple lunch, he pointed to a small glass container of black liquid and indicated we were to pour the sauce over the tofu. Satisfied with the presentation, he backed out the doorway, collided with the reentering hostess who struggled around him to approach us and again offer, "You want woman?" Bob and I both laughed and shook our heads, no.

Although the food was plain and tasteless, except for the salty soy sauce, it took the edge off our hunger. I began to plan what remained of our afternoon.

"I wouldn't mind a bath and massage." Memories of my Japanese experiences were never far from my thoughts.

Bob countered he would rather look around the grounds and see what was going on. He left to explore. I looked for our hostess.

Out in the hall, I closed the door to the room, turned, and was confronted again by the business-like matron.

"You want woman?"

"Yes. That would be nice." I made some hand gestures to convey I would like a bath and massage. "Is that possible?"

Taking me by the arm, she led me into another room where she deposited me, left, and closed the door.

This language stuff is killing me. Guess I'll wait a few minutes and see what happens before I give up and go looking for Bob.

A soft knock brought my attention to the slowly opening door. "My woman" had arrived. She waited in the doorway. A plain, even drab individual whom I took to be around thirty-five. Dressed in a manner that would attract no one's attention, she looked as if she probably carried out a variety of assignments in the lodge. She waited. The pleasantness of her smile helped to make up for my disappointment in not finding someone comparable to my earlier Japanese acquaintances.

With some communication difficulty she established that bathing was the custom there, and a massage was possible. In fact, if I read her correctly, she was available for the afternoon, at an agreed upon fee, to be enjoyed as I wished.

Well, my, my. One doesn't often find this kind of opportunity after weeks at sea. But I still don't quite understand the drill.

Sensing my confusion, her manner became protective. She held my hand and led me as one would a child, down the hallway, past the earlier entrance where the young man and woman had again taken up their loafing. We continued on toward a sunlit, translucent glass door at the end of the hall. The gripping odor of sulfur was closing in on us. Instead of entering the large door before us, she led me to the right and into a doorless, musty undressing area where she began removing her clothing, indicating I should do the same. My blues off and hung on wall pegs, I sat on a damp, raw wood bench to remove my shoes and socks, then stood wearing only my shorts.

Not good enough--skivvies had to go too. *Geeze, what if someone walked by? We'd better hurry to where ever it is we're headed.*

Each of us was now completely nude. There's something about that kind of social encounter that produces feelings of arousal in "male types." The timing was inappropriate for this sensual signaling, and I attempted to "concentrate" the unwanted reaction away, with distracting thoughts of steamed carrots and turnips--all with little success. But I was able to arrest *further* escalation--for the moment.

Again, my mistress took me by the hand, guided me out of the dressing room, and back before the lighted doorway I had seen earlier. With her free hand, she pushed the varnished wood-trimmed glass door and proceeded inside, with me in tow. The murmur of measured conversations in the room quickly melted into an awkward stillness. We stood, side by side, she holding my hand. I focused my eyes past rising vapors, onto faces of other occupants--many other occupants, and wondered how they appreciated our display of frontal nudity. We must have looked something like a rendering of Adam and Eve, standing naked, hand-in-hand.

But this was not Paradise. About fifteen people, water up to their chins, or resting, sitting on the edge with their legs dangling into the odorous water, looked across an expanse of steaming water toward me and my companion. The surface area of the irregular shaped bath looked equal to that of a generous-sized living room. My eyes met with those of young, old, men, women, and a handful of beautiful, black-haired, brown-eyed children.

As if hydraulically controlled, smoothly and without interruption, "Mr. Johnson" eased down into his conventional configuration. It was difficult for me to believe my partner had not known of the room's arrangement before we arrived. But she showed no reaction to the other participants and guided me, as if we were alone, towards the sanitarium-like smell of the caldron.

The patter of conversations resumed as I held the rail and descended the concrete steps, easing into the hot water. *I wonder how often these waters are changed. What interesting human contaminates am I immersing myself into? I know what little kids do in heated water. I'll keep my lips tightly closed and my head above the surface.*

I stole glances all around and realized no one seemed interested in the newcomers. The others socialized among themselves, enjoying the mineral therapy. That was fine for them, but my upbringing dictated *private* bathing. I could think only of how I could get out of there, attracting minimum attention.

My companion compounded the discomfort I was suffering, from our lack of privacy, by playfully attempting to cuddle. She approached and moved her hands like flitting swallows over my submerged body. This was not her first experience in underwater therapy.

But it was useless. The whole scene reminded me of the familiar dream where I am nude in a public place with no means for covering myself. I became more self-conscious and uncomfortable, and determined I wasn't going to take a lot of time trying to explain my feelings to Miss Magic Fingers.

Whispering something like, "Let's go," I climbed from the water, offering them my back, and headed toward the exit, not waiting to see if she was following.

I'm out of here.

She looked confused when she found me alone in the stark dressing area. Hurrying back into my clothes, I could think of no way to salvage the situation. She was perplexed, wanting to oblige, but not knowing how to approach me after my "peculiar" behavior.

I took a five dollar bill from my wallet and extended it towards her. Not touching it, she leaned forward to examine the denomination and murmured something indicating the aborted exercise required additional remuneration. I returned the five and took out a ten. She reluctantly accepted, then began offering some sort of suggestion for further one-on-one activity. I didn't completely understand, but it didn't matter. The place was too wacky for me.

I took off looking for Bob and our cab, not waiting to further discuss her fee or any other alternative arrangement. I wanted to be off the hill, away from the in-over-my-head party. I found my buddy dozing in the back and climbed in beside him. The driver approached from the shade of a bushy pine and pushed off. Bob rubbed a knuckle into one eye and drawled, "How did it go for you? Believe it or not, I had five more offers of 'a woman' while I was nosing around. I've never felt so desirable."

After a moment of pouting, I blurted out, "I feel used. Violated. We're just raw meat in a showcase as far as they're concerned."

We laughed all the way down the hill's winding road, secure that there was still plenty of time to catch our eight o'clock train.

LAST JAPANESE LIBERTY

Riding aft, deep in our wake, the USS HOLLISTER followed the OZBOURN up the eastern side of the islands forming Japan's irregular coastline. Relieved from duty in Formosa, then later from Korean waters, we began our long voyage home.

Our immediate destination, the port of Yokosuka, was a short train ride away from the inviting intrigue of Tokyo. A chance to see the sights of this major Asian capital started me plotting. I hatched a scheme.

The port stop would be short, just a couple of days. It was my last chance to explore Japan. I wanted to remain overnight. It would be my first, all other liberties had expired onboard at 2400, midnight. Cinderella liberty was part of General Mac Arthur's policy for members of the U.S. forces since the Japanese occupation began.

I filled out a dream sheet, a request for special liberty, 48 hours--two full days off. A visit to my newly invented "Uncle Raymond," with an imaginary civilian job at the Tachikawa Air Base, 30 miles outside Tokyo, would be my excuse to gain time for the story book sights I'd read about.

Typically, after long ship deployments with infrequent opportunities for time off, the mood of those in charge was to grant as much recreation time for the crew as demands of the vessel's assignment allowed. For my "family" visit, the special liberty was approved. Of course I would have to remain inside "Uncle Ray's" quarters during curfew hours, as Military Police would arrest any enlisted personnel running around after midnight.

My plan was simple. I'd catch the Tokyo train from Yokosuka as soon as I could get off the ship, enjoy the sights until evening, then find a room in the city at some military-sponsored facility. Next day I'd continue exploring, then catch the evening train back to the ship. I was getting excited--on my own with all that time.

During R & R, in and out of southern Japan over the past year, we'd learned of impressive Army and Air Force clubs in Tokyo. There, enlisted men could find good chow, inexpensive drinks, music, performances, and pretty ladies--in downtown locations, not out on some lonely base. I stopped the first GI I ran into outside the Tokyo train station and got directions to a club.

The Navy's idea of an enlisted "club" was, at best, a gutted Quonset hut, but more often just a piece of shade and a case of cold beer. A real club, with civilian-like appointments, lighting, entertainment, and sit down eating off white china, enjoying the luxury of silverware and table cloths, was not available through the U.S. Navy's efforts. But the Air Force, that was a different story. Word had it that the first thing built after an air strip, was a club. And members of all services were welcome in each other's clubs.

The Air Force in Tokyo did not disappoint. I checked out the club's facilities, then at the recreation desk bought a seat on an afternoon city bus tour. Seeing the bridges constructed of natural, round stones, the walls, streets, and ancient buildings fascinated me. Their masterful construction and the calmness conveyed by their style projected an Eastern beauty. Inside a quiet temple, beneath its fired-tile roof, the soothing background sounds of cascading, splashing water were shattered by a jarring report from the huge bell struck by a rope-suspended log. The sound waves vibrated across the carefully raked grounds and through the adjoining neighborhood.

Later that first evening in the city, I was served chicken cordon-bleu in the club dining room. My Japanese waiter never took his eyes off of me, he anticipated my simplest need. This sort of attention was new to me, even if I had been in The States. Apple pie ala mode, with two giant scoops of French vanilla, forced me to finally push myself away from the table. I'd hardly finished when hidden musicians began playing and, just two tables away, the stage curtain opened. An unseen voice announced a full-on USO variety show.

Solo singers from home, blonde and buxom, along with beautiful local Japanese, shorter and darker than their stateside sisters, all wore long, glittering evening gowns. They took turns singing favorites like *That Old Black Magic, I'll Never Smile Again, and Sleepy Lagoon.* The brass section came forward and tore apart *And The Angels Sing,* to three encores. In the last session the sax player got so caught up with his enthusiastic young audience, he laid down on his back, and played as he kicked his feet into the air. Every one of us was up cheering and whistling. Without missing a beat, dancers rushed on and performed several high kicking numbers to the blaring music. The curtain closed and I just stared, caught up in all the action.

I had never seen such live entertainment. I recognized this as a special time, and I was loving it. I could feel my heart pumping through my jumper. I followed the others as we applauded until the curtain opened again and the entire group came out for their bows. The curtain closed for the second time. I thought everything was finished, when the lights dimmed and a small spot focused against the burgundy backdrop at the left side of the stage .

A young fella with long curly hair, wearing a tuxedo and a large, droopy black bow tie, trotted to center stage holding a cigarette in one hand and a glass in the other. The bright light followed, staying fixed upon him. For a half hour this fall-down-funny comic had us all crying, we were laughing so hard. He knew the sort of humor the young crowd of lonely servicemen enjoyed and he delivered it from both barrels. He kept me so riled-up I paid no attention to being alone. It didn't matter. I realized that the evening had relieved a lot of tension and stress I'd built up over the past months.

But I had let time slip away. When I realized I needed to start looking for a military-sponsored bed, there was none. I had waited too long. No one offered any help. With less than an hour before midnight, I went out into the night to find a cab and try to locate a place to hideout till morning.

I wanted to appear knowledgeable to the driver and, as detailed communication with Japanese always led to frustrating language problems, I asked him to take me to the only name I knew. The famous Imperial Hotel was internationally-known for its architect, Frank Lloyd Wright.

When the cab arrived before the impressive dark gray building, a smartly uniformed doorman hurried over to the compact Japanese pre-war car and opened its back door. But before I could unfold one leg to struggle out, he extended a straight arm, ending just inches from my face. It seemed my uniform presented a problem. I couldn't understand what he was trying to explain, and I didn't have time to wait and listen. I figured the defeated Japanese hadn't learned the U.S. system yet--where, in America, we are all equal. I paid the cabbie and worked my way past the agitated doorman, who fell-in right behind me jabbering all the way to the lobby.

Inside, a wide expanse of marble stretched out separating me from Hotel Reception. The deskman wore formal tails and looked like a member of a wedding party. He hurried around the desk to intercept me. Excitedly, he tried his broken English, but I was having no better luck understanding him than the doorman, who had now taken a position shoulder-to-shoulder beside him. They took turns trying to get their message out, and encouraged me, through their body language, to leave.

Finally the words "Officer Billets," spoken as distinctly as the worried formally dressed Japanese was able, connected with me. As if to celebrate the linguistic success, the deep-toned lobby clock bonged off midnight. By now I was very uncomfortable. Tokyo is an immense city. My pocket map showed an impossibly complex grid of streets that appeared to have evolved in a haphazard web over hundreds of years, and I was completely lost somewhere in it. Desperate, I emptied all of my military script onto the counter and through sign language conveyed my need for a place to sleep that was within my means. Where could I go? What could I do?

The doorman motioned me outside and hailed the first cab from the short line formed at the beginning of the hotel drive, just off the street. Headlights from the small vehicle threw their beams forward and it eased toward the entrance. The driver and the doorman spoke at length. Each of them used the word *roykan* several times. A *roykan* is a smaller, traditional, informal country type inn, although not necessarily located outside a city.

I jumped out of the way when both back doors of the cab suddenly sprang open, remotely released by the driver's lever from the front seat. Mr. Doorman hustled me into the tiny rear compartment. I think he had the idea that, considering our two uniforms, he somehow outranked me. The door slammed. He hurried to the other side and slammed that door. Then stationed himself in a pose that threatened to push me back if I attempted crawling out.

Now it was the cabbie who couldn't make me understand why *he* was upset. Finally, exasperated, he half-turned toward the back seat and, continuing his explanation, unceremoniously pushed me down toward the floorboards while he maneuvered his little smoke belcher out the circular drive. I did understand "Catchie MP. Catchie MP." I did not want to meet any Military Police, not in General Mac Arthur's backyard.

From my cramped position down low on the floor, keeping out of sight, I became aware that the city lights were growing dimmer. They no longer illuminated the cab's interior, and gradually it became totally dark. We had left the main streets. I hoped this fellow hadn't had any unpleasant war experiences in the Pacific, seeing me as an opportunity for payback time. For the next quarter hour we eased through a maze of twists, slowing and turning our way along the narrow passages.

At last the cab jerked to a stop. We had arrived at the cabbie's proposed solution. I raised myself just high enough to peek through my door window and watched the driver run up steps to one of the doorways in a block of low, dark dwellings joined side by side. The form of a lady appeared and remained silhouetted as the driver hurried back and opened my door. *"Ryokan, ryokan. Haeyaku."* He nervously helped me out. Obviously, the fellow didn't want to be associated any longer than necessary. He was an accessory to a serious violation of the Military Governor's Occupation Law.

I bounded the steps two at a time, disregarding the little voice in my head that cautioned me *this could be trouble.* I passed my bowing hostess as she shuffled back, inviting me in with her gestures. She silently eased the door closed and motioned me to follow. But first my shoes. Several other pairs rested on a low shelf by the entry. She took mine as I removed each one, and arranged them into the group.

I relaxed. I was in. Things were settled.

I followed her down the quiet hallway, each of us making swishing sounds with our shoeless feet as they caressed the *tatami* mats covering the floors. She stopped and slid open a *shoji* partition, exposing a pleasant little cubby. It looked inviting after all the fuss of getting there. I began to feel the fatigue of a long day in Tokyo.

She pulled quilts from a closet onto the floor and a fresh pillow filled with buckwheat husks, I heard the packed husks scratching against each other as she arranged the bedding. I thanked my hostess. She backed from the room, head down, bowing.

Moments later, ready to switch off my lamp and slip between the inviting comforters, I heard a light tapping on the bamboo that framed the screen entrance. I opened the *shoji* screen a crack and saw my benefactress holding a steaming bowl of *miso* soup cradled between her two dainty hands. She extended it toward me. Her head remained lowered while I took the refreshment from her. More bowing.

When involved in these exercises of courtesy and bowing with the gracious Japanese, a Westerner feels his body wanting to respond in kind. But I restrained myself. There was too much mystery for me to choose the proper occasion and employ the correct movement--depth of bow, number of bows, duration of bow. I thought I'd better stick to American ways and to leave it to the knowledgeable, rather than risk offending.

The translucent screen slid closed.

The soup tasted wonderfully rich, its effect almost medicinal. Salty, in a pleasant way, it was too hot to drink right down, but too tasty to wait. With no utensils, I blew and sipped the tangy clear liquid directly from its bowl. I hadn't enjoyed a bedtime treat like that since Grandmother's warm milk and cookies.

The next morning the patter of little steps passing in the hallway eased me from a restful sleep. Totally refreshed, I threw back the heavy comforter and reached to unfold a fresh *yukata* laid out the previous evening. In my blue and white-checked oriental wrap I felt very much a part of my surroundings. I began a search down the hall for a WC. My *yukata,* though short on my six foot frame, was a welcome change from the years of wearing only government issue.

Back in my room something special awaited--a steaming hand towel. My hostess held it toward me using chop sticks. I brought it toward my face and deeply inhaled a fresh hint of citrus. While my bedding was taken away to create more floor space, I luxuriated in the Japanese morning custom. I pressed the towel tight against my eyelids and held it there, enjoying its warmth. Then I groomed my face, neck, and ears, finishing by using it to massage my scalp. *We can learn from these people.*

A timid young boy about ten years old, wearing a dark blue school uniform jacket buttoned high to just beneath his chin, appeared at the entry balancing a tray--an opportunity to see the special Western guest before he left for his day at school. The traditional student's nautical cap with anchor sewn onto the front, poked out from beneath his arm where he had temporarily stored it. His coal black hair was cropped close to his scalp, and his eyes searched about the compact room for a spot to set the tea pot and cup. Socially hesitant, but eager to show off his English, he offered, "Good morning, sir--what is the weather?" I laughed, figuring he had just emptied his bag of English phrases, and glanced toward his beaming mother. She was enjoying her accomplished little treasure.

Speaking slowly and distinctly I answered. "I think the weather will be fine. Thank you for the tea."

A younger sister walked slowly by the open *shoji*, smiling shyly and sneaking peeks at me in my odd fitting *yukata,* envying her brother's excuse to enter. I winked at her. She giggled and ran off up the hall. Brother hesitated as if thinking of another English offering, laughed, turned and hurried after his sister, happily chattering in Japanese. Mother backed out, again bowing, and slowly closed the paper screen, leaving me alone.

I poured steaming tea into the small, handleless cup and, feeling natural with both hands around the delicately decorated artifact, I raised it to breathe in the aroma of fresh brewed leaves. Easing myself onto the large flat pillow resting on the floor, I began to think through my remaining day. Some Ginza shopping, then long walks through the ancient sections of the city. I had realized earlier on the bus tour that these sights demanded a slower, up close pace. The Japanese give the most common places and things a special touch of beauty. Nature is brought into every part of life. My last day I would just feast my eyes.

It was barely light the following morning when I manned the phones on my Special Sea and Anchor Detail, high up on OZBOURN's bridge. We were getting underway. Mt. Fuji was slowly disappearing behind us as we steamed through the opened submarine nets that guarded Yokosuka's harbor. Fuji's snow-capped volcanic cone had been the first thing I'd seen in coming to Japan months earlier, and now it would be my last.

The XO looked up from his chart of the harbor, setting down his dividers on the navigator's table.

"Did you find your uncle okay, Spittle? Did everything work out all right on your 48 in Tokyo?"

"Great. Thank, you Sir." I quickly turned away to find something else to busy myself.

I took a position forward, on the open bridge near the skipper. The brisk morning breeze made my eyes water. The past two whirlwind days replayed through my head.

A potentially dangerous time had developed into a very rewarding experience. I had been truly blessed with the makings of warm memories to carry away from this enchanting place and its delightful people.

MAKING HOMEWARD TURNS

It was a time for getting caught up on things. There would be no mail for weeks. Ship's office work, the kind put aside awaiting an open spell, came out. All over the ship sailors turned-to preparing for our return home.

I had the duty the evening of the second night away from Yokosuka. After chow I checked aft in the XO's stateroom to pickup his rough copy for the next Plan-of-the-Day. He glanced up from his cluttered desk, knowing why I'd come.

"I'm finishing it. I have it right here for you." Pushing his chair back and turning toward me, he assumed that lofty gaze probably brought on by stress and fatigue.

"Spittle, remember what Napoleon said he could accomplish if he had enough colored ribbon to pin on his soldier's chests?"

Yeah, right. Does he remember I didn't finish high school? What do I know, Napoleon?

"Your ship's office people are going to have a job organizing this, but medals and ribbons are wonderful for morale. I want the men to be able to get the ribbons they've earned as soon as we hit The States. The medals will come from Bureau of Naval Personnel, so the requests go in the first mail to leave when we hit Pearl."

He extended the hand written instruction to the crew that would appear in tomorrow's POTD. All OZBOURN WestPac deployments that merited recognition, along with their inclusive dates, and the associated medal were noted. Each member would be responsible for initiating the paperwork to receive "his medal" for participating in particular campaigns.

As I walked the inside passageway toward the office, I stopped beneath a light to read the medals' announcement over carefully. I was beginning to get worked-up. *Medals. I'm going to get a medal. No, not just one medal. I'm okay for this Korean Service Medal.* I read on through his notes.

I qualify for this Navy Occupation Medal. And China Service Medal. Holy cow, I'll really have some ribbons. And my Quarterly Marks are high enough for the Navy Good Conduct Medal. All that fruit salad on my chest. Now you're talkin'.

221

Back in the ship's office I began typing the Plan-of-the-Day. When I came to the part about the medals I got so excited I stopped what I was doing, left the desk where I'd been working on the stencil, and went to the other typewriter. I began planning the mechanics of getting the medal awards job started the next morning. Four separate sheets, for crew members to write their names if they felt qualified for the different medals were ready to go and I penned my own name at the top of each sheet.

The work would involve verifying each claim against individual service record entries, checking that each man had served aboard during the designated times. But thoughts of that task couldn't dampen my excitement. There had been no other Navy work I'd ever been assigned that gave me so much job satisfaction as setting up the awarding of those medals. Napoleon was onto something.

Thirteen days of uneventful steaming, punctuated by the brief stop in Pearl Harbor for refueling, gave the ship's officers and crew time to work at getting the tired OZ shipshape. Nearly every Plan of the Day included copies of congratulatory messages from commanders up the chain of command:

```
From:        Commander Task Group 95.9
To:          U.S.S. OZBOURN DD-846
Info:        Commander, Destroyer
             Division ONE HUNDRED TWELVE

    Bearing the brunt of the enemy's reaction
to our vital effort in stopping his
communications through Wonsan you and your
gallant ship have performed your duties most
commendably in keeping with the highest
traditions of the Naval Service.      Well Done.

        Signed:   Rear Admiral Allan E. Smith
                  United States Navy
```

Messages received while underway reported our Commodore, Captain Roeder, was awarded his second Legion of Merit. Our skipper, Commander Akers, and the boat officer during the downed pilot's rescue, Lieutenant Moriarty, were each awarded Bronze Stars. An enlisted quartermaster, O'Brien, won the Navy Commendation Medal. Ike Voles, our laundryman, boat coxswain for the pilot rescue, received a Letter of Commendation. We were all proud of our ship and saw ourselves as a tightly knit unit who had done our job well.

Finally the big day arrived. Wednesday, April 11, 1951, we steamed past Point Loma's lighthouse, the attendant's white-washed cottage with the Stars and Stripes waving beside it, and entered San Diego harbor. We glided past two mammoth carriers tied up off our starboard side at North Island Naval Air Station, past a nest of destroyers to port, and on toward our docking area across from Coronado Island.

The ship's new paint included colorful battle ribbons, elevated on the bulkhead near the bridge. All brass was highly polished. Multicolored pennants snapped in the wind, giving off reports like pistol shots, complementing the smartness of the crew assembled along the main deck in their best dress blues. Everyone was topside, feeling proud, caught up in the excitement. CONUS. Home.

The fleet tug nudged us up close to a wharf teaming with families and friends of crewmen. Crowded below us, the welcomers stretched their necks back searching for a familiar face among the blue jackets pushing three and four deep, wherever they could get a hand-hold along the ship's port side. Children of all ages jumped up and down, waving excitedly. They bumped into adult legs, and stepped on feet of parents too busy searching faces to notice.

The first monkey fist, secured to the end of a messenger thrown off the bow, hit and bounced along the dock's heavy wooden timbers--the signal for the Navy band. High energy sound from shiny brass instruments heightened the thrill. Tubas, trumpets, and saxophones reflected the bright morning sun as they blared out *The Stars and Stripes Forever*. Seaman on the dock scrambled to pull the heaver mooring line and secure it, then ran to gather other messengers sailing across like streamers.

My body felt the concussion, through to my core, as the base drummer swung with an energy that threatened to push a hole through the hide of the large drum faces balanced before him.

I knew I would have to wait for liberty before I could get home and enjoy *my* welcome--married men were always first over. But I shared the feelings of my shipmates as they ran down the lowered gangway into the arms of those waiting.

I kept my eyes straight ahead, wiped the tears with the back of my hand, and tried to swallow away my emotion.

FROM TIN CAN
TO HEAVY METAL

Ship's Barber Merrill Hansen, best buddy on tours aboard
U.S.S. ROCHESTER and U.S.S. OZBOURN

EVERYTHING ONBOARD
BUT A BOWLING ALLEY

We'd been home a few weeks and OZBOURN was undergoing repairs at Mare Island Naval Shipyard when the message arrived. My request for a transfer to the heavy cruiser ROCHESTER had been granted. My orders were to report aboard the USS ROCHESTER CA-124 by midnight the following Friday. I wasted no time routing my drive through Inglewood, to manage a brief visit home on the way south. Only a few hours to chat and I was off again toward San Diego.

It was easy to locate the heavy cruiser from the road. I could see it as I drove along the bay. She was lying directly off downtown San Diego, dwarfing smaller destroyers and destroyer escorts, most everything else scattered about the harbor except the unglamorous tenders, and the carriers far across at North Island. She stood alone in her sleekness.

Seeing seaplanes secured onboard and ready for launching caught my attention. I wasn't used to that on a combatant vessel. This was some ship.

If I checked in during working hours I could store my gear and get a liberty card. Unless there was the duty to deal with, I could return home for the weekend.

But wisps of smoke curling from ROCHESTER's single funnel got me thinking, nudging an idea into shape. I found a phone booth and called the San Diego Harbor Master.

"Is the ROCHESTER in port? I have orders to report aboard. When does she get underway?"

I could picture him high up in his glassed in observation space near the foot of Broadway, sailing schedules at his elbow and a hawk's view of the dozens of gray hulled vessels filling his front yard.

After a moment the voice on the other end answered. "ROCHESTER is departing for Long Beach at 1200 today."

Leaving at noon? Hummmmmmm. Going directly aboard meant there'd be no weekend liberty because we'd be underway. My car would be left in San Diego. My orders allowed me until midnight. If the ship sailed without me I could report to the U.S. Naval Station, San Diego, get weekend liberty with new orders cut to report to the

ROCHESTER in Long Beach the following Monday night--taking that day for travel. That would give me three days off.

I parked where I could watch the activity in the harbor, found myself a walk-away order of fish and chips, settled into the car's passenger seat, and chuckled as I sprinkled vinegar over the thick cut, golden fries.

Sure enough, at noon that imposing gray beauty sounded three whistles, a blast from her horn, shifted the ensign from aft, and slowly steamed right past me toward the harbor entrance. I had missed my ship. Damn. I was learning how to work the system, and feeling pretty smug about it.

My plan had worked perfectly and when I finally reported aboard, in Long Beach the next week, I immediately searched out my barber buddy from the OZBOURN, Merrill Hansen. We had requested transfers together and he had preceded me. I found him at his work station, in a real barber shop. Three black leather, genuine barber chairs, that pumped up and settled down with the touch of a lever, large mirrors, sinks, and plenty of lighting set a scene out of place with my image of a fighting ship.

I smiled at him in his light-blue smock. "Chicken, what a change from you having to carry a stool around the decks of a tin-can. This looks like good duty."

"Frank-san, I wondered if you'd ever get here. Welcome aboard." With his arm around my shoulders, he introduced me to two barbers lounging in their large chrome trimmed chairs, waiting for their next customer.

"Cover for me, Lou, I'm going to buy my pal a malt."

As we walked away from his shop he playfully messed my hair. "You need a haircut, Buddy. A good haircut."

"Yea," I joked, "I'll check later to see if Lou's busy."

Up a wide passageway, we walked what seemed like blocks through the ship's 675 foot length. We exchanged news of happenings since we'd last seen each other aboard the OZBOURN weeks earlier, chattering excitedly back and forth till we approached a short counter separating the gedunk stand from the customers in the passageway,

Merrill offered, "What flavor you want? We've got 'em all."

"Are you kidding me? Real malts? What the hell is this place, a ship or a hotel? Chocolate, thanks."

As a barber, Merrill was acquainted with his fellow Ship's Serviceman running the store. Because the two men were buddies, our malts were made from scratch and so thick with ice cream Merrill turned his cup upside down without spilling. We took our gedunk topside and forward to the forecastle. From the huge triple 8-inch mount, the holy-stoned wooden deck stretched out toward the bow, looking farther than the length of a football field.

Everything I'd seen so far dazzled me with its size and open space--space to work, space to live, space to recreate. After two years aboard a cramped destroyer, I shook my head in disbelief at each new discovery during my first week aboard. The entire 1142-man crew could muster on the fantail of the vessel, whose beam spanned 71 feet. A real brig housed individual barred cells. Officer's staterooms, the wardroom, sickbay, and the mess decks, were all much more comfortable than a destroyer's. Three tremendous turrets positioned nine 8-inch guns. Twelve 5-inch, twice the number of OZBOURN's heaviest armament, took care of lighter assignments. Yet, despite her size and fire power, she could make 33 knots.

I reminded myself that destroyers were designed for speed and maneuverability, to chase down submarines and launch torpedoes at surface targets while at flank speed--designers had to monitor weight and space. This big baby only needed to arrive and she could begin taking care of business.

There had been barely enough room for two small desks jammed side by side in the OZBOURN ship's office. Here the office space accommodated many desks, even the luxury of large work tables, and ample room all around them. You could actually *walk across* the office space. On a destroyer you eased into the space like slipping into the cockpit of a fighter plane.

I'd been aboard just over a month when the ROCHESTER left the West Coast for Hawaii. The challenge of the transition into a new work assignment excited me and the job held my interest. In the past I had performed all the different office tasks as one must on a smaller vessel. Here there was only one responsibility, the Personnel Diary. As Diary Yeoman, I entered all our crew members' comings and goings, their changes in rate, job codes, and the like, on a daily basis. Copies were mailed each day to Bureau of Naval Personnel. I maintained an accurate onboard count, with numbers by different ratings. Staffing information was frequently requested from me by the ship's administrators. I enjoyed the responsibility, plus the recognition I sensed from the people I served, and those with whom I worked.

Adjusting to my new shipmates reached a comfortable level the morning a fellow yeoman walked behind me while I pored over the work on my desk. I came screaming out of my chair. He had flipped his finger against my neck, directly onto what he called a "double yolker"-- angry teenage pimples most of us suffered with. We all teased each other over them. I soon joined in the thumping of neck zits and became an accepted member of the gang.

On the third day underway for Pearl Harbor, after the evening movie, I headed for the ship's office. As I opened the door I immediately sensed something very different inside. Soft music played. All the interior lights were off, but before I reached in to switch them on I caught glimpses of flickering candles positioned about the workspace. As my eyes became accustomed to the darkness, I made out moving forms. Couples were dancing. Frank Sinatra was singing *This Love of Mine*, and these clowns, all guys of course, were partying, dancing in the dark. *Oh, Mama.*

"Hey, Franko. Come on in and have a little torpedo juice with pineapple."

I couldn't see who offered the invitation, but I knew I wasn't interested in dancing with some boys' school loser. *How do you decide who leads?* It seemed too whacky for me, these guys had only been underway less than a week. They couldn't all be gay. Could they? This had to be some kind of a prank. I didn't wait around to learn more, but backed out into the passageway, easing the door closed, and hightailed it to my berthing compartment.

The little junior prom was never mentioned. That suited me just fine.

WHAT WE HAVE HERE IS AN EPIDEMIC

They were not Navy issue, but then nothing about him reflected the military. Resting on his nose, the large glass lenses, encircled by heavy tortoise shell, made me think "owl" each time I looked into his face. Their prescription brought his black pupils, centered in the oversized glass, down to a size where they reminded me of b-b's from my boyhood Red Ryder rifle.

Why would anyone willingly present such an appearance? The guy is goofy enough without having that working against him. But, that's The Professor for you.

His Christian name was Evelyn Westcott. Scuttlebutt had it his uncle was an Admiral and that's how he'd gotten into the Navy with his bad eyes. His sight wasn't all that bad, it was just the crazy glasses he needed for reading and chose to wear continuously. Most of us called him Professor. A few others, the types who always need to stand on top of someone so they can feel a little taller, called him Owl--to which he'd regularly respond, "Ah, shut your pie-hole."

While the rest of us carried paper-backs or comic books crammed into our rear pockets, The Professor always had a hard bound book he was currently reading. He'd hand carry it everywhere, too large to slip into a back pocket of his dungarees.

At mail-call, instead of cookies, his packages contained health supplements. He had a little pitch for each pill. Vitamin E--"Massive doses, take 'em and you'll live past a hundred, easy." Little dark pills he called Saw Palmetto-- "When you guys are sittin' in the home wearing diapers and dribblin' porridge down your chins, me and my healthy prostate will still be out doin' business." Selenium capsules--"One a day, helps your body reproduce healthy cells. You know, ten years from now you'll be a whole new person with all new cells. Ya want that new person to be one hundred percent, don't ya? Selenium man, selenium."

Each morning when he reported to his work area in the Fire Control Shack, he'd take off his white hat, dig three pills from his shirt pocket and place them into the hat. From the full canteen of water he kept at the work-site, he'd wash them down one at a time, sending his head back after each pull on the canteen like a bird looking up and swallowing. Nearby shipmates slowly shook their heads. No one showed much interest in sharing his home pharmacy.

We never saw him eat cookies-from-Mom when others offered them around. Nor did he take desserts or pastries from the chow line. We all knew he ate only one meal a day, always at noon. In the morning he drank hot tea made from bags sent from home--the little tag at the end of the string advertised "Morning Thunder." He carried a fresh bag to the mess hall each morning in the pocket of his dungaree shirt.

Every few weeks he'd put himself onto a three day fast. Only hot water and a piece of fruit at noon, another at bed-time, if it was available.

At breakfast, coming off a fast, he yawned over his steaming mug of Morning Thunder, "I suppose you could call me an ascetic."

He was a disciplined man who had earned the reputation of being a crackpot.

The Professor merrily presented himself, to all who would listen, as the world's greatest authority. And most of us who hadn't graduated from high school were convinced he might well have been. He could speak for hours on any topic. We learned he'd been recalled to active duty from his hometown reserve unit when the Korean War began. He claimed to have left in the middle of his graduate studies at U of I in Urbana, Illinois. His "area of concentration," as he called it, was "the biological digressions of Northern Hemisphere prehistoric primates." That, I figured, he made up. But he was one smart son-of-a-gun.

Those who called him Owl said he was all bullshit. We who called him The Professor went along with him and even enjoyed his frequently offered observations. He related to everyone as his intellectual equal, never talking-down to us. I felt he really believed we understood him most of the time and I guessed expounding was his way of trying to stay amused in the alien nautical atmosphere where he'd been dropped. For me he offered a refreshing diversion and an introduction into the world of varied thinking.

It was The Professor who had hounded me to order the materials from the Education Officer to prepare myself for the General Education Development Test. He worked with me and was a stern taskmaster. He was a pretty good teacher because I passed the test on my first try, and he assured me I could get into any college in the country on the strength of it. He had my future all laid out--pass the GED test, after discharge enter college on my GI Bill, major in education, and become a school teacher.

"Frank, before you know it you'll have your teaching credential and a job in some pretty little schoolhouse working with those wonderful kids. Buddy, when you're the teacher and you close the door on that classroom, you can make it anything you want. You are empowered."

Any argument I offered about my insecurity, inability, or lack of education, he shot down. He'd go over "the plan" again, in detail, defending it to the letter. At twenty-one I couldn't have known how influential and prophetic he was.

For two weeks the men of the heavy cruiser USS ROCHESTER CA124 had been the major players in an epidemic, a disease whose very name gave each "dying" man additional grief--Shigella Flexner.

I spent so much time in the head, I only left because someone else hurried in and demanded my spot.

When my mom hears about this she'll have kittens.

The symptoms were diarrhea and vomiting--repeatedly. Nearly every crew member was suffering. The U.S. Public Health Service sent a team from the mainland. Everyone was restricted to the ship for fear of infecting the population of Honolulu.

It was so bad that when one went to the head he always chose a place with a vacant seat beside him. This provided a place for vomiting. It was a highly contagious disease. Part of the containment procedure required several metal wash bowls in the head be filled with chemicals for rinsing washed hands before leaving. A guard was posted in each of the ship's heads 24 hours a day to insure the crew's compliance.

Every few days groups of us would be assembled. Lined up, with our trousers and shorts dropped around our shoes, we were directed to bend over and spread our buttocks. A corpsman, with a clean cotton swab in one hand and a fresh petri dish in the other, plunged the swab into our rears, withdrew and deposited the residue. After moving it around the bottom of the petri dish in a brisk circular motion and replacing the lid, they rushed it to Atlanta, Georgia, for evaluation.

On one of my frequent trips to the head, the only open spot I could be safe if I vomited was one stool away from The Professor. I wasn't in the mood for conversation, feeling so near death, but I took it. After allowing me a minute to settle in, The Professor began.

"Frank, how many words do you know for excrement?"

"Well, if excrement is what I think it is, then there's 'shit'."

"And dung," added Professor.

"Poop." I offered

231

"And crottels." It was beginning to take on the rhythm of a tennis match.

"Crap." *I can't keep this up.*

"And fumets," returned the expert.

"Manure." My reservoir was getting low.

"And spraints." The smile squeezed his eyes into even smaller openings.

"Turds. That's the best I can do, Professor." I wasn't going to offer "do-do."

"Frank, my lad, you passed your GED test last month. That gives you a High School Equivalency status. I expect a better performance. You left out feces, scats, and droppings."

"You win, Professor. You really know your shit."

We both laughed. He was having a fine time.

"You know, it's nothing for an elephant to drop a steamy turd weighing forty to sixty pounds."

Where the hell does he get this stuff?

A moaner from the far end of the row attempted to put a stop to it. "Hey, Owl. Put a sock in it."

Another malcontent urged, "Give it a rest, will ya Owl?"

The braying continued from other sitting participants. But the Professor's expression showed he hadn't finished the topic. I tried to nudge him onto another course. "I'm so sick, I'm losing sixty pounds in water every day, it's either coming up or going down and out. Man, I can't take much more of this."

The Professor wasn't going to let his captive audience off the hook. "The B.M. you're praying for is one that's eighty percent water, that's the normal stool, eighty percent. The B.M.'s we're leaving here are greater than ninety-eight percent water. A person can't live long producing that without some kind of remediation. So they give us electrolytes. Aren't they yummy?"

I tried to hold my end of the conversation. "I guess that's why the federal docs came all the way out here." It was hard to concentrate with my stomach cramping.

His face took on a serious look. "Listen, you've got eleven-hundred guys here, so sick they can hardly move. That's a lot of concerned citizen-relatives back home for congressmen to contend with."

I smiled at the thought, "If it takes my mom to get this thing cured, then let them tangle with her. I can tell you, they'll lose."

The bored guard, cap pushed to the back of his head, arms crossed, leaning against the head's doorway, rapped his night-stick against the bulkhead and growled, "Okay people, I'm in here for four hours, it's time for a courtesy flush.

"All together now."

THIS COULD BE TROUBLE

The feeling of a sauna engulfed me as I stepped off the ladder, topside, into the humid island morning to report to my muster station. Hawaii meant Tropical Routine, turning-to earlier and securing early to beat some of the worst heat of the day. I looked across the water of Pearl Harbor at gray-hulled Navy vessels of every description. The number 846 on the bow of a destroyer tied up a short distance away came as a surprise. All of the pals I'd served with for two years and hadn't seen since being transferred to the heavy cruiser ROCHESTER were there on that "can." I didn't want to miss a chance to visit my old shipmates before returning to the mainland for my discharge. When liberty was called, I strode down the gangway wearing my favorite uniform, dress whites, and hiked on over to where the OZBOURN was tied up. It was quite a walk even though the two ships were not far apart straight across the water. Once aboard, I assembled a group of my old shipmates, and off we went to the Base Enlisted Men's Club.

We spent the evening drinking beer, laughing, and telling lies to each other. When the club secured we all returned to the OZBOURN for egg sandwiches, aided by Eugene Howie, our galley connection. Later, talking together on the fantail, the time came for me to return to my ship. We could see it tied up across the water. I recalled the long walk over and joked that I might be better off swimming back. When the laughter and jeering challenges subsided, in typical Navy fashion, money appeared and bets were offered.

"Hell, I'm going to do it," I challenged.

The bets were covered and held by a man the yeoman guaranteed didn't have orders to be transferred soon.

I tied my shoes to my belt loops. My liberty card would be needed to board the ROCHESTER, so I removed it from my wallet and handed my watch and wallet to my buddy, Tom Corrothers. Folding my white hat, I pushed it into the front waist band of my trousers, climbed over the rail, stood a moment looking down into the water, and dove in.

Despite jokes about Seaman Second Class--Non Swimmer, I was, in fact, an excellent swimmer. Years in the Southern California surf and diving from the piers had prepared me for this moment. Determined to take my time and keep my eyes on the ROCHESTER, I did a slow, deliberate breast stroke. But I was not prepared for the strange looking debris gliding past me--trash, oil slick and what might have been some floating feces. There were few harbor water pollution restrictions.

The dark water reflected, in sparkling dancing lines, the myriad of lights from the vessels tied up at the many docks about the famous harbor. In time I arrived at the stern of the ROCHESTER and, looking up, realized how much higher that fantail was above the waterline than I had considered. Although there were metal ladder rungs welded to the stern, the bottom rung was too high to reach, designed to be accessed from a boat, not the surface of the water. A chief wearing khakis was fishing off the fantail and couldn't believe his eyes when he spotted me splashing around his line.

"What the hell are you doing down there?" he hollered.

I wanted to project a low-profile image and down-play the situation as much as possible. "I'm okay", I replied nonchalantly, "Just fell off the dock." That was to be my story. Fell off the dock after arriving at the ship *by taxi*.

I swam around to the face of the dock, but the water level was too low for me to secure a hand hold and climb up. I used scissor kicks to propel myself upward, but each time I missed I slid down the oil covered facing. I wasn't concerned about my uniform. The whites were ruined, but I wouldn't need them any longer. I was a short timer, my enlistment up in a few weeks. Besides, I still had two additional sets.

Defeated at attempts to leave the water directly onto the ROCHESTER or onto the dock, I swam to the stern of a nearby destroyer. The screw guards, constructed down close to the water to perform their function, offered a reachable route up. I climbed onto the starboard screw guard. Standing on it, I pulled myself up onto the fantail. Before me, sitting on a capstan, a sentry rested holding an Ml rifle, butt on the deck, supporting his hands and bowed head. He jumped up like he had witnessed a scene out of *The Sea Monster From Hell*. I must have looked frightening with the harbor sludge all over me.

Before he could gather his senses, I quickly offered that I had fallen off the dock, and without waiting for his observations, or reaction, I walked forward toward amidships and the destroyer's gangway. Walking past the watch I reiterated "Fell off the dock" and kept moving past their gaping mouths.

Coolly, I walked across the dock toward the high switched-back gangway of the ROCHESTER. I untied my one remaining shoe from the belt loop, the other had torn off in my dive, put it onto my left foot and sauntered up the gangway. Saluting the stern-mounted ensign, and the OOD, standing some distance away, I dropped my soggy liberty card into the waiting box. Again I offered in passing, as the watch standers looked quizzically at my appearance, "Fell off the dock." This was obviously the solution to this kind of situation--keep moving, stay cool, proceed as if everything is normal. With an awkward gait, caused by a missing shoe, I made my way toward my berthing compartment, feeling their incredulous eyes following my unsteady stride and starboard list. Wet clothes went into the laundry bag. I took a quick shower; put on clean skivvy shorts and shirt, and was in the sack when the ship's bell struck five times.

Slipping into a deep sleep, I was relaxed, secure in knowing I had pulled it off. Tomorrow I would revisit the OZBOURN and collect my bets.

LOCK HIM UP

Someone was shaking me from a sound sleep, asking if I was "Spittle."

"Yeah," I mumbled.

In the glow of the red night light that always prevented complete darkness in the berthing compartments, I made out his white hat and brown duty belt.

"The OOD wants you," he spoke in that sympathetic tone lower echelon peers reserve for each other. I quickly dressed and the messenger led the way back up to the quarter-deck.

I stood before the OOD as he held a clipboard in song book position. Large dark perspiration stains at the arm pits of his khaki shirt contrasted the shiny gold oak leaves on his collar. He frowned and glanced down to the board.

"How did you get back to the ship tonight?"

"Took a taxi, Sir." I lied.

Perusing the clipboard, he indicated, "Says here, you swam."

"I can explain that. Getting out of the taxi I lost my balance, fell off the dock. So I was swimming a bit before I could get back up onto the dock." *Pants on fire.*

Accusingly, "Says here you swam from the OZBOURN."

This was beginning to look bad. *What the hell does he have on that clipboard?*

"Yes sir. Actually I fell off the OZBOURN. I had a few beers earlier and things sorta got away from me, I guess."

Oh what a tangled web we weave.

Looking at me with disdain he rasped, "Says here you dove off the OZBOURN."

I'm screwed. This guy has the goods on me. One last try. "Well, yes Sir. I fell, and while in the air thought, what the hell, I may as well dive. You see I'm from Southern California and I have done a lot of diving and swimming. I ..."

"Let's go," he interrupted, turning and walking away from me.

I should have known that Southern California stuff wouldn't make a dent with this guy. He walked ahead, toward the forward part of the ship, taking determined strides. He didn't look to see if I was following. His manner communicated that he damned well knew I was behind him. Down a passageway, dimly lit by night lights, he stopped at a ladder, dropped the chained sign reading "Officer's Country," and proceeded up. At a door with white lettering on a black background that announced, "Executive Officer," he knocked with consideration, just loud enough to be heard.

The XO's stateroom, Oh No! I knew that this no nonsense second in command, bucking for a fourth stripe, would have me for breakfast. The door opened fully, exposing a little guy wearing only a white skivvy shirt, shorts, and his Navy-issue glasses. His hair out of control, he stood, arms akimbo, bare feet planted solidly on the cool steel deck. I began to eat a heart sandwich. *This guy is tough at any time--but at three in the morning?*

"Excuse me Commander. This man can't seem to remember the truth about his activities this evening." The OOD handed XO the clipboard. He took it, but continued riveting his eyes into mine until I looked away, fearing he might think me insolent. *Boy, I hate that being stared down.* Standing before him, I couldn't keep my knees from shaking. I was helpless, no match for the executive officer of a heavy cruiser. He held my future in his hands, and I was fresh out of lies. *Should I share with him that I had received the Good Conduct Medal a year earlier? Bad idea.*

He read from the mysterious paper, glancing up occasionally. His scowl grew, telegraphing his displeasure. I sensed his notorious short fuse about to sputter.

The XO had heard enough. As he barked the order his mouth and jaw took an odd little twist, looking as though he might have been kicked by a horse sometime in his pre-military past.

"Lock him up!"

The words hit my beer-fogged mind like a bucket of ice water. He wasn't going to deal with this *deviate* now, not at this hour. He had chosen confining me to the ship's brig as the most expeditious short term solution to continuing his interrupted sleep.

Sparking and fizzing, gesturing with his hand, he directed the OOD toward the bulkhead-mounted phone, and growled, "Call the Sergeant of the Guard."

The only good news was that the brig, which consisted of three individual cells, was aboard our ship. I would not be taken to a "disciplinary barracks" on the Naval Base. Those hell holes are the source of some scary stories. Our cells were positioned so the bars faced toward the "free-world," a passageway carrying regular foot traffic. Anyone out there could, and usually did if their business brought them by, come in close for a look. But only from a distance; security was always guaranteed by a barrel chested Marine with a burr-head haircut. As a free man, I always took a peek in the morning, as did my shipmates, to see what the evening's escapades had generated in the way of new jail birds. The openness of this small brig discouraged most of the inhumane treatment that military prisoners are sometimes subjected to by their custodians.

Marines ran the brig. Jarheads have no love for Swabies. They took a perverse delight in having their charges "sound off" for the entertainment of any passers-by.

I set down *God's Little Acre* beside me on the narrow bunk and stood. I sounded off in the manner I'd been instructed.

"Spittle, Frank H., Personnelman Second Class, 568 51 44, incarcerated October 8, 1951."

No-side-burns snarled, "Try it again dog meat, I CAN'T HEAR YOU!"

Shoulders back, head up, eyes forward, heels together, toes forming 45 degrees, I maximized the volume to the delight of the morning spectators. Of course I knew most of them, and they encouraged the corporal to demand another performance. I felt like a circus animal.

Chow times proved to be particularly degrading. A lone marine guard escorted the prisoners to the mess deck. He stood at parade rest behind them while they ate. Often there was only one confined man from our little naval community of about 1100 ROCHESTER crew members. In this case, I was the lone attraction. Sailors who absent-mindedly approached the table with their trays of food, were directed away by the no-nonsense guard. And naturally, the prisoner was not allowed to speak. I felt the eyes of the entire mess hall on me and I lost my youthful appetite for favorites like ground beef and tomato gravy, served on a shingle, or the Navy's airy prune whip dessert.

I'd noticed the Marine wore a lonely blue ribbon on his chest, a marksman's award he'd earned on some remote firing-range in Camp Pendelton. I fantasized about making a break for it, Jimmy Cagney style, but didn't want to be the excuse for him to unload the full magazine from his .45. He'd probably enjoy demonstrating his skill.

During the next few days there was plenty of time to think. *Man, this can not be.* In five years I'd never been in serious trouble. A few Mickey Mouse violations; late for quarters, hitch-hiking, topside without a hat. These earned me several hours of extra duty or restriction from liberty for a few days.

My most serious offense had been shirking duty, the old lawn mowing assignment years earlier at the Corpus Christi Air Station. Cleaning grease traps in the base galley had been my extra duty punishment. The worst part of the squalid grease traps had been the smell, it would gag a maggot. I stared at the gray bulkheads of my small cell there on the ROCHESTER and wondered why the service now hires civilians to maintain those foul smelling receptacles on shore. There's a never ending source of naughty sailors that could keep them flowing and spotless.

My experience as a legal yeoman, during my first year in the Navy, taught me something of the procedures leading up to the awarding of disciplinary punishment. I suspected that, because I hadn't been called to Captain's Mast the first morning after being locked up, the XO must be working overtime putting together charges that would make an example of the Los Angeles goof-off, Spittle.

I remembered too, a few weeks earlier, with the crew mustered on the fantail before our first liberty in Honolulu, this martinet, our new XO, had addressed us in a no-nonsense way. His manner showed he felt discipline violations took him away from his vitally important primary responsibilities and he made it clear that he was determined not to be detracted by any mischievous crew members. I wondered at the time if that authoritarian bellow was his normal voice, or one he reserved for "addressing the men."

He ordered that the good people of Honolulu were not to be subjected by *his* ship's crew, to any "conduct to the prejudice of good order and discipline"--that all inclusive legalese the military uses to nail just about any bad behavior. I wasn't aware of the "good people of Honolulu." The ones I'd met were B-girls, photo scam artists, or tattoo parlor proprietors on seedy Hotel Street. That's where most of the sailors I knew spent their liberties.

Should there be any deviation, this man would personally kick butt--his determined glare convinced me.

But I had become the character he had warned against, the clown he had been waiting for. He was the kind who would make good on his promises. *I had better put my sea lawyer experience to work, pronto, if I want to get out of this mess without serious consequences.*

We had on board a Lieutenant Commander who was a regular Joe, an officer in the image of the hero in the *Mr. Roberts* play. He showed, by his casual relationships with enlisted men, that he never quite learned the lesson--there are officers and there are enlisted scum and the two don't mix socially. Our trails had crossed more than once in the ship's office when he had been assigned to defend some messed-up individual who had been awarded a court martial.

That afternoon I got a message to him: Should I be court martialed, I would like him to defend me.

He came down to the brig early the next morning.

SWIMMING IN AN UNAUTHORIZED AREA

"Well, dog bite my pecker, if that isn't the damnedest sea story I ever heard." The Lieutenant Commander's Georgian mannerisms and expressions, coupled with the boyish twinkle in his eye, were the first friendly gestures extended toward me since the whole crazy mess began.

"You bet I'll defend you, if it comes to that." He laughed. "And have some real fun doin' it. I'd just love to tie a can to the ass of any ol' boy who tries to make a federal case out of this little fraternity escapade. But I doubt if you're goin' to see more than a butt chew. It's pretty hard for me to take any of this too seriously." He grabbed my shoulder firmly with one hand and gave it a shake. "Let's give it a day or two to let the fat rise to the top. But I'll tell you right now, I don't think this dog'll hunt."

I wasn't convinced. "I've got to tell you, Commander, I'm gettin' pretty nervous over this whole thing."

Now, with both hands on my shoulders, he looked me in the eye and lowered his voice. Son, back home people say I could talk a dog off a meat truck." He winked and was gone.

A ray of hope. Not everyone thought I should be stood against the wall. What the hell had I done, anyway?

I learned later, that on the night of the swim my OZBOURN buddies became concerned after I'd been gone an hour. They speculated on the dangers our drinking bout might present to a late night swimmer. Their solution was to climb up to the OZBOURN bridge and convince the signalman to send a visual light message to the signal bridge on the ROCHESTER. The message asked the receiver to go down to my bunk and determine if I had arrived safely. The protocol on the ROCHESTER was much more formal than on the smaller destroyer, where everyone knew everyone else and the crew resembled a family. For some reason the ROCHESTER signalman elected to route the message to the OOD, as if it were official traffic instead of an informal request for cooperation. There the odyssey began.

On the third day after my Pearl Harbor swim I was taken from the brig to Captain's Mast, where I would learn my fate. I stood at attention before the Skipper, dressed in sparkling whites and spit shined liberty shoes. But I would have felt much better with a fresh haircut.

Our CO, a four striper, looked every inch the authority figure. His crisp white uniform, white shoes, and open shirt with silver eagles on each collar point, were a perfect complement to his patrician appearance of neatly combed, cut short, gray flecked hair. He resembled Cary Grant. He stood behind a podium. A second class yeoman in undress whites, holding another damn clipboard, took a position at his left. At his right was the XO, wearing the look of a pit bull ready to tear my face off.

I realized that standing there before him was very serious business, and I couldn't have felt more uncomfortable.

"Petty Officer Spittle," the CO's voice was solemn, "you are charged with some serious offenses. In swimming from the OZBOURN to this ship you caused a vessel nearby to call a Man Overboard exercise in the middle of the night. They put a boat into the water. The safety of others was jeopardized by your thoughtlessness. When confronted, it appears you lied, lied to a superior officer." He turned to the XO, "Please read the charges to Petty Officer Spittle."

The XO read, "Specification 1: On October 8th, 1951, at or about 0100, the aforementioned man did knowingly and willfully swim in an unauthorized area, to wit the main channel at the U.S. Naval Base, Pearl Harbor, Hawaii. Specification 2: On October 8th, 1951, at or about 0200, the aforementioned man did appear in an unclean uniform before the Officer of the Deck aboard the USS ROCHESTER, one Lieutenant Commander T.L. BATES, United States Navy."

Wow! Even I knew that those two Huck Finn offenses would never land me a court martial. I couldn't believe they hadn't included a spec. for lying, but they must have had their reasons. Like, "Let's get his ass off this ship as soon as possible and be done with this nonsense before we're all made the laughing stock of CruDesPac."

"What have you to say for yourself?" asked the Captain.

The XO shifted, waiting for the next lie. I was sure this really gripped his butt since it was his task to prepare the charges for the Captain and he wanted them to stick. I knew he would have come up with something much more creative if he could have found anything more serious in his three days of searching the Uniform Code of Military Justice.

"It's all true, Sir. I used bad judgment." *There. Repentance.* I hoped that would satisfy the CO. The tropical humidity was making me feel shaky and lightheaded. I'd been standing at attention for a long time. Standing at stiff attention.

"Very well. I assign you to three days confinement in the ship's brig." The yeoman made some notations in the Punishment Log. "The three days you have served while waiting for Mast will satisfy the sentence." The CO turned, and with an "Attention on deck!" from the yeoman, he left us.

The XO and the yeoman dropped their shoulders, unlocked their knees and relaxed a bit. I didn't dare. In the cramped, makeshift area of the passageway intersection that was used each working morning for dispensing punishment, the XO stepped closer to me. I could see a little vein throbbing on his left temple. "You are one lucky sailor, Spittle. You have orders from CinCPac to report to Naval Base, Treasure Island, California, for separation due to expiration of enlistment. Wait for a Space-A flight at Hickam Field. Go to early chow and be off this vessel by 1200 hours, or I'll slam-dunk your ass back into the steel bar hotel where you belong." He motioned to the yeoman, who handed me a manila envelope. I looked inside and found my orders, service record, health and pay records--I was gone.

"By 1200 sailor.   Off my ship!" the XO terminated the proceedings.

Whatever happened to the traditional send off, the old "Smooth sailing, fair winds and following seas," crap? I guess they reserve such nicety for officers and those who have served with more honor than a midnight swimmer who appeared in an unclean uniform.

"WE'LL TELL YOU WHEN"

Author, El Camino College,
California, 1953

CONTAGIOUS

The gurgle of soft moaning drifted from every direction of the darkened ward. I was in the midst of 45 seasoned warriors, suffering and tossing on their crisp hospital sheets.

Lieutenant Anderson, angelic in her starched white nurse's uniform, glided on rubber-soled shoes along the softly lit aisle between our beds, stopping to dispense a pain pill to the crew-cut marine two beds down.

As she passed on her way back toward the nurse's station I offered a low voiced greeting, hoping for a little attention.

"Good morning, Miss Anderson."

"Shut up, Spittle," she hissed. "If you wake these clowns and get them yakking, I'll brain you. I mean it, shut up. It's an hour and a half before reveille."

"Don't be that way, Andy. You know I'm your favorite."

Approaching my bed, she reached out and excited me by brushing her smooth palm against my cheek, then seized a chunk and squeezed until my eyes watered..

"You're contagious, sailor boy. Now be good and later I'll see what I can do to get some three-minute eggs for your breakfast."

She left. I'd been awarded my morning's ration of care.

A good sport, she was more civilian nurse than Navy lieutenant, showing the skill of a seasoned ringmaster handling our group of delinquents. We all carried on like summer camp cabin mates.

In the gastrointestinal ward of the U.S. Naval Hospital at Oakland, California, men with ulcers, problems with their small or large intestines, or hemorrhoids, were gathered together. I had been in the ward for three weeks. I was past my discharge date, but couldn't be released into the vulnerable civilian population until the docs determined I was negative for Shegillea Flexner.

Weeks earlier, on Treasure Island in the San Francisco Bay, my military life became dramatic. I was two days into the discharge process when a messenger passed through the barracks calling my name. I accompanied him to the duty officer, who took me by jeep to the base dispensary. Since it was late Sunday afternoon, we had to wait a half

245

hour before the duty doctor arrived. A young man strode into the waiting room wearing a Hawaiian print shirt, shorts, and rubber flip-flops. The base Duty Officer rose and handed him the clipboard holding a dispatch.

"Sorry to pull you in on a Sunday, Doc."

Doc didn't respond, just read the large type of the message as he ran a hand through his short cropped hair. He glanced up toward me, read some more, and quizzically looked me over again. The board dropped to his side and he whistled softly, more an exhale through his pursed lips.

"How do you feel?" He gave me a gaze as if surprised to see me standing.

"I'm fine. What's happening here, Sir?"

"When was your last bowel movement?" *What a hell of a way to begin a relationship.*

"This morning."

The First Class Corpsman got up from behind his desk, came and stood beside the doctor, glancing over the dispatch. The doctor cut the Duty Officer free and directed me to follow him and the corpsman as they led off into one of the quiet hallways leading away from the reception area.

They both stopped before a door marked "Quarantined," and turned toward me. The doc opened the door, reached in and switched on the light, but didn't enter. The sparse, plain room contained one bed, one chair, a desk and a lamp. About as cheery as a monk's cell. The doctor proceeded to put me into shock by issuing the corpsman a string of frightening precautions.

"He'll be served all meals in here." He indicated the interior of the room. "Bring several of the compartmentalized, metal chow trays from the galley. They are to remain here in the room, not go to the scullery. I'll have to figure out later how in the hell to dispose of them safely. When he is served, don't allow the serving ladle to touch the tray. If it accidentally makes contact, leave it here in the room.

"Bring in a portable commode." Looking serious and very professional he instructed me, "Do not use the head through that door," he pointed to his right. "That water goes into the bay. Shegillea Flexner is highly contagious, I don't want San Francisco coming down with an epidemic.

"I can't believe you feel okay, that you're not suffering. When did you last have any symptoms?"

So this is what they're up to, the epidemic on the cruiser.

246

"I've been fine for over a week."

"Well, the dispatch from Honolulu says your last smear came back positive. We'll send you to Oak Knoll Hospital tomorrow morning. They'll get to the bottom of this. Until then do not leave this room. If you need anything, press the summons button. It's clipped to your bed sheet there on the side. Wash you hands frequently, particularly after using the porta-potty. If you begin to feel any of your earlier symptoms, call Petty Officer Pilgrim here, immediately. Are you married?"

"No, Sir."

"Good. We won't have to worry about family members coming down with this. I've never seen a case of Shegillea, but the book makes it sound terrible. Were you very ill before?"

"Everyone on the ship wished he was dead."

"Wow." The doc took on an expression that said he felt his medical knowledge base had just doubled. "Try to get a good night's sleep. I probably won't see you again, I'm off tomorrow. Good luck." He started to extend his hand, but immediately withdrew it and slid both hands deep into his pockets.

"Yes. Well, good luck."

Thank you Father Damian. A nice welcome to your little island colony. I hope nothing falls off while I'm your guest.

He was gone. The corpsman was gone. I didn't even have anything to read. I couldn't leave to go to the rec. room and watch TV. I was contagious. I was quarantined. I sat in the chair and stared at the gray wall, feeling like a leper. My morale had bottomed out. I was supposed to be discharged from the Navy in two days, and now I was headed for the Naval Hospital instead. It didn't look like I'd be making my discharge date.

Can they do this? What a joke, hell yes they can do this. This is the Navy, they can do anything they want.

Once settled into the routine in Oak Knoll Naval Hospital, there was a less serious concern for my condition, on the part of the medical staff, than the doctor at Treasure Island had earlier shown. I was out of quarantine, even allowed to leave the ward for fresh air and sun. I'd go from watching TV in the lounge, to reading, or playing cards and board games with other patients.

Daily, at 0800, each person in the ward, if able to stand, stood at attention beside his hospital bed for sick-call. A doctor, nurse, and two corpsmen moved as a group down the center aisle, stopping at each little campsite to examine the chart that hung on the foot of the bed.

I wanted out of the Navy. After two weeks I was fed up with my laid-back hospital duty of eating, B-S-ing, and the competing in an ongoing game of monopoly, that we stored away under my mattress with everything remaining in place for the next round. I was over my enlistment and being home sounded much better than vegetating in the hospital. I still hadn't shown any of the terrible symptoms I'd experienced weeks earlier in Hawaii on the ROCHESTER.

When the doctor finished examining my chart he neither added nor invited any dialogue other than his initial "Good Morning." I was determined to make the little group of white gowned decision-makers resolve a couple of my issues before they moved on in the way they did each morning. After all, didn't I hold some bargaining power? My enlistment had expired. I was as good as a civilian. Who did these guys think they were fooling with?

I began my well-practiced proposal. "Sir?" The doctor halted and did an about-face. The corpsman behind him almost kissed him in their Larry-Curly-and-Moe near collision.

"Sir, I need to be discharged. Not just from the hospital, from the Navy." I hurried on, not wanting to lose my momentum. "I feel great. I have, ever since I got here. My enlistment has expired. I'm a civilian. If there is nothing else to test, nothing to treat, may I please go home and get started with the rest of my life ?"

He took up the chart to examine again. This time it looked as if he actually read the damn thing. The doc handed it to Lieutenant Anderson, the ward nurse. "Schedule Spittle for a proctoscope exam in the Treatment Room at 1000 tomorrow."

He faced me and pulled himself erect. In a slow, direct, condescending tone he counseled, "Son..." *When they start that way, I always tune out.* "You are not a civilian until you're discharged, even if it's a year from now. If the results of tomorrow's exam come back negative we'll ship you out of here first thing. Until then you're still in the Navy. Be grateful for the government's excellent medical care."

When they'd finished with the last sailor at the far end of the ward I went to stand at the nurse's station, ready to quiz Nurse Anderson.

"Andy..."

"Lieutenant Anderson to you, Frankie."

"Come on, Andy, I'm the guy that got your car running. I'm the guy who keeps you amused when you're on the ward. Cut me some slack. If you hold me here much longer I really will be sick. Just what is this proctoscope exam, anyway?"

A smile curled the outer edges of her mouth. She teased, "You'll see, tomorrow."

"Why can't you tell me now?" Her *I know something you don't know* look made me desperate.

"Tell me now, or I'll go get Seaman Chao laughing again and he'll soil himself. You know what that means for you. Look, I won't bother you the rest of the day. Okay?"

She dug into her front pocket, produced a ring of keys, and searched through them. Finding one she liked, she raised her eyes. "Come with me, Petty Officer Spittle."

Lieutenant Anderson moved toward the rear entrance to the ward, where she unlocked an adjacent door stenciled in black regulation lettering, "Treatment Room." I followed her into the chilly, impersonal compartment as she switched on the light, then proceeded across toward a tall glass-faced cabinet. Carefully reaching in with both hands, she removed an elongated wooden box, turned and placed it onto the examining table, using a motion that suggested presenting some precious artifact for me to enjoy.

Again, the devilish smile. "Are you ready?" Her eyes actually twinkled.

Holding me in her gaze, she maintained the suspense by slowly removing the top from the box.

I looked down past the opened top. Cradled in a black, velvet-lined indentation, rested an eighteen-inch-long chromed cylindrical device, about an inch and a half in diameter, glistening. She didn't need to tell me the anatomical destination for this ghoulish contraption.

Oh my gawd. I can't let them do this to me. No way.

Laughing now, she pointed out features of the thing as if it were a sports car centered on a showroom floor. A light at one end illuminated the pathway for another apparatus to remove a tissue sample. On the other end of the monster, which was looking larger every minute we stood there, light reflected from an eyepiece through which the operator views and directs the procedure.

My tone even surprised *me*. "There is nothing in the United States Navy that could get me to submit to that thing. I'm a civilian. I'm not kidding, Lieutenant. You can tell them I absolutely refuse that monster. They can punish me any way they want, but I just won't go along with this."

I was warming to my subject. "My first stop will be the chaplain, then request mast, a letter to my congressman, and then the president. I'm calling the American Civil Liberties Union. I mean it." I stormed out and went for a walk on the grounds. I needed some air. My entire body was shaking.

I determined I would stick to it. No way would I be violated with that damn thing. For the remainder of the day each time our trails crossed nurse Anderson telegraphed that special smile. I didn't sleep well that night.

At sick call the next morning the medics walked right past my chart. No greeting, nothing.

Maybe they realize they've taken this too far. They must appreciate a guy's got to take a stand, somewhere.

After they'd made their rounds, nurse Anderson returned to my bed with a small tray covered with a linen towel.

No cute smile. This morning she was the all serious nurse. "Sit down please." She indicated the chair beside my bed. "The doctor has ordered an injection."

Good. A shot instead of that proctoscope thing. She must have said something to them. Good. I rolled up my sleeve.

She wiped my arm with a cold, damp piece of cotton, picked up the syringe and watched as she held it at eye level and discharged a short squirt into the air before leaning to administer my shot.

Okay, this is more like it. I'll have my discharge papers and be out of here in a day or two.

I attempted to stand, but Miss Anderson placed her hand on my shoulder. "Just stay in the chair until I return. Don't try to get up for a few minutes."

The pleasant feeling of warm, soothing oil moved up from the base of my neck, slowly seeping its way throughout my head. I felt the beginning of an out-of-body experience. My world was without care. I was content.

Two corpsmen wearing undress whites came to each side of the chair and helped me to my feet. They steered me toward the Treatment Room where the doctor and nurse Anderson waited.

Now it was my turn to give a knowing smile to Anderson. The doctor rested his hand on a white piece of furniture and asked me to kneel on it in a praying position. I felt no concern for the upcoming procedure. In my drug induced state they could have pushed a Louisville Slugger up my butt, and it would have been okay with me.

As I knelt, the doctor lightly directed my upper body forward until I was in a Z position, my head rested on my folded arms. The kneeling apparatus was then tilted forward and held in position by the first class corpsmen who stood near my head. I was in an extreme sunny-side-up pose. Doc directed Anderson and the other corpsmen to spread my cheeks while he smeared me with a chilly lubricant.

Then the sensation of being entered. But it was okay. I was cool. In fact, I was still smiling.

The next few seconds burned into my mind like a permanent brand: Dynamic movement, attention demanding racket, and intense excitement among my caregivers, all came together in one explosive flash.

WHAM. I felt myself fly backwards into my original upright kneeling position. The support contraption had violently shifted. I heard the silver projectile clang to the deck.

The doc was raging. "Gawd damn it, Forsythe. Are you trying to rip this guy apart? A simple job like holding on and you can't handle it? Gawd damn it."

When I turned my head the first person I saw beside me was Nurse Anderson, her eyes wide open like a cartoon character. She was motionless, her expression frozen.

"Lieutenant, get this scope cleaned up." Doc was in his full Navy Commander mode.

"Forsythe, one more screw up from you and I'll have your crow. I'll tear it right off your arm, you nitwit. You'll be a slick sleeve striker all over again.

"Gawd damn it."

"Are you all right, son?" He patted my shoulder. His face showed legitimate concern.

I smiled. "Can I have another shot?"

He patted my shoulder again. "We don't want to send you home a junky."

Looking toward his statue-like staff, he directed, "I'm going to have a cigarette. Come to the porch entrance when you're ready for me."

First Class Corpsman Forsythe asked if *he* could go have a cigarette. The doctor drew him into his cold stare, turned his head slowly from side to side and again moaned, just audibly.

"Gawd damn it."

He turned and walked out.

The medical crew crisply answered, in unison. "Yes Sir."

Terms like malpractice and litigation didn't enter my mind. At that moment the doc was more concerned than I. I was still smiling.

We resumed the exercise a few minutes later. The tenseness in the treatment room was thick, like heavy fog. But everything seemed to proceed okay. Forsythe held on this time. The doc had his look-see and took a tissue sample.

That morning's potential seriousness didn't hit me until the following day. Had anything interrupted the descent of the silver missile as I sped downward with it protruding half out of my rear, I'd have been torn to my navel.

Years later, each time I kneel in church, the Treatment Room scene plays and my hands get clammy.

So much for the government's excellent medical care.

I'M OUT

For the first time in five years I was completely free. No expiration of liberty to worry about, no assignment to a location I hated, no unpleasant individuals directing me on tasks I didn't choose--none, ever again.

Outside the hospital grounds the line of dusty cars parked along the shoulder of the road extended out of sight. I easily found my '37 Ford coupe, it had the best styling among the pack. I pushed and crammed my seabag into the trunk before I could force the deck lid closed. The large envelope containing my discharge papers got tossed onto the passenger's seat, the little civilian lapel pin awarded to discharged veterans, a golden eagle the guys called "the ruptured duck," landed on top. I doubted I would ever wear it.

Back pay, reimbursement for unused leave, and the equivalent of train fare to my point of enlistment, Los Angeles, all in cash, was buttoned into my inside jumper pocket. There's something exciting about hundred dollar bills in discretionary money to a guy who had been earning one hundred thirty seven dollars a month. Life was good.

Experience taught me my car wouldn't start after sitting gathering dust since I'd been admitted to the hospital. But I offered up my usual little prayer and reached for the starter button that had been retrofitted up to the dashboard. Click, click, click--no luck. At least I was parked on a slight incline. I could coast down. By habit, I always searched for that kind of a spot when parking--a free rolling start. I went to work, turning my back to the trunk, squatted to grab the bumper in both hands and, digging in my heels, leaned into it. Several quick trips to the open window to realign the steering wheel and finally I had muscled the car into the street. It began to coast slowly on its own.

The next part was always a little tricky. The doors opened forward, hinged in the rear. The drill dictated I hurry around from the rear, awkwardly maneuvering past the open door to jump behind the wheel. It meant carefully pirouetting to enter, butt first. I worried that if I fell, or the door knocked me over, I'd be left sitting in the street watching my pilotless car coast on, faster and faster.

My suicide exercise behind me, I sat safely behind the wheel as the car picked up momentum. I really wasn't dressed for the task. In my

253

woolen blues, after the donkey work of pushing the car by myself, I was damp with sweat. But I forced all of my concentration to the mental check-off list. You only get one chance when you're rolling downhill: Pull choke out half way, gas pedal down one third, shift into second gear and slowly release the clutch until fully extended.

If she doesn't start by the bottom of the hill I'm in deep caca.

Sputterrrr--good sign. Depress clutch again, pump the gas pedal--not too much.

The engine caught while I continued finessing just the right ration to the carburetor. By pushing in the choke nearly all the way, and easing as much gas pedal as she could handle before warming up after her long rest, it all came together. We were cruising along the street under our own power. I settled back into the seat and began to breathe easy as I pointed her toward Coast Highway and the 500-mile trip south to Inglewood. Wind from the open window cooled my face. I was on top-of-the-world. Being a civilian for the past two hours was a good fit.

During the day-long drive the sun sparkled off the surface of the Pacific, its energy urging me homeward. I sang every Frank Sinatra song I knew, some more than once, each with my own special styling.

It had been dark several hours when I coasted into the space beside Mother's little trailer house, hand painted blue and white by this indefatigable woman. She had lived here alone for the past few years, after the end of a second marriage no more satisfying than her first. Her door opened as if she'd been standing just behind it, waiting.

Out stepped my little five-foot Mom.

"Hi Mom, your Jackass is home--for good."

And she began to cry. "Get in here, Mister," she sniffed, "There's a nice supper waiting for you that I've been keeping warm in the oven."

I moved to her, bent down and took her in my arms, holding on a little tighter and a little longer for the years we'd missed. Neither of us moved to let go.

She lifted her head toward my face. "I'm sorry for crying, Honey. I'm just so happy you're home."

She took me by the hand, led me inside, directly to the table. Sitting me down, she took a pot-holder and from the oven produced a plate with my favorite, meat loaf. After spooning on a huge portion of mashed potatoes, she covered them with meaty dark brown gravy. There were waxy pale green limas beside a couple of thick slices of her fresh-baked bread. I brought a piece of bread to my nose and inhaled. Yes, this was home.

She poured me a second glass of milk, I guess she figured I'd had enough time to settle in after the long drive and she couldn't wait any longer.

"Now, you were saying in your letters, Honey, about college and wanting to teach children. I was so tickled. You're sure an ambitious little cuss." I stood a foot taller than she, but I was always her *little* something--cuss, boy, jackass.

"But I don't understand how all this works. Don't you have to finish high school before you can go into college?"

"No, Mom. I took care of that in the Navy, the GED test and all. I can start right in when the new semester begins. The GI Bill will pay for tuition, books, supplies, and give us a check for about a hundred dollars every month. I'll have to get a job, I know the check won't be enough, but we can make this work."

Mom's face broadcast her excitement. "Don't you worry. I know a few tricks for stretching a budget."

My plan of action was ready. "I'm going to the Post Office next Monday about work. Being a veteran will help me get on, they're civil service. Maybe I'll wear my ruptured duck."

Mom's eyebrows showed she'd just remembered something. "Speaking of Monday, before I forget, the park manager here is getting concerned about the length of my grass in the strip alongside where your car is parked. You probably noticed it when you got out. Before Monday, could you take the old lawn mower from the shed and cut that grass for me?"

My memory jolted, resurrecting the past lawn mower experiences that plagued me right up into my Navy career. "You're not trying to get me to reenlist, are you?"

As always, she only heard want she wanted to hear. She continued, not missing a beat. "My Son, the Teacher. I'm so happy and proud. I could burst."

The wadded tissue came out from her apron pocket again, and she took off her glasses to dab at the tears. Smiling, crying, laughing, and wiping her eyes, she got up from the table and went to her Bible next to the lamp. She removed a clipping from beneath the cover and handed it across the table.

"I loved this so much. I saved it for you."

A teacher in Winnetka, Illinois, Miss Lola May, had written some special words about my chosen teaching profession: "A hundred years from now it won't matter what kind of car I drove, the house I lived in, or how much money I made. But the world might be a different place because I was important in the life of a child."

I set the clipping down, looked into Mom's brimming eyes, and we both cried. *Damn, is this what living at home is going to be, crying all the time?*

For the next two years, studying at El Camino Community College, Mom and I shared the little trailer and put on a team effort to move me through college. Later, in Santa Barbara, at the University of California, the *experts* finished the job, molding me into a certificated school teacher. Through it all, between classes and assignments, I kept myself busy. I carried mail, sold men's clothing, worked in the college bookstore, dug ditches for the City Water Department, hashed at the Sig Ep fraternity house, swept classrooms, delivered newspapers, checked groceries, and was a part-time fireman, living on campus at the university fire house.

Finally the day Mom and I had planned for, worked and sacrificed for, arrived. A wired twenty-seven year old, dressed in his new herring-bone sport coat, wearing his graduation watch, and his first new glasses since Navy issue years earlier, stood before a roomful of squirming ten-year olds at James Kew School, in Inglewood.

My own fifth grade class.

I soon realized that motivating youngsters whose concerns had nothing to do with long division, their minds pondering the likes of recess, lunch, and three o'clock dismissal, would test my mettle every day. But each time a student shot up his hand to answer a question, and begged "Teacher, teacher," I knew I'd made the right career choice.

My good fortune continued. Into my life came Darlene, a very special lady who agreed, with me, to spend the rest of our lives together. Two little girls, Alison and Jennifer, were soon running through our home. God had fulfilled my dreams.

After my daughters had begun school and learned a bit about their world, they began to show interest in my teenage Navy years.

"What did *you* do in the war, Daddy?"

Well kids, I was a typist. I was a darn good typist.

GLOSSARY

aft; after	Toward the rear section of the vessel.
airedale	Slang for Naval aviation personnel.
arigato	Japanese, meaning "thank you."
Asiatic	State of mind that demonstrates abnormal behavior. Originally exhibited by Navy men on duty for extended periods in the Far East, during Yangtze River gunboat era.
bare-a-hand	Hurry.
bell-bottom	Extra material is added to the pants' trouser bottoms giving them the appearance of "belling out" above the shoe.
B-Girl	A female working in a bar who earns a commission from drinks customers purchase for her.
below	Down-stairs. Below the main deck.
billet	A position; job; an assignment.
boot	A recruit in training.
boot camp	Basic training base for new recruits.
brass	Officers.
brass monkey	"Cold enough to freeze the balls off a brass monkey." An old nautical term.
bridge	Command center for the ship when underway.

bulkhead	Wall.
bunk	A sleeping platform designed to accommodate a mattress.
can	A particular combatant vessel--a destroyer.
captain's mast	Ceremony where the captain awards punishment for infractions of rules. If the seriousness warrants, the captain may award a court martial where the individual is tried for his offense and awarded a punishment greater than the captain may assign at mast.
charge sheet	Paper that outlines an accusation of violation of the Uniform Code of Military Justice.
chit	A small piece of official paperwork. An authorization; a receipt; a voucher, etc.
chow	Food; a meal. "Shipping-over chow." An expression of praise for a particularly good meal.
C.I.C.	Combat Information Center
CINCPAC	Commander in Chief, Pacific Fleet
Cinderella liberty	Liberty that expires at midnight.
clothes-stops	Cotton strings, approximately 12 inches long, designed to tie wet clothing to dry on a line.
Company Commander	The individual in charge of a company made up of recruits.
con	Control. As to "have the con" = in charge.

CONUS	Continental Limits of the United States.
CPO	Chief Petty Officer, E-7. Comprising "middle management," chiefs are the backbone of the Navy and have the respect and authority to execute any assignment.
crabs	Blood sucking body lice. Attach eggs to their host's hair strands.
crow	The rate badge worn on the sleeve of enlisted uniforms. Comprised of an eagle with chevrons beneath and a rating insignia centered between them. "I'll take your crow." An expression used by a superior to threaten an individual for poor performance.
CruDesPac	The Command for all Cruisers and Destroyers in the Pacific Fleet.
davit	Small crane projecting over ship's side; used for hoisting and lowering boats.
deck ape	An individual who's shipboard assignment has him working topside.
Deck Court Martial	The lowest level of military court martial assignable in 1947. Summary and General Courts Martial completed the possibilities.
Detailer	Office in Bureau of Naval Personnel concerned with assigning individuals to open billets throughout the service.
deuce	Two. Seaman deuce is slang for Seaman Second Class.
dogged	A hatch secured (with handles) to maintain watertight integrity.

down below	Downstairs.
dream-sheet	A prepared application sheet for a request of some sort, i.e.. transfer, leave, school.
EM	Enlisted Man.
enlisted man	An individual whose rank is below that of an officer. E-1 through E-9.
ensign	The United States flag. An officer of rank O-1.
extra duty	A punishment. Extra hours of work to be performed after regular working hours. Typically chores of the most undesirable nature, i.e.. cleaning grease traps in the galley or chipping and scraping rusted paint.
fart sack	White mattress cover constructed as a sack.
field stripped cigarette	A manner of disposing of a finished cigarette. Torn apart, the tobacco is allowed to sprinkle about. The paper is rolled into a tiny ball. The discarded parts are hard to notice on the ground.
fish	Torpedo.
flight ops	Flight operations; launching or landing of aircraft.
foreskins	Slang for creamed chipped beef.
forty-five (.45)	Forty-five caliber. A military hand gun, semi-automatic with a clip of ammunition inserted into the grip area.

fruit salad	Slang for "ribbons" worn upon uniforms denoting medals awarded.
galley	Place where food is prepared. A kitchen.
gangway	The plank type arrangement for pedestrians boarding ships from docks or adjacent moored vessels.
gear	One's belongings or the equipment for accomplishing a task.
G.E.D. Tests	General Education Development Tests. Success here was generally accepted in the civilian world as equivalent to a high school graduation.
gedunk	Sweets, malts.
glory bars	Slang for "ribbons".
goldbricker	One who shirks his duties.
Gold Star Mother	One who lost a child in military service during WWII.
grinder	Black topped area set aside for marching.
gyro repeater	An instrument, usually located on the open bridge of a vessel, connected to a gyrocompass. Used for taking bearings.
haeyaku	Japanese, meaning "hurry up."
hai	Japanese, meaning "yes."
helm	Steering mechanism for a vessel. The wheel.
helmsman	Individual who mans the helm.

holy stoning	Scraping the wooden deck with an abrasive piece of material, pushed with a swab handle.
honey bucket	Any container for human waste. Size could be from a pail to a truck-load.
Irish pennant	An untidy loose end of a line. A piece of thread on clothing.
jarhead	Sailor slang for a Marine.
JOOD	Junior Officer of the Deck. See OOD.
joto	Japanese, meaning "very good."
kieyie brush	Wooden backed, stiff bristle brush (approximately 8 inches by 3 inches) designed for scrubbing clothing.
knot	A unit of speed equal to 1 nautical mile per hour.
ladder	Any stairway.
lay to	To remain stationary.
liberty	Free time, off duty, that allows one to leave the ship or base.
Lucky Bag	A place where all lost clothing, clothing of deserters, and clothing of individuals, released from service (other than Honorable Dischargees who keep their clothing), is taken. Personnel may come here to purchase items at fire sale prices.
MAA	Master At Arms. A petty officer performing duties concerned with keeping order on the ship.

mescal	Alcoholic beverage made from cactus (agave) juice.
mess	Having to do with food serving.
mess cook	Server; scullery hand; cook's helper.
messenger	A light line used for hauling over a heavier rope.
mid-watch	Assignment from midnight until 4 A.M. Especially unpleasant because of boredom and possible fatigue.
monkey fist	A knot worked into the end of a heaving line to form a heavy ball to aid throwing the line across water.
Murphy	Slang for potato
Mustang	An officer who has advanced through the enlisted ranks.
muster	To gather for roll call and announcements.
nautical mile	6080.20 feet. About one fifth longer than a statute mile.
night stick	Hand held club (approximately 30 inches long and 1 1/2 inches in diameter) often carried by watch standers.
obi	Japanese traditional waist wrap-around to hold a yakata (gown for men or women).
oksa	Japanese, meaning "wife."
Old Man	The commanding officer.

OOD	Officer of the Deck. In charge for a certain period during the day.
peacoat	Heavy wool, double breasted overcoat. Navy blue, wide collar, length to mid thigh. Worn by enlisted men.
piece	Weapon; gun.
pilot house	Enclosed structure aboard ship, bridge area, where the helmsman and other watch standers execute their duties when ship is underway.
piss and punk	Slang for bread and water.
plan-of-the-day	A schedule, published daily aboard ship, of the day's routine.
Pollywog	An individual in a crossing the equator ceremony who has yet to be initiated.
poontang (or poon)	Slang for sexual intercourse.
quarters	Assembly for muster by divisions.
rack	Bed. See bunk.
R and R	Rest and Recreation. Intervals planned by military commands for the mental and physical refreshment of the troops.
ration	A meal.
regs	Regulations. As in Navy Regs.
report	Placed on report = being charged with some infraction of rules. Those on report face Captain's Mast for disposition.

request mast	Each working day the captain of the vessel, or base, will hear from any subordinate who has a special request that he has not been able to satisfy through lower channels.
ribbons	1 1/4 inch colorful cloth bars made of the material that suspends medals they represent. Worn on an individual's left breast.
ryokan	Japanese country-inn.
saki	Japanese rice wine. Served both hot and cold, depending upon the weather.
salt	Slang for an experienced old-timer with many years in the Navy.
scuttle-butt	(1) Conversation; rumor. (2) A drinking fountain.
seabag	Canvas, cylindrical bag (approximately 42 inches high and 18 inches in diameter) used by enlisted personnel to contain personal gear.
sea gull	Slang for chicken.
Seaman deuce	Slang for Seaman Second Class.
sea-store cigarettes	Especially packaged to be sold in Navy stores (aboard ship and out to sea). In 1950 cost was eight cents a pack.
secure	(1) Finish the work at hand (2) to make secure.
seventy-two	A 72. Three days off. A seventy-two always includes Saturday and Sunday.

shakedown	An underway testing of systems aboard a vessel.
Shell Back	One who has crossed the equator and been initiated in the ceremony.
shillelagh	A club-like arrangement made of canvas and stuffed with wet toilet paper. Used to beat initiates in the equator crossing ceremony.
shingle	Piece of toast.
shit can	Slang for a trash can.
shoji screen	A sliding, light-weight partition creating rooms in a Japanese home.
short-time	A paid for interlude, producing the favors of a prostitute for one session rather than an extended period of time.
sickbay	Medical facility.
sick call	A designated time for people to report their physical ailments at sickbay.
slip the anchor	An emergency procedure. The anchor chain is separated on the deck and allowed to slide overboard, remaining at the bottom with the anchor.
smoking lamp	A condition allowing or prohibiting smoking, i.e.. the smoking lamp is lit = smoking allowed; the smoking lamp is out = smoking prohibited.
snipe	An individual whose shipboard assignment has him performing below decks, in the engine room or fire room. An engineer.

SOS	Shit-on-a-shingle. A popular breakfast dish made with tomatoes, ground meat, onions, pickles, and seasoning; poured over a piece of toast (the shingle).
stanchion	A physical, upright support.
stand-by	n. A person who takes another's assignment. v. To be ready.
steaming	Proceeding under ship's power.
steaming chair	A large chair on the bridge, reserved for the captain (when he is present).
striker	A seaman, airman, or fireman working toward petty officer third class in a particular rating, i.e.. Yeoman Striker, Cook Striker.
swabbie	Marine Corps slang for sailor.
tailor-mades	Uniforms made by civilian tailors. Gabardine material cut to be form fitting, zipper down the side of jumper, and accentuated belled bottoms. Very popular, but often banned as "out of uniform."
tatami mat	Woven matts covering the floors of Japanese homes.
tin can	The particular combatant vessel--a destroyer.
tit	Slang for a chicken's breast, white meat.
topside	Upstairs.
turn to	Commence working.

USO	United Services Organization. Off base facilities staffed by civilian volunteers serving food and beverages. Servicemen came to relax while on liberty, enjoying reading and writing areas, dances and entertainment.
VD	Venereal Disease. A sexually transmitted disease, i.e. gonorrhea, syphilis.
wardroom	The area where ship's officers congregate, eat their meals, hold meetings, or just relax.
watch	Assigned period, i.e.. 4 hours. One is *on watch*, has *the watch*, and is delighted to learn that some disagreeable incident "Didn't happen on *my watch*."
Watch, Quarter, and Station Bill	A posted assignment breakdown showing the responsibilities of each member of the crew during emergency and routine drills. An individual might have a dozen different assignments depending on the particular contingency. Individual's berth numbers and locker numbers also appear here.
WestPac	Western Pacific.
working girl	A prostitute.
yeoman	A clerical person.

About the author of
Sailor, Write Your Mother

After receiving his Honorable Discharge from the Navy, Frank Spittle pursued his B.A. degree at the University of California, Santa Barbara, and his M.A. from California State University, Los Angeles.

His interest in sea service was rekindled after twenty years of civilian life. He joined the Coast Guard Reserve, rising to the rank of Chief Warrant Officer before retiring.

For thirty-one years, teaching kept him challenged while he and his wife Darlene reared two daughters, Alison and Jennifer.

He now resides in Laguna Hills, California, where he writes, speaks, and enjoys frequent international travel.

P.O. Box 3421
Laguna Hills, CA 92654

ORDER FORM
Enjoy more of Frank's humor
and crackling fiction
Ocean Breeze Productions
P.O. Box 3421
Laguna Hills, CA 92654

Client _____

Address _____

_____

_____ copies *Sailor, Write Your Mother!*
A Teenage Boy Comes of Age Despite the
Rigors of the United States Military
@ $16.95   _____
   CA - add tax $1.40 per book   _____
      *   *   *

_____ copies *Can You See Me Now?*
Manual for a Deranged Boyhood
@ $18.95   _____
CA - add tax $1.56 per book   _____
      *   *   *

_____copies *The Trailer Two Spaces*
      Down   A novel
@ $19.99   _____
   CA - add tax $1.65 per book   _____
      *   *   *

Shipping and Handling @   _____
$3. **per book**

                    Total $_____

Please make checks payable to:
Ocean Breeze Productions

Any questions? Phone: **949-581-8377**

To order additional copies of
Sailor, Write Your Mother!
complete the information below.

Ship To: (please print)

Name_____

Address_____

City, State, Zip_____

Day Phone _____

Please send me:

____ copies of *Sailor, Write Your Mother!* @ $16.95 each $_____

Postage and handling @ $3.00 per book $_____

CA residents add $1.36 tax per book $_____

Total Amount Enclosed $_____

Make Checks Payable to Ocean Breeze Productions

Send order form and payment to:
Ocean Breeze Productions
PO Box 3421
Laguna Hills, CA 92654

5K   Edwards Solstice
1954 - Feb 20
10 P.M. - 12 m.   in L.A.
Feb 19-21 Aliens "Frank Edwards
Tech -
Policy - Secrecy 2 mo...

~56
Orange - Red.   18.61
1600

Sun -
moon cycles & eclipse
Truman 83 days
1947 Roswell
Washington   UFO
                    War?   Decoy
NOS 1961
1963 - Cosmos - NOV 11 Share - UFO
NOV 12 - NOV 22 Killed
March 16 1967 -   Salis missiles off line
Nixon 1971 - NOV 1971 -
1974 - Gleeson by himself to Homestead
Leave - 6-8
Bill Clinton - Hubell #2 1993
died 1976 - GB 1977
                61 1947